The World Encyclopedia of Comics

Edited by Maurice Horn

VOLUME 6

THE CONTRIBUTORS
Manuel Auad (M.A.), *The Philippines*
Bill Blackbeard (B.B.), *U.S.*
Gianni Bono (G.B.), *Italy*
Joe Brancatelli (J.B.), *U.S.*
MaryBeth Calhoun (M.B.C.), *U.S.*
Javier Coma (J.C.), *Spain*
Bill Crouch (B.C.), *U.S.*
Giulio Cesare Cuccolini (G.C.C.), *Italy*
Mark Evanier (M.E.), *U.S.*
Wolfgang Fuchs (W.F.), *Germany*
Luis Gasca (L.G.), *Spain*
Robert Gerson (R.G.), *U.S.*
Denis Gifford (D.G.), *Great Britain*
Paul Gravett (P.G.), *Great Britain*
Peter Harris (P.H.), *Canada*
Hongying Liu-Lengyel (H.Y.L.L.), *China*
Maurice Horn (M.H.), *France/U.S.*
Pierre L. Horn (P.L.H.), *U.S.*
Slobodan Ivkov (S.I.), *Yugoslavia (Serbia)*
Bill Janocha (B.J.), *U.S.*
Orvy Jundis (O.J.), *The Philippines*
Hisao Kato (H.K.), *Japan*
John A. Lent (J.A.L.), *Asia*
Richard Marschall (R.M.), *U.S.*
Alvaro de Moya (A.M.), *Brazil*
Kalmán Rubovszky (K.R.), *Hungary/Poland*
Ervin Rustemagić (E.R.), *Yugoslavia*
John Ryan (J.R.), *Australia*
Matthew A. Thorn (M.A.T.), *Japan*
Dennis Wepman (D.W.), *U.S.*

The World Encyclopedia of Comics

Edited by Maurice Horn

VOLUME 6

Chelsea House Publishers
Philadelphia

Acknowledgments

The editors of *The World Encyclopedia of Comics* wish to extend their sincere thanks to the following persons: Bill Anderson, Jerry Bails, Larry Brill, Mary Beth Calhoun, Frank Clark, Bill Crouch, Leonard Darvin, Tony Dispoto, Jacques Glénat-Guttin, Ron Goulart, George Henderson, Pierre Horn, Pierre Huet, S. M. "Jerry" Iger, Jessie Kahles Straut, Rolf Kauka, Heikki Kaukoranta, Roland Kohlsaat, Maria-M. Lamm, Mort Leav, Vane Lindesay, Ernie McGee, Jacques Marcovitch, Victor Margolin, Doug Murray, Pascal Nadon, Harry Neigher, Walter Neugebauer, Syd Nicholls, Tom Peoples, Rainer Schwarz, Silvano Scotto, Luciano Secchi, David Smith, Manfred Soder, Jim Steranko, Ernesto Traverso, Miguel Urrutía, Jim Vadeboncoeur, Jr., Wendell Washer, Peter Wiechmann, Mrs. John Wheeler and Joe Willicombe.

We would also like to thank the following collectors who donated reproductions of art from their collections: Wendy Gaines Bucci, Mike Burkey, Tony Christopher, Russ Cochran, Robert Gerson, Roger Hill, Bill Leach, Eric Sack, and Jim Steranko.

Special thanks also to Michel Mandry, Bernard Trout, José Maria Conget of Instituto Cervantes in New York, Four-Color Images Gallery, Frederik Schodt, David Astor, Alain Beyrand, Manuel Halffter, Dominique Petitfaux, Annie Baron-Carvais, Janice Silverman.

Our appreciation also to the following organizations: Associated Newspapers Ltd., Bastei Verlag, Bulls Pressedienst, Comics Magazine Association of America, Editions Dupuis, ERB Inc., Field Newspaper Syndicate, Globi Verlag, The Herald and Weekly Times Ltd., Kauka Comic Akademie, King Features Syndicate, Marvel Comics Group, San Francisco Academy of Comic Art, Strip Art Features, Walt Disney Archives and Walt Disney Productions.

Finally, we wish to thank Don Manza for his photographic work.

Chelsea House Publishers
1974 Sproul Road, Suite 400
P.O. Box 914
Broomall PA 19008-0914

Typeset by Alexander Graphics, Indianapolis IN

Library of Congress Cataloging-in-Publication Data

The world encyclopedia of comics / edited by Maurice Horn.
    p. cm.
    Includes bibliographical references and index.
    ISBN 0-7910-4854-3 (set). — ISBN 0-7910-4857-8 (v. 1). — ISBN
0-7910-4858-6 (v. 2). — ISBN 0-7910-4859-4 (v. 3). — ISBN
0-7910-4860-8 (v. 4). — ISBN 0-7910-4861-6 (v. 5). — ISBN
0-7910-4862-4 (v. 6). — ISBN 0-7910-4863-2 (v. 7)
    1. Comic books, strips, etc.—Dictionaries. I. Horn, Maurice.
PN6710.W6 1998
741.5'03—dc21   97-50448
                                          CIP

"Sor Pampurio," Carlo Bisi. © Corriere dei Piccoli.

SORANG (Spain) *Sorang*, Enric Sío's first color comic, conceived on an idea by Emili Teixidor and developed by Jaume Vidal Alcover, was originally designed for an adult and exclusive publication. The restrictions imposed by its actual vehicle, the weekly comic book series *Vector 2*, led to a complete overhaul of the script, which was taken over by Sío after page 25.

The theme of *Sorang*, which unfolded over a one-year period starting in October 1968, explores the possibility of a submarine society made up of the remnants of successive shipwrecks who regain life after a nuclear explosion. This aquatic group is ruled by Queen Materia, who has a matriarchal regime in which communication is not verbal, but telepathic and visual. Materia's henchmen abduct two land-dwellers from the beach—Max and Julio (the last one a scientist)—to work for the queen. Julio succeeds in isolating words through a scientific process, and converts each of them into an effective weapon in his struggle against the aquatic people. The original script ended with the elimination of Materia and the transformation of the denizens of *Sorang* into a normal people capable of communicating through different languages.

Sío, however, decided to change the ending and its implications; Julio realizes that he cannot fight effectively against those who dominate the image. His enemies do not use the language code and therefore are impervious to words. This situation forces him to give life to his own images, thus fighting the people of the abyss with their own weapons. In the resulting confusion, the people of Sarong destroy one another and the queen is disintegrated. In the final analysis, Julio has fought against a dead world that never existed, a world of ghosts.

Graphically *Sorang* meant total creative freedom for the author. He could eliminate perhaps for the first time in the history of the world's comics the black line which delineates the drawings, working exclusively with masses of color. Sio intended to adapt the techniques of advertising, design, and especially photography to the comics. The author's obsession with the photographic process known as pseudo-solarization is evident in the extraordinary color distortions which, while adding meaning to the language of the comics, have a double drawback: on the one hand Sío attempts to send a message in each page, conceived as a harmonic and plastic whole; on the other hand he obtains a demythifying, destructive, and antiheroic dimension.

In the ultimate pages of the strip, however, Sío rediscovered the value of black, which he had practically eliminated from his tonal range, contrasting it with collages of color photographs and monochromatic panels.

L.G.

SOR PAMPURIO (Italy) *Sor Pampurio*, created by Carlo Bisi, appeared in the pages of the *Corriere dei Piccoli* from 1929 to 1941. This illustration of the life and times of an upper-middle-class Italian family appeared in the period when it was still possible to think of the good life, before history and war had overtaken the Mussolini regime.

Pampurio, along with his wife, son, and maid Rosetta, is always looking for a new home. His frantic weekly chase not only represents the slightly mad aspects of house-hunting but symbolizes, on a higher level, everyman's dream of peace and quiet. Pampurio is always burdened with everyday problems, such as how to spend his free time, how to find money for the holidays, and how best to dispose of the old furniture in the country house. These problems are not very important, but in Pampurio's compulsive frenzy, we are reminded of our own tendencies to overblow the simple incidents of daily life.

Pampurio was sketched in a hasty, cartoony style by Bisi, who gave him an egg-shaped head surmounted by two wooly tufts instead of hair. His wife and son were similarly drawn in the linear, one-dimensional way that most befitted the protagonists' single-minded obsessions.

G.B.

SPECTRE, THE (U.S.) *The Spectre* was created by writer Jerry Siegel and artist Bernard Baily and made its first appearance in National's *More Fun* number 52 for February 1940. In a world populated with superpowered studs, even the Spectre was extraordinary. He was as close to God as the comic books got. He had the power of just about every superhero combined, and you could be killed just by staring into his skull-pupiled eyes.

The Spectre was really policeman Jim Corrigan. While trying to save his fiancée, Clarice Winston, he was encased in cement and drowned. He was returned to earth, however, and told he could not have eternal rest until he wiped out all crime on the planet. As a ghost, the Spectre could exist outside of Corrigan's body, which neatly handled the often-sticky alter ego problem. And incredibly enough, the Spectre could talk directly to God. Over the years, the Spectre and Jim Corrigan changed. After a while, his powers were reduced and other changes were developed in the Corrigan/Spectre relationship. Apparently, it was becoming impossible to write a strip about a demigod.

Artistically, *The Spectre* was a dark and ominous strip. His green and gray costume set the pace and Bernard Baily handled the feature ploddingly, letting the incredible Spectre's powers take the forefront.

The Spectre lasted in *More Fun* through February 1945, issue number 101. He also appeared in *All-Star* from the first issue, Summer 1940, through the 23rd issue (Winter 1945). In the 1960's rush to revive superheroes, *The Spectre* was one of the last reborn. After three outstanding Gardner Fox/Murphy Anderson issues of *Showcase*, however, he was awarded his own book in November 1967. The title did not sell, however, and it lasted only ten issues, through June 1969. True to form, the ghost did not die and was revived again in *Adventure*, beginning in January 1974, issue number 431. He later came back in his own title in 1987 to 1989; a third ongoing series started in December 1992.

J.B.

SPEED TARŌ (Japan) *Speed Tarō* was created by Sakō Shishido in late 1930 for the Yomiuri Sunday Manga, then passed to the Yamiuri-Shōnen Shinbun in May 1931 before being discontinued in early 1933.

Speed Tarō was a google-eyed Japanese boy with slanted eyebrows and an indomitable spirit. One day as he was driving in his favorite car, he came upon a gold-smuggling plot but was captured by the criminals. They were nationals of a foreign country, the fictitious Dorumania, and Tarō was secreted away to their country. There Tarō escaped and took an active part in the ensuing fight between Dorumania and its arch-rival Kurokodaya, in a plot thick with suspense, thrills, and unpredictable twists.

Sakō Shishido had studied art in the United States for about nine years (while working at the same time) before starting his career in comic strips in Japan. He had carefully studied and mastered the techniques of the great American comic strip artists and his strip, *Speed Tarō*, was like a breath of fresh air for Japanese children used to traditional plots and storytelling; Shishido used modern storytelling devices (framing, composition, space manipulation) and his trip ushered in the new age of Japanese comics.

H.K.

SPIDER-MAN (U.S.) *Spider-Man* was created by writer and editor Stan Lee and artist Steve Ditko and made his first appearance in Marvel's *Amazing Fantasy* number 15 in August 1962. Known alternately as the web slinger and your friendly neighborhood Spider-Man, the character is the embodiment of the comic book antihero and the best-known comic creation of the 1960s. By March 1963, the feature was appearing in its own title, and *Spider-Man* has been the strip Marvel has most often utilized in new formats and commercial ventures. *Spider-Man* symbolizes the Marvel philosophy of superhero comics: a super-powered individual, beset with personal problems and hang-ups, battles for truth, justice, and the American way, often questioning himself and what he is fighting to uphold.

As originally conceived by Lee and Ditko, Spider-Man (and alter ego Peter Parker) was just another hung-up high school student who happened to be bitten by a radioactive spider. And although the spider endowed Parker with superhuman abilities, it did not straighten out his personal drawbacks. Over the years, Spider-Man has been through a horde of lovers; has a cloying Aunt May who's had an infinite number of heart attacks; has been sought by police and J. Jonah Jameson, a newspaper publisher who, for some unexplained reason, hates Spider-Man; has grown six arms and later lost them; and even had a junkie friend whose father was his deadly enemy, the Green Goblin. Lee's scripts, loaded with action and inventive villains as well as pathos, were instant hits among teenaged readers. *Spider-Man* eventually became a symbol of the uncertainties of the youths of the 1960s.

The artistic contribution of Steve Ditko is hard to overestimate. His grotesque-looking characters, sharp layouts, and fast pacing made him a perfect illustrator for the strip. His superior renditions catapulted Ditko to prominence and many other achievements, but many consider his *Spider-Man* work the best of his long career. Ditko left the strip in the spring of 1966 and the assignment was given to John Romita. His version was much slicker and cleaner; he once said that Lee was never happy with his handsome version of Peter Parker and he drew the strip while it was at the height of his popularity.

Lee and Romita both left the strip early in the 1970s. Promoted to publisher in 1971, Lee handed the scripting chores to Roy Thomas and later to Gerry Conway. By 1970, Romita was assuming responsibility for Marvel's art direction and drew fewer and fewer *Spider-Man* stories. By late 1972, he was all but completely replaced by Gil Kane, Ross Andru, and others. Although the feature continued to sell well, much of the Lee-Ditko-Romita magic had disappeared.

As Marvel's premiere creation, *Spider-Man* has appeared in many other media. A record of *Spider-Man* adventures was released in 1973, and over the years, paperback books, posters, dolls, cartoons, and toys were also marketed.

Among the many artists who have worked on *Spider-Man* from the mid-1970s on, mention should be made of John Byrne, Steve Austin, Todd McFarlane, and Erik Larsen; while writers have included Roger Stern and Peter David. The character has also give birth to a number of spin-offs (*Spider-Man Adventures*, *Spider-Man Magazine*, *Spider-Man 2099*, even *Spider-Woman*).

"Spider-Man," Jim Mooney, John Romita. © Marvel Comics.

In addition the Register and Tribune Syndicate started distribution of the *Amazing Spider-Man* newspaper strip in 1977.

J.B.

SPIEGELMAN, ARTHUR (1948-   ) American cartoonist Arthur ("Art") Spiegelman, the son of two survivors from the Auschwitz concentration camp, was born in Stockholm, Sweden, on February 15, 1948, and immigrated with his parents to the United States in his early childhood. He studied cartooning in high school and became a professional at age 16, drawing illustrations and cartoons for the *Long Island Post.* Despite the opposition of his parents (who wanted him to become a dentist) he opted for an artistic career and majored in art and philosophy at Harpur College.

After he left college in 1968, he decided to join the burgeoning underground "comix" movement. Over the next decade he became a regular contributor to a number of underground publications, including *Young Lust, Real Pulp, Bizarre Sex,* and *Sleazy Scandals of the Silver Screen,* with such creations as "Ace Hole, Midget Detective," "Nervous Rex," and "Cracking Jokes" under a variety of pseudonyms ("Joe Cutrate," "Skeeter Grant," and "Al Flooglebuckle"). At the same time he drew bubblegum cards for Topps and cartoons for *Playboy.*

In parallel with his cartooning career Spiegelman edited several underground comic magazines: *Arcade* (with Bill Griffith) and, starting in 1980, *Raw,* with his wife Françoise Mouly. In the pages of *Raw* he published not only his works and those of other under-ground cartoonists (Charles Burns, Gary Panter, Justin Green, and others) but also helped reveal to his comics-loving audience important talents from foreign shores (e.g., Ever Meulen from Belgium, Jacques Tardi of France, Joost Swarte from Holland, and Argentina's José Muñoz, among others).

Spiegelman's career really took flight with the publication of *Maus.* It originated in 1972 in the comic book *Funny Aminals* (sic) in the form of a three-page allegory in animal guise; drawing upon the experiences of his parents as concentration-camp survivors, it was a harrowing tale of cruelty, with the Jews represented as mice and the Germans depicted as cats. He later expanded this premise into a full-blown graphic novel, which he drew from 1980 to 1986 with the Jews again presented as mice and the Germans now called "the Katzies" (a bit of funnybook facetiousness, which in this context should have been resisted at all costs). Published in book form in 1986 as *Maus: A Survivor's Tale* by Pantheon, the work earned its author fame and a grant from the Guggenheim Foundation to complete the tale with *Maus II: From Mauschwitz to the Catskills,* which came out in 1991, again to great acclaim.

Basking in his newfound celebrity status, Spiegelman has considerably reduced his comics output since that time, aside from an occasional book review in comic strip form. He has illustrated one obscure novel and drawn a number of covers for the *New Yorker* (where his wife happens to work as cover art editor). To an interviewer he confided that he was looking for

Art Spiegelman, self-portrait.

Dan Spiegle, "Hopalong Cassidy." © Mirror Syndicate.

a "story worth telling" on a par with *Maus*. It remains to be seen.

M.H.

SPIEGLE, DAN (1920-   ) Dan Spiegle is an American cartoonist born December 10, 1920, in Cosmopolis, Washington. When he was 10 his family moved to northern California. In his second year of high school he sent a sample comic strip to King Features, which politely turned it down: from this moment Spiegle vowed to become a cartoonist. After graduation and a series of small art jobs, he enlisted in the navy at the start of World War II (he spent most of the war designing plane insignias and drawing cartoons for the base newspaper).

Discharged in 1946, Spiegle enrolled at the Chouinard Art Institute of Los Angeles on the G.I. bill. During his last year at Chouinard (1949), he was introduced to movie actor Bill Boyd who was looking for an artist to draw a projected strip based on his Hopalong Cassidy interpretation. Spiegle got the job and *Hopalong Cassidy* started appearing the same year, distributed by the Los Angeles Mirror Syndicate. *Cassidy* was sold to King Features in 1951, and Spiegle continued to draw the strip until its demise in 1955. He then tried his hand at a pirate strip, *Penn and Chris*, but it was rejected by all major newspaper syndicates (only in 1972 did it see the light of print in a small fanzine).

Spiegle then shifted to comic book work, and in 1956 he started his long collaboration with Dell Publications, working on a variety of comic book titles from *Maverick* (Spiegle's own favorite) to *Space Family Robinson* and *Magnus, Robot Fighter*. When Russ Manning left Dell to draw the *Tarzan* newspaper strip in 1967, Spiegle took over *Korak*. He has also done the comic

book versions of a number of Walt Disney movies and contributed many illustrations to *Mystery Comics Digest*. His credits in the 1980s and 1990s have included *Indiana Jones* for *Dark Horse*, *Crossfire* for *Eclipse*, and a number of Disney adaptations (*Pocahontas*, *Roger Rabbit*, etc.)

Dan Spiegle is a solid craftsman, unexciting but enjoyable, and his work displays an understated but obvious sense of fun.

M.H.

SPIRIT, THE (U.S.) Will Eisner created *The Spirit* on June 2, 1940, as a weekly seven-page feature, part of a comic book-sized Sunday supplement carried in the comic section of a score of American newspapers. *The Spirit*'s historical importance (as distinct from its artistic excellence) lies in its bridging of the gap between the comic book and the newspaper strip: the feature was distributed by the Register and Tribune Syndicate which also ran a *Spirit* strip in daily newspapers for about two years, from October 1941 to February 1944.

Eisner drew and wrote the feature from its inception till 1942 when he was called into service. During his four-year absence his work was carried on by Lou Fine and others. In 1946 Eisner took the strip back and was to draw it until 1950, when he decided to go into business for himself. *The Spirit*, now drawn by Wallace Wood, lingered a while longer before finally bowing out on September 28, 1952.

The Spirit covered the identity of Denny Colt, a criminologist whom everyone thought dead, and who used his disguise (a simple eye mask!) to fight crime from his hideaway in Wildwood Cemetery. At first he was not that distinguishable from the hordes of other hooded crime-fighters who were cluttering the comic pages. What made the Spirit unique was the depth of characterization and the sense of human involvement that Eisner was able to bring to his hero.

The Spirit's acolytes were more conventional: the harassed hapless Commissioner Dolan; his lovely blonde daughter Ellen, enamored (naturally!) of the hero; and Ebony White, the Spirit's sidekick, character-

"The Spirit," Will Eisner. © Will Eisner.

"Spirou," Jijé (Joseph Gillain). © Editions Dupuis.

ized midway between pathos and stereotype. On the other hand Eisner succeeded in delineating his auxilary characters, whether they be dyed-in-the-wool villains, slinky femmes fatales, or uncomprehending bystanders, with a sure hand and deft sense of humor, and graced them with Dickensian names such as Mortimer J. Titmouse, Humid S. Millibar, Carboy T. Gretch, Wisp O'Smoke, Sparrow Fallon, Plaster of Paris, and Autumn Mews.

The setting of the strip was Central City (in actuality New York), disquieting, squalid, but majestic in its formidable presence and its towering aloofness. In its seven-page narrative each Spirit episode constituted a self-contained short story, but the weekly unfolding of the tales revealed a peculiar rhythm, a cadence evoking not so much the prose narrative as the prose poem (even down to the suggestion of blank verse in the text). In this aspect The Spirit probably has few counterparts in comic history.

The Spirit was often reprinted in comic book form (in Police Comics in the 1940s, in its own book published by Quality Comics in the 1950s and by Harvey in the 1960s.) Since the late 1970s Kitchen Sink Press has been reprinting the old Spirit episodes with an occasional new story.

M.H.

SPIROU (Belgium) Spirou, created by the Frenchman Robert Velter (signing "Rob-Vel"), appeared in the first issue (April 21, 1938) of the comic weekly that bears its name.

Spirou was a bellboy at the Moustic Hotel and his adventures were not very remarkable at first. In 1939 he acquired an animal companion, Snip the squirrel, and together they underwent a series of adventures that took them all around the world. (Rob Vel was obviously trying to imitate the formula that had contributed to the success of Hergé's Tintin.) No less obviously the strip was floundering, and it temporarily disappeared in 1943 when the Germans banned the publication of Spirou magazine.

Spirou reappeared, along with the magazine, in October 1944, shortly after Belgium's liberation, under the signature of "Jijé" (Joseph Gullain). Jijé gave the strip a better visual organization and the benefit of his undeniable graphic qualities. He also provided Spirou with a sidekick, Fantasio, whose easygoing nature and levity were a welcome relief from the hero's earnestness.

But it was André Franquin who was to develop Spirou into a major feature. Succeeding Jijé in 1946, Franquin launched Spirou into his most unforgettable adventures, and created a gallery of secondary characters second only to Hergé's. One should mention Zantafio, Fantasio's megalomaniacal cousin, the eccentric inventor Count of Champignac, and best of all, the marsupilami, the most likable, versatile and fanciful animal ever to grace the comic page since Segar's jeep.

In 1969 Spirou was taken over by Jean-Claude Fournier who unfortunately possesses neither Franquin's graphic virtuosity nor his unbridled imagination. In 1979 he was replaced by Nicolas Broca and Raoul Cauvin who, in turn, were succeeded by Yves Chaland the next year. Chaland gave the spunky little bellboy a new, retro look that lasted only one story. Tome and Janry took over the character in 1981 and have been able to conserve him to this day.

Spirou's popularity steadily grew after World War II. Most of the episodes were reprinted in book form by Dupuis. Spirou, however, never enjoyed the success of Tintin or Asterix, partly because of a lack of direction (the series always hovered between humor, fantasy, and adventure without settling on any one theme), and partly because of the different (and sometimes incompatible) authors who worked on the strip.

M.H.

SPOOKY (U.S.) Bill Holman's Spooky, as a cat, appeared in the first Sunday Smokey Stover episode (called "Smokey") of March 10, 1935; Spooky, as a strip, first opened on April 7, 1935, as a four-panel gag row at the bottom of a Smokey full page, later becoming the half-page it remained for years on May 12, 1935. Spooky was a shaggy, shabby, black cat with white paws, whose red-bandaged tail was her trademark. (Her sex was established early, on May 12, 1935, when she presented a dismayed housewife with a brood of eight kittens.) Unlike Al Smith's equally female Cicero's Cat, Spooky never developed human-

"Spooky," Bill Holman. © Chicago Tribune-New York News Syndicate.

ized characteristics although it is evident from time to time that she can read and understand human speech and remained from first to last a fantasized feline who began her career in Cash U. Nutt's fire house, and then became a roving vagabond for the purpose of Bill Holman's often surrealistic slapstick.

Basically, *Spooky* was designed and distributed as a Sunday filler strip, something which could be conveniently dropped for the inclusion of advertisements in the Sunday sections. It is unlikely that any paper, even the feature's home papers, the *New York Daily News* and the *Chicago Tribune*, whose combined syndication circulated the strip at its outset, printed more than two-thirds of the episodes drawn, and most papers printed even less, although *Smokey Stover* itself ran regularly everywhere. Early in 1945, *Spooky* was dropped as a half-page, and was added to the *Smokey Stover* third-page as, once again, a single row of panels, making a full Holman half-page for those papers wishing to run it as such. In this last form, *Spooky* ran for another ten years, finally disappearing from print in the mid-1950s. An amusing gag strip, *Spooky* was not collected in any separate books but was reprinted in several comic books of the 1940s and 1950s.

B.B.

SPRANG, RICHARD (1915-   ) While certainly not an artist of the first rank—only a good journeyman purveyor of comic book fare—Dick Sprang is among those fortunate cartoonists who have lived long enough to see fame suddenly come to them thanks to a revived comic book market and the irresistible pull of nostalgia. Born in Fremont, Ohio, in 1915, he started his artistic career at age 15, painting signs, billboards, and movie posters in his hometown. Upon graduation from high school in 1934, he went to work as staff artist for the *Toledo News-Bee* daily newspaper, a position he held for two years.

Coming to New York City in 1936, he became a freelance artist, mostly illustrating pulp-magazine stories for the major publishers of the day. This led him almost naturally to comic book work, starting in 1941, when he was assigned by the editors at DC Comics to illustrate a *Batman* script. From that time on there was no looking back: for the next 20-odd years Sprang was

to draw countless comic book pages for DC, occasionally working on some *Superman* titles, but mainly concentrating on *Batman*.

After he took over *Batman*, Sprang did not tamper with the Caped Crusader's original image. "I didn't change him any more than that," he later stated. "Shortened his ears a little bit, and so on." His compositions, however, displayed a greater dynamism, and the action was depicted with a greater deal of telling detail. It was his covers that made him really stand out: these were crowd-pleasers portraying Batman and some of his more colorful foes, such as the Joker, Catwoman, and the Penguin, in unexpected settings (often having nothing to do with the story inside). Since Sprang labored in utter anonymity, like most of his comic book colleagues at the time, his budding renown went unnoticed by him.

In 1963 he left the comic book field, seemingly for good, and pursued a career as a rancher, guide, and surveyor in the West (he had moved to Arizona as far back as 1946). A chance encounter in the mid-1970s led to his rediscovery as one of the early pioneers of the medium. Soon he was making appearances at comics conventions and in 1987 was asked again to draw illustrations and covers for some of the *Batman* titles. Now in his eighties he is busier than ever turning out painted re-creations of his classic covers and limited-edition lithographs for the fan market, thereby illustrating the adage that everything old is new again.

M.H.

SPRINGER, FRANK (1929-   ) An American cartoonist born in New York City on December 6, 1929, Frank Springer is a master of realistic cartoon technique. After earning an art degree from Syracuse University in 1952, Springer served a tour in the U.S. Army. From 1955 to 1960 he served as George Wunder's assistant on *Terry and the Pirates*. He was also an assistant and influenced by the styles of Stan Drake on *The Heart of Juliet Jones* and Leonard Starr on the story strip *On Stage*.

Basically a freelance cartoonist, Springer has drawn a wide variety of adventure and action comic books for Dell, DC, and Marvel. He drew both sports and editorial cartoons for the *New York Daily News*. He worked on *Space Ghost*, a Hanna-Barbera Saturday morning animated television show. In 1979 he took over drawing Field Syndicate's *Rex Morgan, M.D.* for awhile bringing some of the most interesting artwork ever to that story strip begun in 1948. He collaborated with Marvel's Stan Lee and drew the syndicated soap opera strip *Virtue of Vera Valiant* for its year of existence. Springer, who has been president of the National Cartoonists Society, currently draws *The Adventures of Hedley Kase* for *Sports Illustrated for Kids*.

However, his most lasting fame is not from his excellent work in comic books, which were often unsigned, or comic strips, which he was usually ghosting for others, but for *The Adventures of Phoebe Zeit-Geist*. Influenced by the success in Europe of sexy cartoon albums, New York City's Grove Press not only published the American version of Jean-Claude Forest's *Barbarella* and Guy Pellaert's *Jodelle* in 1966, but launched its own sexy Perils of Pauline-style strip that year, *The Adventures of Phoebe Zeit-Geist*, which was serialized in its periodical *The Evergreen Review*.

Written by Michael O'Donoghue and drawn by Frank Springer, *The Adventures of Phoebe Zeit-Geist* in their entirety were published as a book by Grove Press in 1968. While sexy cartoon albums were not a novelty in Europe, *Phoebe Zeit-Geist* was a sensation in the United States. Springer used his realistic style to delineate in detail the brunette twenty-something Phoebe's vain attempts to keep her clothes on and virtue in place. She was successful at neither.

Although generally unknown outside the military, Wally Wood was at the same time writing and drawing his *Sally Forth* for the tabloid *The Overseas Weekly*, marketed exclusively to U.S. military personnel. Both Phoebe and Sally owe their inspiration to the success of *Barbarella.* Of the two, Sally, given Wood's years of being a *MAD* magazine veteran, was funnier and lacked the pretensions of O'Donoghue's script. However, Frank Springer's *Phoebe Zeit-Geist* art shows what the result would be when a master of newspaper story strip art takes a walk on the wild side. His *Phoebe* artwork also brought him story strip work published in *Playboy* and *National Lampoon.*

As distinguished as Springer's career has been, his place in history as a cartoonist will forever be linked

with the often nude, bound, and spanked beauty Phoebe Zeit-Geist.

B.C.

SPY SMASHER (U.S.) Writer and editor Bill Parker and artists C. C. Beck and Pete Costanza created *Spy Smasher* in February 1940, and it first appeared in Fawcett's *Whiz* number 1. In reality rich playboy Alan Armstrong, Spy Smasher was a creature of the recently declared World War II. He was an undying patriot, an accomplished aviator, and, most importantly, a crusader. A larger-than-life Spy Smasher appeared on the cover of *Spy Smasher* number 2 proclaiming Death to Spies in America!

Most of the strips were typical of the patriotic overkill being churned out during the 1940s. Spy Smasher's sole desire was to search out and destroy the enemies of America. Fifth columnists and traitors were his prime targets. Strangely enough, the best stories in the series came when the character turned against the country and took on Captain Marvel. Brainwashed into hating America, Spy Smasher went on a rampage, kill-

Frank Springer and Michael O'Donoghue, "The Adventures of Phoebe Zeit-Geist." © the authors.

"Spy Smasher," Ken Bald. © Fawcett Publications.

ing, maiming, and destroying, all in an attempt to overthrow the country he once loved. He was eventually defeated by Captain Marvel, but the battle lasted four monumental issues (*Whiz* numbers 15 through 18). Spy Smasher was later pardoned for his crimes and sent back into the battle to protect America. Even though these stories took place in 1941, before the United States was officially involved in the war effort, it was novel to see an American hero allowed to turn traitor even temporarily, and even when brainwashed.

The artwork, while consistent, was never outstanding. The only other art of consequence besides creator Beck's was the work of Charles Sultan during 1941 and 1942. In fact, the most interesting artistic feature of *Spy Smasher* was his constant updating of uniform. Over the years he went from a World War I flying suit to a typical set of superhero's togs.

Spy Smasher ran into great trouble after the war years, however. A strip steeped in flag-waving patriotism during a time of crisis, the story line was lost without a foreign enemy to fight. After a brief attempt to rechristen the strip *Crime Smasher* and have the hero battle everyday criminals, the feature was dropped after its March 1953 appearance in *Whiz* number 83.

At the height of his popularity, however, *Spy Smasher* was an important member of the Fawcett stable. From 1941 to February 1943 he even had his own comic, *Spy Smasher*, which lasted 11 issues. Kane Richmond starred as Spy Smasher in a 1942 motion picture serial released by Republic Features.

J.B.

STANLEY, JOHN (1914-1993) American comic book writer and artist John Stanley was born March 22,

1914, in the Harlem district of New York City. Throughout his career, Stanley was a very private person and remained reluctant to discuss his past. As a result, information about him is sketchy and much of what comic book historians have written about him has since proven inaccurate. It is known, however, that Stanley attended two art schools, one of them the Art Students League, and that he began his career with various freelance cartooning jobs in New York, including selling several gag ideas to the *New Yorker* magazine.

In 1945, Stanley helped launch Western Publishing Company's *Little Lulu* comic, a feature with which he was affiliated for 14 years. Stanley wrote virtually all of the *Little Lulu* stories, drawing his scripts up in storyboard form. The penciled art for the comics, handled by others, was based on Stanley's layouts, a practice not uncommon in animation-type comic books. He usually did finished art, penciled and inked, for covers. Stanley's *Little Lulu* stories are fondly remembered for their simplicity and humor. Often, the simplest childhood problem would mushroom into a crisis of chaotic proportions. Stanley produced an incredible variety of stories featuring Lulu and the neighborhood youngsters.

While writing *Lulu*, Stanley also did stories and some art for a number of other Western publications including a regular feature, *Peterkin Pottle*, which ran in *Raggedy Ann* comics during the late 1940s. He kept no records of this work, which ranged from humor to adventure, and his fans have had a difficult time determining any further information.

In 1962 Western Publishing Company severed its affiliation with the Dell company and continued its books under the Gold Key logo. Stanley went with the newly formed Dell company and did stories and art for a variety of new comics including *Thirteen*, a teen comic, and *Melvin Monster* (1965-1966). He worked intermittently for Dell, also accepting some work doing storyboards for television cartoons. When the new Dell company cut back its titles and relied heavily on reprints, Stanley did some work for the Gold Key company: the first (and only) issue of *Choo Choo Charlie* (1969) and the first issue of *O.G. Whiz* (1971), a book about the exploits of a young boy who became president of a toy company.

O.G. Whiz was Stanley's last known work in comics. In subsequent years, he worked at a company that manufactures plastic rulers as head of the silk-screening department. He died from cancer on November 11, 1993.

M.E.

STARMAN (U.S.) *Starman* was created by writer Gardner Fox and artist Jack Burnley and first appeared in National's April 1941 issue of *Adventure Comics* (number 61). In reality playboy Ted Knight, Starman received his great powers from a magnetic wand that harnessed, as Fox put it in the original tale, the mysterious powers of the stars. Starman's costume was rather pedestrian: red and green tights. The costume's only variation was an odd cowl which covered only the back of his head.

Fox's scripts, though constantly competent and fast-paced, were never as original as many of his other efforts. In fact, *Starman* came across as just another superhero strip. His magic wand, which gave him the ability to fly, was never innovatively used.

On the other hand, artist Jack Burnley was one of the best artists in the National stable. Heavily influenced by Alex Raymond's work on *Flash Gordon*, Burnley's work was always smooth and refined. His draftsmanship was always excellent and his anatomy clean. While the astral avenger was never one of National's big heroes, he was always well-drawn. After Burnley departed to illustrate *Superman*, Mort Meskin (1942), Paul Reinman (1943), George Roussos (1942-1943), and others took his place.

A member of the Justice Society of America, *Starman* appeared in *All-Star Comics* from December 1941 through Winter 1945 and lasted in his solo feature through March 1946's *Adventure Comics* number 102.

When National authored a general revival of 1940s superheroes in the middle-1960s, *Starman* was exhumed and appeared in two issues of *Showcase* along with the *Black Canary*. It was revived twice again: in 1988 to 1992, and then in 1994 in a series that is still ongoing.

J.B.

STARR, LEONARD (1925-   ) An American artist born in Manhattan on October 28, 1925, Starr attended the High School of Music and Art and during World War II took courses at Pratt Institute. After the war Starr entered the comic book field, going to work for Fawcett and other publishers. Among his titles were *Human Torch*, *Sub-Mariner*, and *Don Winslow*; he rose from background work to inking and complete production.

Without the benefit of full training, the busy Starr grew proficient, fast, and slick but began to see deficiencies in his work that others may not have seen. He began studying with Frank Reilly at nights and concentrated on advertising work, with (inevitably) Johnstone and Cushing and other agencies. All the while he submitted story strip ideas to syndicates. In 1956 one of many was accepted and *On Stage* debuted in February of the following year, distributed by the Chicago Tribune-New York News Syndicate.

Contrary to publicity releases, Starr displayed no abnormal love of the theater while growing up. His preoccupation was art, and the work of his idols, Raymond and Caniff, is very clearly seen in his work. Starr's art is perhaps the most attractive and compelling of today's story strips. Tackiness and conformity are absent while a visual verve and mature story line consistently command attention. Starr has agonized no less than any of his fellows over the newsprint crunch and the decline of the story strip. Answering the first challenge, he has reluctantly resorted to street-scene wide angles and figure close-ups. And, in answer to the contemporary war against story strips, he experimented with humorous continuities for a period in the early 1970s.

Starr has won the Best Story Strip award from the National Cartoonists Society as well as its Reuben (1965). He has also served as vice president of the NCS. His work remains premier in his field and his integrity has never faltered.

Starr abandoned *On Stage* in 1979 to write and draw the revived *Annie* strip, to which he has given a more contemporary tone and a more visually appealing look. In 1980, in collaboration with Stan Drake, he developed the short-lived *Kelly Green* series of graphic albums; and in 1984 he acted as story and head writer of the *Thundercats* animated television show.

R.M.

STAR SPANGLED KID (U.S.) In the golden age of comic books during the 1940s, script writing was formularized, and one of the unbreakable rules of the business stated that the costumed hero was an adult and the sidekick was a teenager. Batman had the teen-aged Robin, Captain America had young Bucky, Toro rode the heated coattails of the Human Torch, and so on. About the only strip to break away from tradition was the *Star Spangled Kid* feature which premiered in National's *Star Spangled Comics* number 1 in October 1941. Created by writer Jerry Siegel, who helped create *Superman* several years earlier, and artist Hal Sherman, the hero of the strip was the Star-Spangled Kid, who in reality, was teenaged heir Sylvester Pemberton. His assistant was Pat Dugan, an ex-pugilist who had considerable mechanical skills and great strength. Together brainy Sylvester and the dim-witted Pat set forth to stop the Nazis, which was a formula Siegel chose not to break.

The duo had a unique origin, however. Sylvester Pemberton, a rich heir who had brains and strength, and Pat Dugan attended a patriotic movie together and helped break up an attempted Nazi disturbance. They learned of impending Axis plans for other domestic upheavals, and each set out separately to make the flag come alive. The Star-Spangled Kid came up with a red, white, and blue uniform, star-spangled of course, and Stripesy (Pat Dugan) managed a red, white, and blue striped costume. Each then set out independently to help destroy the fifth column activists and were rivals early on before they decided to team up to fight the Nazi menace. Sylvester hired Pat as his chauffeur, and Pat responded by modifying the Pemberton limousine into a 1940's version of a James Bond car. It had a bubble top, wings, rockets, and even helicopter blades—ludicrous, but well-conceived for the gimmicky strips of the 1940s.

Writer Siegel also populated the early strip with several exciting, if admittedly outlandish, villains. Among them were Moonglow, a scientist who was bombarded with moon rays and had his mind warped and his head turned into a type of light bulb; the Needle, a skinny ex-circus performer who used a deadly needle gun; and Dr. Weerd, a Jekyll-Hyde-type villain.

Artistically, the strip was never particularly outstanding, even though cocreator Sherman's work between 1941 and 1944 was above average for the war years. He was eventually succeeded by illustrators like Joe Kubert (1943), Lou Cazeneuve (1944-1945), Win Mortimer (1948), and several others.

In all, the *Star Spangled Kid* appeared in the first 81 issues of *Star Spangled Comics* until November 1948. The characters also appeared in *Leading* 1 (Winter 1942) through 14 (Spring 1945) as members of the short-lived *Seven Soldiers of Victory*, and in *World's Finest* issues 6 (Summer 1942) through 18 (Summer 1945).

J.B.

STAR WARS (U.S.) John Lucas's immensely successful *Star Wars* movie trilogy was largely based on comics iconology in general (and on *Flash Gordon* in particular), so it is not surprising that the comics would in turn make the theme their own.

Shortly after the first film's release Marvel came out with a *Star Wars* comic book, which lasted from 1977 to 1986. The first issues followed closely the plot of the original film, as Luke Skywalker, Han Solo, Princess Leiah, and their small band of freedom-fighters battled the evil Empire and its chief henchman, the black-helmeted Darth Vader. This adaptation, excellently illustrated by Howard Chaykin, proved very popular with the readers. The stories, initially written by Roy Thomas and later by Archie Goodwin, soon started to stray off-base, only following Lucas's original concept when the next two films in the trilogy (*The Empire Strikes Back* and *The Return of the Jedi*) were released in the early 1980s. Among the many artists who worked on the series, mention should be made of John Byrne, Frank Miller, Bill Sienkiewicz, Walt Simonson, and Al Williamson.

In 1991 Dark Horse started publishing a new line of *Star Wars* comic books. Mostly released as limited series (with such titles as *Dark Empire, Empire's End,* etc.), with Tom Veitch as principal writer and Cam Kennedy as main artist, these have enjoyed a fair amount of success so far.

A *Star Wars* newspaper strip also saw the light of print, distributed from March 1979 to March 1984 by the Los Angeles Times Syndicate. It was initially scripted by Brian Daley (the author of a number of *Star Wars* novels) and illustrated by Russ Manning and later by Alfredo Alcala. The duo of Archie Goodwin and Al Williamson took over in 1981. (The Goodwin-Williamson strips were reprinted by Russ Cochran in 1991, and as trade paperbacks by Dark Horse in 1994-1995.)

M.H.

STEEL STERLING (U.S.) *Steel Sterling* was created in February 1940 by artist and writer Charles Biro and made his first appearance in MLJ's *Zip Comics* number 1. The red-and-blue clad Man of Steel was really John Sterling, an experimenter who plunged his body into a cauldron of molten metal. Somehow, that gave Sterling the powers of invulnerability and flight. Whenever he ran or flew, the word zip would trail off from his boots.

Biro, one of the great creators of the 1940s, populated *Steel Sterling* with a coterie of fine supporting characters. Although girlfriend Dora Cummings was a run-of-the-mill love interest, Clancy, a fat, red-headed cop, and Louie, a skinny dimwit, soon developed into the Laurel and Hardy team of comic books. Later in the series, the fire-breathing Inferno was added as Steel Sterling's assistant. His popularity was so great, however, he was given his own feature after three issues. Artistically, Biro was famous for his inventive, but straightforward storytelling techniques.

After Biro's departure in 1942, the strip faltered despite the best efforts of artist Irv Novick and writers Otto Binder (1942-1944) and Bob Kanigher (1942). Throughout his career, Sterling fought an array of stereotyped Axis villains, but the particularly ruthless Baron Gestapo was popular enough to rate several return battles.

Steel Sterling appeared in *Zip Comics* until the Summer 1944 issue (number 47), and also appeared in all nine *Jackpot* comics from Spring 1941 to Summer 1943. Along with the other MLJ characters, *Sterling* was revived briefly in 1965.

J.B.

STERANKO, JAMES (1938-) American comic book artist and writer, James Steranko was born November 5, 1938, in Reading, Pennsylvania. A self-taught artist, Steranko entered the comics industry in 1966 while moonlighting as an ad agency art director (1964-1968) and movie illustrator (1966-1968); his first three creations the *Spyman, Gladiator,* and *Magicman* adventure features for Harvey were short-lived failures.

Steranko then moved to Marvel in December, 1966 and began working on *Nick Fury, Agent of S.H.I.E.L.D.* with writer-editor Stan Lee and artist Jack Kirby. After several issues of uninspired inking, Steranko improved and soon took over not only the penciling and inking, but also the writing and coloring. *S.H.I.E.L.D.* was set in the present and starred Nick Fury who was concurrently appearing in a World War II Marvel comic as the leader of a paramilitary, supersecret organization. The early stories were routine spy fare, but Steranko took the series away from its James Bondish orientation.

James Steranko, "Tower of Shadows." © *Marvel Comics.*

Building from his earlier material, which showed heavy influences of the Jack Kirby dynamic style, he added touches of Eisner, Krigstein, and many others and developed his own unique cinematic techniques which made *S.H.I.E.L.D.* possibly the best written and drawn strip of the decade. His innovative and intricate layouts, pop art-inspired drawings, and crisp storytelling captured the comic book world and netted him three fan-issued Alley awards in 1968. He was certainly on his way to becoming one of comic books' greatest illustrators. But, after the feature moved from *Strange Tales* to its own book in June 1968, Steranko's time-consuming work forced him to miss deadlines. He was finally taken off the book after December 1968's seventh issue, and the book folded a year later.

While drawing *S.H.I.E.L.D.* and for a time after he was removed, Steranko also created several well-received stories for *Captain America, X-MEN,* and for the horror and romance titles. But he continually had problems meeting the comic book industry's often oppressive deadline schedule, and all but abandoned the field in 1969. He formed the Supergraphics Publishing Company, and, in recent years, has produced two volumes on the comic book's history, many comic-oriented products, and introduced a magazine about the comics industry, *Comixscene.* The magazine gutted most of its comics material in 1973 and changed its name to *Mediascene.* He divided much of his time to the publication of the magazine (later renamed *Preview*). His last comic book work was on *Nick Fury vs. SHIELD* (1988), but he has done a number of covers, notably for *Ray Bradbury Comics.* He also produced two graphic novels, the movie-inspired *Outland* and the thriller *Red Tide.*

J.B.

STERRETT, CLIFF (1883-1964) The gifted creator of *Polly and Her Pals,* Cliff Sterrett, was born December 12, 1883, in Fergus Falls, Minnesota, into a middle-class family which put him through 12 years of school at Fergus Falls and nearby Alexander. Aware of his artistic ability, Sterrett left home to attend Chase Arts School in New York at 18. After two years of intense study there, he landed his first job in 1904 on the *New York Herald,* where he did spot news illustrations, decorative borders for photographs, sketches of interviewed celebrities—in fact, anything but cartoons, which were all the young Sterrett wanted to do. From the *Herald,* however, he went to the *New York Times* in 1908; after two dull years drawing visiting kings for the *Times,* and a further stint on the *Rochester Democrat and Chronicle,* Sterrett finally had his big chance—a job doing not one but four daily comic strips on the *New York Evening Telegram* in early 1911.

Sterrett's earliest *Telegram* strip was called *Ventriloquial Vag,* but he quickly added and developed three more: *When a Man's Married, Before and After,* and *For This We Have Daughters?,* drawing all of them for simultaneous publication in the six-day-a-week *Telegram,* like a one-man comic strip syndicate. The latter strip, about an avidly courted college-age girl and her deeply middle-aged parents, became the most popular with readers of the *Telegram*'s syndicated comics across the country, and Hearst discerned a rising star in the young cartoonist, hiring him in late 1912 to work for his National News Syndicate.

Sterrett carried over the characters and concepts of *Daughters* into his new Hearst strip, first called *Positive Polly,* then a bit later *Polly and Her Pals,* which opened on the *New York Journal*'s daily comic page on December 4, 1912. A year later, Hearst felt Sterrett had earned a Sunday page, and put his *Polly* in the four-color supplement of the *New York American.*

Sterrett added a second, one-row strip at the top of his weekly page on June 21, 1926, featuring a dog and a cat team called *Damon and Pythias* (the title being changed to *Dot and Dash* on September 5, 1926). This feature was replaced on July 1, 1928, by a quarter-page strip called *Sweethearts and Wives* (which was a resumption of Sterrett's old daily strip *Before and After,* and which took a humorously pessimistic view of man and woman trapped into marriage), the title of which was changed to *Belles and Wedding Bells* on June 22, 1930.

Sterrett's own domestic life seems to have been almost ideally happy, and it is obvious that he liked his family since he was one of the first Hearst strip artists who was permitted to draw at home rather than in the cartoonists' offices at the publisher's New York papers. Enlarging on this privilege, he moved to Ogunquit, Maine, in the early 1920s, where he and his family developed their taste for music by learning innumerable musical instruments.

One of the few strip artists (another was Roy Crane) honest enough not to sign his work when, because of illness or other problems, he had to have it ghosted, Sterrett dropped his signature from the daily *Polly* strip when he decided to cut his workload in half in 1935 and assigned the daily feature to another artist (as he had done a bit earlier with the Sunday *Belles and Wedding Bells*). He continued to draw the Sunday *Polly* until his complete retirement in 1958. After his wife's death in 1948, Sterrett went to live with his wife's sister, Dorothy, until his own death on December 28, 1964. Held by some to be second only to George Herriman as a graphic innovator on the comic page, Sterrett is inarguably one of the most important strip artists of all time.

B.B.

STEVE CANYON (U.S.) Shortly after leaving *Terry and the Pirates,* Milton Caniff created *Steve Canyon* for Field Enterprises as a synchronized daily/Sunday feature on January 13, 1947. The strip appeared simultaneously in 125 newspapers throughout the United States, a rare feat for a beginning feature.

As Caniff himself described him in a *Time* interview in December 1946, Steve Canyon was to be a sort of modern Kit Carson, the strong silent Gary Cooper plainsman type. . . . He'll have lots of gals, one at every port. True to his creator's word Steve Canyon cut a dashing figure from his first appearance. A former air force captain, now head of a shaky airline company Horizons Unlimited, Steve accepts the most dangerous missions. In his adventures, which take him to the most remote corners of the earth, he comes up against an assorted string of ruffians, gun-runners, drug traffickers, international spies, Nazi fanatics, and Communist agents. Many of them turn out to be women, eternally dangerous, and eternally in love with the hero, such as Copper Calhoun, the she-wolf of Wall Street, Steve's most relentless adversary and pursuer.

With the outbreak of the Korean war, Steve reenlists in the air force and, as Colonel Stevenson B. Canyon, he is sent to the hottest spots of the Cold War: from Korea to Turkey to Greece to Formosa to the Middle East, and in more recent years, Vietnam.

"Steve Canyon," Milton Caniff. © Field Newspaper Syndicate.

Another bevy of female enemies lay in wait for him: the one-armed Madame Hook, Captain Akoola of Soviet intelligence, Queen Taja, and others. In-between war adventures, there are more peaceful interludes, the heroine of which often is Poteet Canyon, Steve's pert and high-spirited ward. In April 1970, however, Steve married his old flame Summer Olson, and the strip has been floundering on the shoals of soap-opera melodramatics ever since. Following the end of the Vietnam war, Steve was seen more and more often out of uniform and many of the episodes were devoted to his marital woes (he eventually separated from his wife). Caniff continued to write the scripts but left penciling in the hands of his assistant, Dick Rockwell, reserving the inking to himself. The strip regained some of his erstwhile luster in 1986 with an adventure set in China, a nostalgic journey involving Steve with Caniff's heroes from an earlier era: Terry, Pat, and Connie. *Steve Canyon* was discontinued in June 1988, following its creator's death in April of that year.

As an example of Caniff's art, *Steve Canyon* reached its apex during the early and middle 1950s. But as a body of work, *Steve Canyon* cannot compare with Caniff's earlier and more inspired *Terry* though it generated a great deal of excitement in the first ten years of its existence, when Caniff's powers were at their peak.

Steve Canyon had its own comic book version in the 1940s and 1950s published by Dell and drawn by Ray Bailey, and it was adapted to the television screen for one season in 1958 to 1959, with Dean Fredericks in the role of Steve Canyon.

M.H.

STEVE ROPER (U.S.) One of the earliest brainchildren of Harold Anderson and Eugene Conleys at Publishers Newspaper Syndicate in Chicago was delayed because of the release of another brainchild, the George Gallup survey. But in the interim, the other creation, *The Great Gusto*, was taken in sample form to editors around the country and garnered an impressive advance sale.

But editors liked the half-pint Indian chief medicine man better than the title character, an admitted derivative of W. C. Fields. So *The Great Gusto* never became a comic strip; instead, *Big Chief Wahoo* was introduced, finally, in late 1936.

Allen Saunders, a cartoonist and writer, was the author, and Elmer Woggon, a cartoonist, the artist who proposed the strip. Both had ill-fated features with United Feature Syndicate: Woggon's *Skylark* aviation strip and Saunders's *Miserable Moments*, a copy of Clare Briggs's *When a Feller Needs a Friend*.

The Great Gusto ran a medicine show (the time setting changed from the 1890s to contemporary days with the title change) and Wahoo was his stooge. Eventually Wahoo became wiser and Gusto was phased out (the team of creators had once gone to Hollywood to receive congratulations from the real Fields, who was a fan of the strip). And a pretty Indian maiden, Minnie-Ha-Cha, a onetime nightclub singer in New York, entered the strip as his sweetheart.

The growing popularity of story strips and Publishers Syndicate's constant and excellent polling system to determine client's tastes in comics both led to the demise of *Wahoo* as a gag-a-day strip.

Steve Roper was introduced as a handsome blond photographer for a major news magazine; he parachuted into the reservation. At once he assumed the hero role, much to the chief's anoyance, especially when Minnie-Ha-Cha fell for Roper. Thereafter Wahoo became Watson to Roper's Holmes.

Finally, in 1953, comic artist and versatile ghost Bill Overgard was engaged, and he turned the strip into today's sleek, sexy, very attractive product. He introduced Mike Nomad, based on a character he had tried to sell in a strip, and found a gutsy counterpoint to the new Roper's urbane reserve. Mike drives a circulation truck for Proof.

"Steve Roper," Bill Overgard. © Field Newspaper Syndicate.

"Stonehenge Kit," A. J. Kelly. © Fleetway Publications.

Other major characters in the present-day *Roper* include: Major McCoy, head of the magazine empire; Steve's secretary Honeydew Mellon, a blonde Southerner; Crandall Mellon, Honeydew's uncle and a private eye; Mike's parents, Polish immigrants named Nowak; and Ma Jong, over whose restaurant Mike lives.

Overgard's art is as slick and dramatic as Woggon's was neat and funny. The story line, which has concentrated in recent years on frauds and racketeering, is still written by Overgard, with help from his son, John, a TV newscaster who once scripted *Dateline: Danger*. Today *Steve Roper*, in both story and art, is one of the foremost straight strips in the anemic genre.

Overgard brought in the character of Mike Nomad, a tough private eye in the Mike Hammer mold, in the late 1970s, and the newcomer soon took over the strip, now renamed *Steve Roper and Mike Nomad*. When Allen Sauders retired in 1979, he left the feature in the hands of his son John. Overgard left in his turn in 1983 to create *Rudy*, and he was replaced by Fran Matera, an able if somewhat limited craftsman.

R.M.

STONEHENGE KIT THE ANCIENT BRIT (G.B.)
This stone-age saga began in a small way—a half-page strip in the first issue of *Knockout* (March 4, 1939) but it quickly caught on, perhaps because of its novelty as a comic serial, and expanded into a full page. It later moved to the two-tone back cover.

The hero, a simple, loincloth-clad clod with three hairs on his head, spent his strip defending King Kongo (Kingy for short) of Kongo Kourt from G. Whizz the Wizard (Whizzy the Wizard for short), aided by Glam,

his gal pal. Whizzy used all manner of wacky inventions in his mad plan to usurp Kingy's crown: his Kit Kosher, his Wind Whizzer, his Trap Tripper, his Flea Flicker, not to mention his mighty musclemen, Brit Basher Number One and Brit Basher Number Two (terribly tough twins only identifiable by their attached paper labels). There was also the local fauna to consider: the Coal Chewing Fire Gobbler, the Brontowotsit, and the Crockerdilligator.

Norman Ward created *Stonehenge Kit* and added a new twist in 1942 by making all his characters speak in rhyme. A. J. Kelly took over from Ward on May 18, 1942, and the series continued until May 1944. After three years' retirement, *Kit and Kompany* were brought back by Kelly, and the series, which began again on February 1, 1947, was perhaps their best. "The Search for the Stolen Crown" was followed by the "Quest of the Magic Applecore," the "Kourt of King Arfer," and the "Prehistoric Puff-Puff." Kelly's early death robbed the series of genius, but Hugh McNeill, and later Denis Gifford, continued the strip until November 25, 1950.

D.G.

STONY CRAIG OF THE MARINES (U.S.) Don Dickson's *Stony Craig of the Marines* (also known as *Sergeant Craig*) started its career in the pages of the *Boston Traveler* in August 1937.

Sergeant Stony Craig and his subordinates, the loud-mouthed Wise, the resourceful Fink, and the handsome Hazard, were U.S. Marines stationed in the American settlement in Shanghai. They seemed to be busier fighting the Japanese and their allies than protecting the American administrative headquarters. The similarities with Caniff's *Terry and the Pirates* are obvious (there is even a woman guerilla-fighter, half-Russian, half-Chinese, by the name of Tania). If anything, Dickson was even more emphatically anti-Japanese than Caniff, and he (correctly) foresaw the coming hostilities with Japan as early as 1939. To prepare for the day, Craig and his cohorts, in collusion with Intelligence Service officer Jeremy Blade (who looked like Clark Gable), did their best to harass the Japanese, blowing up their convoys, hijacking their arms shipments, and lending help to the guerillas. In between there were a few romantic interludes involving Hazard and his army nurse love, the blonde and demure Helen.

In 1940 (following the closing of all foreign settlements in China by the Japanese authorities) Craig and company returned to the United States to combat spies and fifth columnists until 1942 when the author left to join the marines. (With *Stony Craig* Don Dickson seemed to have found his métier in more ways than one; he later became the official artist of the Marine Corps and had his combat drawings published in *Life*, the *Saturday Evening Post* and *Collier's*, while his paintings were exhibited at the National Gallery in Washington.) The strip was continued for a while by Gerry Bouchard.

Obscure as it is, *Stony Craig* was an excellent (and prescient) action strip, well-plotted, straight-forwardedly written and drawn in a loose, punchy, and winning style. In a time when story strips are suffering from terminal anemia, it reminds us of how vital and robust the genre once was, before syndicate taboos and strictures started whittling it down.

M.H.

STRANGE WORLD OF MR. MUM, THE (U.S.) Irving Phillips's *The Strange World of Mr. Mum* started its career (as a daily panel, and later as a full-fledged comic strip) on May 5, 1958, for Publishers Syndicate.

Strange indeed is Mr. Mum's world. Browsers sprout wings on their heels to reach the upper shelves of libraries, Rodin's thinker takes time out for calisthenics, Oriental bazaar merchants hold discount sales on magic carpets, visitors from outer space have their spaceship refueled at the neighborhood gas station. Mr. Mum, small, bespectacled, and bald-headed, observes all these (and more) in bemused silence. (Neither does Phillips's protagonist intervene in the weird goings-on he is constantly witnessing—perhaps he is meant to symbolize the helplessness of the individual in a world of uncontrollable forces.)

Of course Phillips's trick consists in his abolishing (or suspending) the laws of time and space (in this he carries Virgil Patch's experiments one step further). We follow Mr. Mum into a fourth-dimensional world where the extraordinary is the commonplace and the exception becomes the norm.

Although often intellectual and sometimes esoteric, *Mr. Mum* is also one of the funniest inventions of the last two decades. It has been reprinted many times in paperback form, but was discontinued in 1974.

M.H.

STRIEBEL, JOHN H. (1891-1967) The noted cartoonist whose artwork on *Dixie Dugan* has been followed by tens of millions of readers for more than 40 years, John H. Striebel, was born on September 14, 1891, in Bertrand, Michigan, and moved a few years later to South Bend, Indiana, where he attended school and obtained his first cartooning job as the front-page political artist for the *South Bend News* at age 14 (within the same week he had been fired as a newsboy by the *News* circulation manager). After attending Notre Dame for two years, Striebel moved on to Chicago, where he illustrated current fashions for the Meyer-Both Syndicate, then transferred his clothing talents to the Marshall Field Department Store, where he drew "Fashions of the Hour" for their advertising purposes. He also found a steady job, after some freelancing, with the *Chicago Tribune* art staff, where he illustrated current fiction in the *Tribune* weekly magazine section and drew the spot art for the new *Potters* weekly narrative feature by an old crony from the *South Bend News*, J. P. McEvoy. His drawing of McEvoy's chief characters, Ma and Pa Potter, and their daughter, Mamie, favorably impressed McEvoy and Striebel was asked to design the jacket for the 1923 book edition of the hit play McEvoy based on *The Potters*.

A few years later, after Striebel had introduced his daily anecdote feature, *Pantomime* (a paneled gag without recurrent characters or balloons, usually involving a child or animal), which ran through most of the 1920s, he was asked to illustrate a comic strip McEvoy planned to base on the heroine of his 1929 novel, *Show Girl*. The heroine, Dixie Dugan, like Mamie in *The Potters*, had parents called Ma and Pa, and McEvoy wanted them drawn just as Striebel had done the *Potter* characters. Striebel obliged, and the strip, called *Show Girl*, was launched in 1929. Slow in getting under way, it took off in the early 1930s. Its name changed to *Dixie Dugan*, the strip ultimately became one of the country's most widely read comic strips.

Also collaborating with McEvoy in illustrating *Show Girl* as a serial story for *Liberty* in 1929 (as well as its two sequels), Striebel continued to work on *Dixie Dugan* until the mid-1940s when McEvoy stepped off the strip and turned the scripting over to his son, Renny.

Following his hobbies of croquet, painting, and playing the violin, Striebel lived in Bearsville, New York, with his wife, Fritzi, and four daughters, until his death in 1967.

B.B.

STUPS (Germany) *Stups*, a creation of German comic artist Max A. Otto, was published in the newspaper *Grüne Post* from 1928 to 1929. The stories, trying to be on the safe side, used both verse below the pictures and speech balloons, speed lines, and other usual comic strip conventions. The strip holds up well even today and is proof of the much-neglected fact that a German comic production existed between the two world wars. Strangely enough, these strips rarely had the success they could have or should have had (with a few exceptions like *Vater und Sohn*), or were lost because of the paper drives of World War II.

Some of these strips were carried over into postwar years but, of course, with no mention of connections to an earlier era which everyone wanted to forget. Thus, Max Otto had another strip, titled *Stips*, in the postwar *Grünes Blatt*. In the 1950s he also drew *Jippi der Indianerboy* ("Yippi the Indian Boy"), a comic strip that for quite a while was included in *Pete*, a weekly dime novel series in a Western setting aimed at younger readers. In 1954 *Das Jippi-Buch* ("The Yippi Book") was published, featuring 48 pages of text and 46 pages of *Jippi* reprints.

"Stups," Max Otto. © Max Otto.

Neighboring Austria had seen an even longer running strip, *Tobias Seicherl*, drawn and written in Austrian dialect by Ludwig Kmoch and published in *Das kleine Blatt*. Originally opposed to fascism, the strip displayed nationalistic tendencies by the end of the 1930s. Nevertheless the strip disappeared just as all of the children's magazines (a number of them produced in Austria and distributed in Germany's department stores) disappeared by 1940. Most of these children's magazines were giveaways either for certain chains of department stores or for products like margarine. While filled with lots of text features, there were also a number of genuine comic strips in magazines like *Rama Post*, *Pa pa gei*, *Kiebitz*, or *Teddy Bär*. Some of them even featured reprints of foreign comic strips like *Prinz Waldemar* ("Prince Valiant") as late as 1939.

Stups may serve as a reminder that it will take a great deal of research to find the missing links of comics history in Germany.

W.F.

STURMTRUPPEN (Italy) In 1968 the Roman newspaper *Paese Sera* sponsored a contest aimed at finding an original Italian daily strip. Franco Bonvicini (who signs his work simply as "Bonvi") won the contest with his comic creation *Sturmtruppen*.

Sturmtruppen was not the first Italian daily strip. One earlier effort was Marco Biassoni's *Prode Anselmo* ("Anselmo the Bold"), published in the newspaper *Il Giorno*; a whole batch of experimental features had also been sponsored by the Corriere Mercantile of Genoa, but none of those ever survived for more than a few months. While many Italian comics were very successful in the form of comic books or in weekly comic magazines, up to this time none of them had ever made it in a big way in the newspaper page. *Sturmtruppen*'s greatest merit lies in its success as a trailblazer; it was followed by a host of others (*Zio Boris*, *Gli Aristocratici*, *Santincielo*, *Et Voila*, *Olimpiastri*, *Pasquino*, *Animalie*, to name but a few). However, *Sturmtruppen* was the first and, in many ways, the most successful one.

The strip, featuring a cast of weird-acting German storm troopers (including a werewolf, a vampire, and several cannibals), takes place in an hallucinatory setting in the middle of World War II. It is replete with dumb Nazi officers and hapless soldiers bedeviled by race theories and blind obedience to their superiors. Of those none is more dumbfounded than Private Schultze on whose head are constantly heaped torrents of abuse and contradictory orders. *Sturmtruppen* not only satirizes militarism and the military mind like Jaroslev Hasek's *Good Soldier Svejk*, it is also a bitter, often sick, black comedy that indicts the whole human race.

Sturmtruppen has been reprinted in book form and was adapted to television by its author. In 1975 Bonvi abandoned the strip because he had grown tired of it (and he refused to have it ghosted), but a revival occurred in 1976. The feature ended for good with Bonvi's death in 1995.

G.B.

SUB-MARINER, THE (U.S.) Created by Bill Everett in November 1939, *The Sub-Mariner* made its premiere appearance in Timely's *Marvel Comics* (later *Marvel Mystery*) number 1. The son of an American naval officer and Princess Fen of Atlantis, Prince Namor was perpetually angry at the human race. One of the first popular antiheroes, the character was awarded his own book in the Spring of 1941, and he also made appearances in *Human Torch*, *All Winners*, and a half-dozen other books.

He was against mankind, which culminated in several classic battles with the Human Torch in the *Marvel Mystery* and *Human Torch* books, which ended during the World War II years. He suddenly became a protector of America and made the seas a dangerous place for Axis aquatic travel. He even developed a love interest, Betty Dean, one of the few humans who

"Sturmtruppen," Bonvi (Franco Bonvicini). © Bonvicini.

"Sub-Mariner," Bill Everett. © Marvel Comics Group.

could reason with the wing-footed hybrid. She was later replaced by Namora, another undersea inhabitant. Prince Namor's phenomenal powers enabled him to fly and consult fish, and and he was equally effective on land and in water. This made him one of the most popular heroes of the 1940s.

Like the other stars of the golden age, however, the Sub-Mariner began floundering after the war. Never resuming his battle against humans, he took to fighting crooks and by 1949 was making his last appearances in *Marvel Mystery* (91, April) and *Sub-Mariner* (32, June). When Atlas began reviving superheroes in 1953, Namor was the most successful of the ill-fated trio of *Captain America, Human Torch,* and *Sub-Mariner.* Making his first reappearance in *Young Men* December 1953, number 24, he also appeared in several issues of *Human Torch* and *Men's Adventure. Sub-Mariner* was also revived, lasting from April 1954 (issue number 33) to October 1955 (issue number 42). When Marvel (formerly Timely and Atlas) reentered the superhero field in 1960, Namor was the first to be revived.

Making his re-reappearance in *Fantastic Four* number four, May 1962, the Sub-Mariner was once again cast as the enemy of society. Marvel returned him to his own feature in August 1965 in *Tales to Astonish* number 70, and he lasted in that book until it folded after April 1968 (issue number 101). The next month a new series of *Sub-Mariner* comics began with issue number 1, and that book lasted through September 1974 (issue number 72). During all these years, however, the Prince could never quite decide who or what he was

fighting for. He was comicdom's foremost schizophrenic.

The definitive artist on *Sub-Mariner* was the creator, Bill Everett. Handling the strip on-and-off between 1939 and 1973, his stylized artwork was always superior to other artists' interpretations. Everett always drew Namor with a triangular head and pointed eyebrows, and they became the character's trademark. Gene Colan, Marie Severin, Vince Coletta, Sal Buscema, and others have handled the strip over the years. Writers like Roy Thomas, Stan Lee, Otto Binder, Everett himself, and even novelist Mickey Spillane have all worked on Namor.

And although he now appears solely as a supporting character, the *Sub-Mariner* has had a long and illustrious career and will probably survive as long as superheroes do. Indeed the man from Atlantis has made his reappearance time and again in his own comic book: in 1984, from 1988 to 1989, and from 1990 to 1995.

J.B.

SUBURBAN COWGIRLS (U.S.) *Suburban Cowgirls* began Thanksgiving Day, 1987, in the newspapers of MPG Newspapers of Plymouth, Massachusetts. By the fall of 1989, after a number of syndicates looked at it, the strip's creators, Ed Colley, who draws, and Janet Alfieri, who writes, were offered a contract by Tribune Media Services. *Suburban Cowgirls* began international syndication October 1, 1990.

The lead characters in the strip are Maxine "Max" Marshall, a thirty-something single mother of two; Angelique, 13; Jesse, eight; and her best friend, Darlene Dillon, also thirty-something, who's been married 15 years and has no children.

The title *Suburban Cowgirls* hails from a night in the mid-1980s when writer Alfieri and a group of women friends decided to join a bowling league as a lark with that as the team's name. The idea was to get out of the house one night a week, away from husbands and kids. They never bowled, but it's a great title for a comic strip about relationships in sububia.

Janet Alfieri graduated from Emmanuel college, a Catholic women's college in Boston, in 1971 with a degree in sociology. Ed Colley earned both undergraduate and masters of fine arts degrees from Boston University; from 1962 until 1989 he was a high school art teacher. Colley drew editorial cartoons for the MPG Newspaper chain and Alfieri worked there as a features writer, reporter, and layout artist. After Colley put the word out that he was looking for a partner to develop a comic strip, Alfieri volunteered. As both have the shared experience of raising families in suburbia, the subject matter of *Suburban Cowgirls* was a natural for them.

In the strip Max wants nothing to do with her ex-husband. It's strongly implied that he was unfaithful in their marriage. She supports herself hosting the morning radio show on a small radio station WMOM-AM, "the radio station that rocks the hand that rocks the cradle." Her counterpoint is best friend Darlene Dillon whom she met in the back row of a low-impact aerobics class. Darlene works as assistant to the president of the local bank in their hometown of Tupperville outside a major city. Darlene's husband, Bob, is the top salesman for a plumbing supply company during the day, but off work he's become a television-addicted beer-drinking couch potato. He's more

NO··· I CAN'T MAKE IT FRIDAY NIGHT.

SORRY··· SATURDAY IS OUT OF THE QUESTION.

LET'S SEE··· HOW ABOUT THE SECOND FRIDAY IN JULY?

HEY, SO I'M POPULAR! OK?

"Suburban Cowgirls," Ed Colley and Janet Alfieri. © Tribune Media Services.

emotionally involved with his hound dog Bo than with Darlene. The couple are in marriage counseling.

Since the strip began, cartoonist Colley, as happens with all strips, has modified the appearance of the characters. If anything he has made the women more attractive and shapely. Max has a wild mop of blonde hair and the more conservative Darlene's brunette hair is perfectly groomed. Bob has remained constant from day one, beer-bellied and bald.

Max favors T-shirts with a message on the front. What started as a gimmick now is an integral part of the strip that fans look for. The daily from January 6, 1997, has no caption but plays off the T-shirts. Max and Darlene seen from the rear pass by a woman in a "Kiss Me I'm Irish" shirt and a man in a "Kiss Me I'm Polish" one. In the last panel Darlene is shown in her "Don't Touch Me I'm Waspish" T-shirt, and Max, the disc jockette, in her "KISS 1996 World Tour" shirt.

While Max turns heads, she searches in vain for a sensitive new-age guy. Darlene loves Bob but longs for romance to return to her marriage. In one daily she thinks he's snuggling up to her on the couch only to find out he's trying to get the TV program guide she's accidently sitting on. Many gags and short continuities revolve around Max's relationship with her kids. Janet Alfieri's writing and Ed Colley's cartoons have family humor and great design. Whether struggling to keep their figures at exercise class or discussing the ironies of life for thirty-something women, Max and Darlene are winners.

These Suburban Cowgirls just want to have fun and make you laugh. They have none of the victim quality of *Cathy* but rather are more everyday women such as the characters in *For Better Or For Worse*, *Gasoline Alley*, *Rose Is Rose*, or *Sally Forth*.

B.C.

SUGIURA, SHIGERU (1908-   ) Shigeru Sugiura is a Japanese comic book artist born in Tokyo on April 3, 1908. Sugiura's father was a doctor, as his older two brothers also went on to become, but the young Shigeru wanted to be an artist. He went to the Taiheiyō ga Kenkyujo school at Shimaya where he studied painting from 1926 to 1930. That same year his landscapes were accepted by Teiten (later Nitten), one of the most famous Japanese art exhibitions. But in spite of his artistic successes, Sugiura had trouble earning a living with his paintings in the Japan of the depression years, and he decided to become a comic strip artist, studying for one year with the celebrated comic artist Suihō Tagawa. Sugiura's first work of

Shigeru Sugiura, comic book illustration.

comic art appeared in the boys' magazine *Shōnen Kurabu*, in 1933.

After 18 years of relative obscurity (during which he contributed ephemeral cartoons to several magazines) Shigeru Sugiura burst upon the comic book scene with *Mohican Zokuno Saigo* ("The Last of the Mohicans"), his first best-selling strip. In 1953 he created the feature which he is best known for, *Sarutobi Sasuke*, a nonsensical comic strip about an inept secret agent by that name.

Sugiura's works are full of surprises which spring at the unsuspecting reader like jacks-in-the-box. In his strips he often makes use of American figures of comic art, screen, and fiction such as Tarzan, Laurel and Hardy, Popeye, the Marx Brothers, or Betty Boop. His art style, whimsical, weird, and almost surrealistic, has contributed to Shigeru Sugiura's appellation as the Japanese Basil Wolverton.

H.K.

SU LANG (1938-   ) Graduated from the Northwest Normal College in 1957 with a major in art, Su worked as a reporter and editor for the *Gansu Daily* in China between 1957 and 1985, and as a deputy general editor at Gansu (Province) People's Art Publishing House and deputy editor-in-chief of Gansu Pictorial between 1985 and 1995; since then he has been the deputy editor for Gansu People's Publishing House. He is a member of the Chinese Artist Association and of the Outstanding Committees of Chinese News Media Cartoon Research Society and Gansu Artist Association. As a nationally known cartoonist, he has been

President of Gansu Cartoonist Association. He is also a Researcher at the Museum of Gansu History.

Although all his cartoons and comics were made in his leisure time, which overburdened his life, Su never stopped making them after he started cartooning as a student in the 1950s. Several thousand cartoons, comics, and prints that were published in the past years were all made either at night or on holidays. His artworks were selected for national or international exhibitions many times, and his art often earned awards. In 1993 Su's cartoon received the highest award in Chinese cartoon circles—the Golden Monkey Award. In 1995 he was again awarded first prize in the National Newspaper Cartoon Competition; in the same year, he won first prize at the Second Black-and-White Cartoon Contest of Worker's Daily with his cartoon *The Shadow Troop*, which ridicules people eager to "serve" those who have power (the symbol of power is the seal in the hand of the man walking in front of the "troop"). The "services," however, are in various ways very convenient to different persons or personalities: some are always ready to light cigarettes for the boss and sing loudly flattering songs, and others are trying to please him with gifts and/or to serve him in bed.

Among Su's more than 10 cartoon and comics collections published, the comic book entitled *Legends Along the Silk Road* is the first of a seven-volume comic book series that was published in three languages (Chinese, English, and Japanese) by the Chinese Literature Publishing House in 1995. Illustrated with more than 500 drawings made by Su in two months, *Legends*

Along the Silk Road includes the history and natural scenery as well as the religions, arts, and numerous tales associated with the Silk Road, all based upon authentic historical records.

H.Y.L.L.

SULLIVAN, PAT (1887-1933) Pat Sullivan was an American cartoonist born in 1887 (or 1888, according to some sources) in Australia. Despite Sullivan's fame as the creator of the extravagantly successful Felix the Cat cartoon character, little seems to be known about his early life. After a disappointing stab at a cartooning career in a number of Australian papers, he left for England in 1908 and worked on the *Ally Sloper* feature for a time. In 1914 he emigrated again, this time to the United States. There he worked as a prize-fighter and vaudeville comedian while trying his hand at comic strips (creating *Pa Perkins* in 1914 and *Samuel Johnson* a little later), not too successfully.

Around 1915 Sullivan turned his sights toward animation, eventually establishing his own small studio: his first recorded effort in this field seems to have been an animated version of *Pa Perkins*. In 1917 Sullivan produced the first *Felix the Cat* short: the success was immediate and spectacular. By the time of Sullivan's death in 1933 more than 100 cartoons had been produced, *Felix* was appearing all over the world in many forms (as a comic strip since 1923), and a catchy little tune had everybody humming: Felix kept on walking/ Kept on walking still.

Pat Sullivan is only marginally connected with the comic strip field but, like Walt Disney after him, his work as an animator proved instrumental in many ways. And, of course, his *Felix the Cat* remains as a memorial to his imagination and talent.

M.H.

SUPERBONE (Italy) Feeling the need for a magazine aimed at the younger reader, Alceo and Domenico Del Duca, owners of the Casa Editrice Universo, decided to republish their old comic magazine, *Il Monello*, but in a more convenient pocket-size format. The first issue hit the newsstands in 1953 with a mixture of comic stories and illustrated tales with captions in octosyllabic verse. It was in this revamped version of *Il Monello* that, starting in issue number one, Erio Nicolo's *Superbone* ("Superbrat") appeared. It ran until the mid-1960s.

Drawn in a blend of realistic and grotesque graphic styles well suited to the spirit of the story, the feature starred an unruly young boy in the *Katzenjammer* tradition who liked to play pranks on parents, neighbors, and strangers alike. Unfortunately for him, however, each of his shenanigans ended up with his receiving a few good whacks of the broomstick wielded by his implacable aunt. Always wearing a pair of knickers and an unruly forelock falling on his eye, Superbone usually got in all kinds of scrapes with the other boys who lived in the village: he always tried to outwit them but they usually had the last laugh as they saw Superbone punished by his aunt.

The strip certainly does not come up to the quality of similar American series, but it is amusing and fresh, and the younger readers enjoy it immensely.

G.B.

SUPERGIRL (U.S.) *Supergirl* was created by editor Mort Weisinger and writer Otto Binder as a back-up feature for the *Superman* strip in Action Comics, com-

Su Lang, "Legends Along the Silk Road." © Su Lang.

mencing with issue number 252 (May 1959). The new feature was initiated after a tremendous reader response to an issue of *Superman*, a year earlier. The August 1958 issue of *Superman* carried a story, "The Girl of Steel," in which Jimmy Olsen used a magic totem pole to wish a Super Girl into existence. The character later sacrificed her life to save Superman's and, when that issue sold exceedingly well, it was decided to create a new Supergirl to be featured in *Action Comics*.

That Supergirl was the last remaining survivor (at the time) of Argo City, part of the planet Krypton. When the planet exploded, the original story explained, Argo City was hurled away on a large chunk of soil that soon turned into deadly Kryptonite. Lead sheeting was used to cover the ground but, years later, a meteor shower punctured the protective lead, unleashing the Kryptonite radiations. Scientist Zor-el (brother of Superman's father, Jor-el) sent his teenaged daughter, Kara, to earth, much as Jor-el had sent his son, Kal-el. In the intervening years, Kal-el had grown up into Superman. Since the new Supergirl was therefore Superman's cousin, it eliminated any possibility of a Superman-Supergirl romance, which would have interfered with the Superman-Lois Lane courtship.

The blonde, teenaged Supergirl was given a brown wig and the secret identity of Linda Lee, a resident of the Midvale Orphanage. For a time, the existence of a Supergirl on earth was carefully guarded, and Linda Lee scrupulously avoided being adopted. Finally, in August 1961, she was adopted by a Mr. and Mrs. Danvers (making her secret identity name Linda Lee Danvers) and, in February of the following year, Superman announced that her training period was over and that the world should know of her presence.

The first *Supergirl* story was drawn by Al Plastino, after which Jim Mooney became the permanent artist until 1968 when Kurt Schaffenberger took over. Stories were supplied by Binder, Leo Dorfman, Edmond Hamilton, and many others. Over the years, *Supergirl* also appeared frequently in all of the other magazines spun-off from the *Superman* feature, including her entry into the Legion of Superheroes. Linda Lee Danvers grew up and enrolled in college.

In June 1969, commencing with *Adventure Comics* number 381, *Supergirl* took over the whole magazine, abandoning the back-up slot in *Action Comics*. Schaffenberger and Winslow Mortimer illustrated the feature until the following year when Mike Sekowsky took over the editing, writing, and drawing. Linda Lee Danvers graduated from college at about this time and, shortly after, Sekowsky was replaced by a constantly changing crew of writers and artists, including Bob Oksner, Art Saaf, Vince Colletta, John Albano, Steve Skeates, and (later) Sekowsky again. In 1972, *Supergirl* left *Adventure Comics* and appeared in a new *Supergirl* magazine, beginning with number 1 (November 1972). It lasted ten issues, after which *Supergirl* became a rotating feature in *The Superman Family* comic book.

In 1982 the publishers revived the *Supergirl* comic book (as *The Daring Adventures of Supergirl*) with Gil Kane as the main artist, but it only lasted until 1984, the year that the *Supergirl* movie, starring Helen Slater, came out. In 1985 DC did the comic book adaptation. There also was a *Supergirl* miniseries in 1994.

M.E.

SUPERMACHOS, LOS (Mexico) *Los Supermachos de San Garabato Cuc*, more simply, *Los Supermachos* ("The Supermales"), is the Mexican comic feature that revolutionized that country's comic industry; it is without precedent or equivalent in other Spanish-speaking countries and stands as a symbol of what a successful political comic should be.

The strip's creator is the cartoonist Rius (pseudonym of Eduardo del Río), who in 1965, gave life to the inhabitants of the mythical town of San Garabato in a series of comic books published by Editorial Meridiano S.A. Following a dispute with the publisher in 1968 Rius left the series, and it passed into other hands. In the meantime, Rius devoted himself to the parallel collection, *Los Agachados*, with even more vigor and authenticity.

Through the characters of the inhabitants of this lost village of San Garabato, who spend their time arguing or taking siestas, Rius expounds subtle social criticism that is valid not only for Mexico but for all other countries where similar social conditions exist, as well. In the strip's vast dramatis personae a number of characters stand out, such as the politician Don Perpetuo del Rosal, and the Indians Chón Prieto and Juan Calzoncin. The latter vainly attempts to communicate his political ideas to his fellow villagers; at times he appears as the major character and gave his name to the movie inspired by the strip, Calzoncin Inspector. A stage play based *on Los Supermachos* was produced in Guadalajara.

L.G.

SUPERMAN (U.S.) 1—*Superman* was created by two 17-year-olds, writer Jerry Siegel and artist Joe Shuster, and made its first appearance in the premiere issue of National Comics' *Action* (June 1938). The quintessential comic book strip, *Superman* carried comic book's first costumed superhero and provided the impetus for the industry's boom in 1940 through 1945.

Based heavily on Philip Wylie's 1930 science-fiction novel *Gladiator*, Siegel's concept of the strip rested heavily on three now-clichéd themes: the visitor from another planet, the superhuman being, and the dual identity. As familiar as these themes were, however, the feature was originally rejected by every major newspaper syndicate in the country. M. C. Gaines eventually recommended *Superman* to publisher Harry Donnenfeld who bought it for $130 and repasted the strip into a 13-page comic book story. By 1941, *Superman* was being advertised as "The World's Greatest Adventure Strip Character" and was appearing in a half-dozen comic books and on radio.

Superman's origin is part of Americana: born on the doomed planet Krypton, Superman was launched into space just before the planet's collapse. Landing on earth, he was adopted by Jonathan and Martha Kent and discovered his Kryptonian heritage endowed him with great abilities. He later came to Metropolis, adopted the guise of a Daily Planet reporter and devoted his life to fighting for truth, justice, and the American way.

As the prototype of all comic book superhero features, *Superman* has received a great deal of psychological scrutiny. While the majority of his superheroic imitators were normal men transformed into superhumans, Superman was born super and adopted the alter ego of the somewhat craven Clark Kent. Critics are constantly analyzing the peculiar juxtaposition of

"Superman," © National Periodical Publications.

"Superman," Wayne Boring. © National Periodical Publications.

Superman, who could easily have been a king, and Clark Kent, who accepted a badgering boss (Perry White), an unceremonious attire, a less-than-brilliant companion (Jimmy Olsen), and the constant irony of being in competition with himself for the woman he loves (Lois Lane).

Despite the great powers originally given to him by Siegel, time strengthened the Man of Steel even further. He eventually developed the powers of flight and invulnerability and several types of x-ray vision. His powers became so immense, however, that green kryptonite was developed. Introduced by Bob Maxwell for the *Superman* radio show, and later incorporated into the comic books, green kryptonite were fragments of Superman's home planet that could kill him. In the 1950s, editor Mort Weisinger expanded the kryptonite

concept to other colors (with varying effects) and added many other facets to the *Superman* feature. And it was Weisinger who considerably altered the tone of *Superman*'s adventures. Whereas Siegel's concept centered around a superhuman battling an almost equally endowed opponent, Weisinger's concept had a godlike Superman perplexed not by the second strongest man, but by fools (Mr. Mxyzlptlk), pranksters (Toyman), and gadgeted mad scientists (Lex Luther).

Artistically, Joe Shuster's crude, almost comedic version faded into oblivion after he left the feature, and, for many years afterwards, the publishers called his work too amateurish to reprint. Wayne Boring's later interpretations became more prevalent and his tight renderings, expressive faces, and stonelike figures made the feature a stalking ground of musclemen. In more recent years, however, the feature has been handled by Curt Swan and Murphy Anderson, and their version is slicker and more pristine than ever before.

The feature's fame has reached into other media, too. A fabulously successful radio show began in 1940 (featuring the voice of Bud Collyer), followed by several series of animated cartoons, a George Lowther novel (1942), several serials, a now-famous four-year television series starring George Reeves, and a Broadway play, *It's a Bird . . . It's a Plane . . . It's Superman!* An anthology, *Superman from the 30s to the 70s*, was published by Crown in 1971. Not to mention thousands of toys, games, giveaways, and a now-defunct museum, Metropolis, Illinois's Amazing World of Superman.

With the dawn of the 1970s, changes in the feature came at a terrifyingly rapid rate as Julius Schwartz assumed editorial control over several of the *Superman* family titles. Clark Kent even left the *Daily Planet* for a television job! But no amount of changes are likely to alter the importance of the *Superman* feature to modern American mythology.

The sinking fortunes of the Man of Steel were revived by the phenomenal success of the 1978 *Superman* movie starring Christopher Reeve. To capitalize on the film's momentum, the editors at DC called on a succession of talented artists, including John Byrne, Joe

Kubert, and Dave Gibbons, to revamp the character. In 1992 Superman died (for the umpteenth time), only to come back the following year; and in 1996 he finally hitched up with Lois Lane. (In 1997 he also changed his costume, but that gimmick only elicited yawns from a jaded public.)

Meanwhile the character's mediatization continued apace, with three more *Superman* movies coming out throughout the 1980s. In 1993 the television series *Lois and Clark: The New Adventures of Superman* started its long run on ABC. There have also been two more animated series, one on CBS-TV from 1988 to 1989, the other on the WB network, debuting in the fall of 1996. *Superman* even inspired a full-scale orchestral work, Michael Daugherty's five-movement *Metropolis Symphony*.

J.B.

2—*Superman* started his career in newspapers in 1939 (January 16, for the daily strip, November 5, for the Sunday page). Distributed by the McClure Syndicate, the feature was at first written and drawn by its creators, Jerry Siegel and Joe Shuster, before being taken over by Wayne Boring in 1940. The strip met with notable success in the 1940s, but its popularity declined in the 1950s and it was discontinued in 1967. It was revived 1977 to 1993.

The *Superman* newspaper strip was decidedly more adult than the comic book version. Its stories were more carefully plotted and its characterization somewhat better defined but, of course, the basic plot and situation remained unchanged.

M.H.

SUPERSNIPE (U.S.) The superhero explosion that did not begin until Jerry Siegel and Joe Shuster created *Superman* in 1938 had become an uncontrollable glut by 1942. Hundreds of titles showcasing hundreds of heroes many of them insufferable bores and uninspired imitations were flooding newsstands. But one company, Street and Smith, a top-notch pulp house turned comic producer, always looked at their comic book line differently. They marketed fewer titles than most, and spent most of their time pushing the comic reincarnations of pulp heroes like the *Shadow* and *Doc Savage*. And, starting in *The Shadow* number 6 for March 1942, began a delightful new series of adventures in a strip called *Supersnipe*.

Created by writer Ed Gruskin and illustrator George Marcoux, *Supersnipe* was actually a parody of the whole superhero craze and of comic books themselves. The strip featured Koppy McFad, an eight-year-old who lived in Yapburg and claimed to have more comic books than anyone in America. Or, as one cover blurb put it, He reads 'em, breathes 'em and sleeps 'em. Notwithstanding the fact that Koppy was only shown with the relatively small Street and Smith output, he did indeed have a lot of comics, and eventually assumed his Supersnipe alter ego to fight crime: real, imagined, and daydreamed. For a costume, Koppy wore red flannel underwear, his father's blue cape, and a domino mask. He never had any superpowers, save for once when a friend rigged up a flying rubber suit for him.

The character was an instant success, and, after an additional appearance in *The Shadow* and several other Street and Smith titles, *Supersnipe* comics began with October 1942's sixth issue. As the stories progressed, Koppy added a troupe of assistants. Among his friends were: Herlock Dolmes, a child who fancied checkered coats and a deerstalker cap and thought himself the youngest, greatest crimefighter in the world; Ulysses Q. Wacky, boy inventor; Wilferd Berlad, nicknamed Trouble, who lived a charmed life; and a self-proclaimed, self-styled girl guerilla named Roxy Adams. Together, Supersnipe and his rag-tag group went on to fight crime in Yapburg and around the world. Never forgetting, of course, that Koppy had the most comic books in the world!

Writer Gruskin who was also the *Street and Smith* comics editor wrote most of the stories in a deceptively simple manner. His characters never lost their charming curiosity, childish logic, and attractive sense of humor. They were simply children having fun, something rarely if ever successfully portrayed in comics. The artist, George Marcoux, originated the *Supersnipe* concept and illustrated the stories tastefully, often using a child's perception. Perhaps his most famous and often-seen cover appeared in June 1943 and depicted the barely four-foot Koppy in full dress holding a pin to a metal statuette of Hitler. Reflected in the mirror was a larger-than-life Supersnipe menacing the real Hitler with a giant stake.

Supersnipe outlasted many of the superheroes it lampooned, last appearing in August 1949's *Supersnipe* number 49. And although the strip has never been revived, it has become a legend of sorts.

J.B.

SUSKE EN WISKE (Belgium) *Suske en Wiske* is one of the longest running comic series to come out of Flemish Belgium. Originally created as *Rikki en Wiske* early in 1945, the first adventure did not see print until late in 1945, after the war had ended. *Rikki en Wiske* was published in the newspaper *De Nieuwe Gids*, later retitled *De Nieuwe Standaard*, finally *De Standaard*. *Rikki en Wiske* owed a lot to Hergé's *Totor* and *Tintin*, as

"Suske en Wiske," Willy Vandersteen. © Willy Vandersteen.

writer and artist Willy Vandersteen had always been a fan of these comics. The first episode plunged Rikki and Wiske, brother and sister, and their aunt Sidonie into a kidnapping affair, and the readers were pleased. Nevertheless, Vandersteen wrote Rikki out of the story because he was much older than Wiske and acted much like Tintin and, in the second story, introduced the orphan boy Suske, who is Wiske's age. Henceforth the series has been known as *Suske en Wiske*. The second story also introduced Professor Barabas, an ingenious if forgetful inventor who kept reappearing regularly.

In story number 31, another important addition to the cast was made in the person of Lambik, who was changed from plumber to private detective and was totally integrated into the adventurous lives of Suske and Wiske. Lambik represents the Belgian element in the comic strip. Besides his eccentricities and a penchant toward drinking, he has the proverbial heart of gold. The adventures of Suske and Wiske, taking place all over the globe, are drawn in a moderately funny style, much like the adventures of Tintin.

The success of the feature has led to reprints in album form starting in 1948. That same year, Vandersteen was asked to work for *Kuifje*, a Flemish edition of *Tintin* that was not doing too well. Hergé suggested that Vandersteen draw slightly more realistically and more detailed and should have style sheets for all his characters to facilitate a changeover to a ghost artist if necessary. *Suske en Wiske* has since spread to many European countries, making its humorous and moralizing tales an international phenomenon.

W.F.

SVIRČIĆ, ZDENKO (1924-   ) Zdenko Svirčić is a Yugoslav cartoonist and academic artist who was born in Split, on November 26, 1924. Svirčić's uncle was a photographer who took many pictures for different museums and reproduced the originals of famous Yugoslav artists. Svirčić was able to study art on these reproductions and to try something of his own. He was very busy painting and cartooning up to the age of 14, when he decided to quit and to try sculpture. World War II soon forced him to leave his new hobby, but after the war he studied at and graduated from the Academy of Plastic Arts in Zagreb.

After graduation he married and became concerned with supporting his family. He began to draw a few comic strip pages based on the famous *Salambo* novel and offered them to the Vjesnik publishing house in Zagreb. However, he got another job in the same house, and in 1954 his first comic strip was published. The scriptwriter was the noted Marcel Čukli. At that time Svirčić most admired Raymond's *Flash Gordon* and Foster's *Tarzan* and *Prince Valiant*. Immersed in comics and illustrations for different papers and books, he no longer had time for sculpture.

Many Yugoslav cartoonists usually drew (and still draw) both realistic and humor strips, but Svirčić has always done only the realistic ones. His most popular comics were *Gusari na Atlantiku* ("The Pirates of the Atlantic") and *U ledenoj pustinji* ("In the Ice Desert").

Svirčić left comics in 1967 because of his low income and because of the generally poor situation of comics in Yugoslavia. He now does mainly illustrations and front cover pictures for different publications.

E.R.

SWAB *see* Burgon, Sid.

SWAMP THING (U.S.) One of the few comic book characters bereft of superpowers to come out of the superhero-besotted 1970s, *Swamp Thing* made his appearance in July 1971 in the pages of DC Comics' *House of Secrets*. It was the creation of Len Wein, who wrote the texts, and Berni Wrightson, who contributed the artwork.

As these things stand, the protagonist's origins were fairly straightforward: Dr. Alec Holland was transmogrified into Swamp Thing when his laboratory, secreted deep in the Louisiana bayous, was bombed by foreign agents and he remained immersed in the marshes for days, only to reemerge as a creature half-vegetal, half-human, incapable of speech but remaining a sentient being under his exterior of roots, moss, and muck. The story caused enough of a sensation for *Swamp Thing* to get his own title in 1972.

Wein developed sensitive, intelligent scripts, dwelling at length on the plight of a human being trapped in an alien body. Other characters came into the story: Matt Cable, a government agent trying to solve the mystery of the swamp creature; Arcane, the obligatory mad scientist out to capture Swamp Thing for his own purposes; and Arcane's daughter Abigail, who fell for the handsome Cable. Interesting as these stories were, it was the artwork that arrested the reader's attention. Wrightson, who had honed his skills on the horror magazines published by Warren, created a mood of suspense, creepiness, and fear in a succession of chillingly evocative drawings. Unfortunately Wrightson left in 1974, followed later in the same year by Wein, and the title fell into the inept hands of David Michelinie, whose pedestrian plots not even Nestor Redondo's excellent artwork could redeem. *Swamp Thing* went into free fall, with the last issue appearing in 1976.

The title was revived in 1982 as *Saga of the Swamp Thing* under a number of artists, including Stephen Bissette, John Totleben, and Rick Veitch. In 1984 British writer Alan Moore took over the scripting, and in his retelling of the creature's origins he averred that Dr. Holland was in fact turned into a "plant elemental." Around this basic premise Moore constructed genuinely gripping tales, enhanced by a lyrical prose often reminiscent of Edgar Allan Poe and Mary Shelley, as in this opening to one of his stories: "At night you can almost imagine what it might look like if the swamp were boiled down to its essence, and distilled into corporeal form; if all the muck, all the forgotten muskrat bones, and all the luscious decay would rise up and wade on two legs through the shallows; if the swamp had a spirit and that spirit walked like a man." Despite its narrative and artistic brilliance, *Swamp Thing* met with only scant success. In 1993 it was transferred to DC's Vertigo imprint, a comic book line aimed at a more sophisticated audience.

M.H.

SWARTE, JOOST (1947-   ) Joost Swarte was born in 1947 in Hemstede, the Netherlands. While he studied industrial design at the academy of Eindhoven from 1966 to 1969, he became self-educated as an artist, especially in the field of comics. Swarte earned his fame as a graphic designer for his book and magazine illustrations as well as for his advertising art. They made him one of the most sought-after contemporary artists in the Netherlands, while his comic works have

"Swamp Thing," Len Wein and Berni Wrightson. © DC Comics.

Joost Swarte, self-portrait.

been few and for the most part have remained works that were at first only treated as of interest to insiders.

Swarte drew comic strips for various Dutch magazines between 1970 and 1980. These were finally collected for book publication under the prestigious title *Modern Art* in 1980. Each of the stories by Swarte is a little masterpiece in itself. The anarchic humor, which sometimes seems inspired by the Marx Brothers, time and again belies the seeming naiveté of his artwork.

Swarte in his regular as in his comic work shows strong influences of what has been termed the school of "ligne claire." In fact, he constantly refers to the epitome of ligne claire-ism, to Hergé. He not only takes this artistic style to its limits, he also uses the imagery of Hergé, even coming up with a very Tintin-like protagonist. One is wont to say he out-Hergés Hergé.

While Swarte obviously has been saturated with ligne claire comics, his storytelling turns what seems simple at first look into utmost ambiguity while at the same time being replete with all kinds of detail. Swarte's comics have long since gone from insider stuff to cult status as they playfully stretch the possibilities of the comics medium and reward readers with a refreshing joyfulness that is hard to find elsewhere.

Swarte also managed to become a regular guest in Art Spiegelman's *Raw* magazine. His art graces many products, books, and newspapers and can even be seen on Dutch postage stamps.

W.F.

SWEENEY AND SON (U.S.) Al Posen's *Sweeney and Son* started as a Sunday page in the same issue of the *Chicago Tribune* as Gaar Williams's famed *A Strain on the Family Tie*, an identical strip in theme, on October 1, 1933. Like the Williams strip, *Sweeney and Son* told of the weekly doings of father and son companions, sometimes at loggerheads, but more often in league together against the looming feminine world of propriety and discipline represented by the mother of the family. Both graphically and in an anecdotal story, Posen's strip was the lighter work of the two features, rarely rising above the simplified art and gag level of such strips as *The Little King* or *Reg'lar Fellers*, and it lacked virtually all of the sense of suppressed savagery and frantic desperation of domestic life that often surfaced in other father-and-son strips, such as Fera's *Elmer*, Crosby's *Skippy*, or Posen's fellow-starter, Williams's *Strain*.

It was a pleasant spot on the Sunday page, however, and the weekly escapades of Pop and Junior Sweeney usually provided a smile or two between the more attentively read *Dick Tracy* or *Little Joe*. Aside from the two protagonists, and Mom Sweeney, no other major characters entered the strip over the years, nor was there any narrative continuity of any consequence. Posen's style was attractive, with the same dancing movement that made his earlier daily strip, *Them Days Is Gone Forever*, so visually enjoyable. There were no separate book collections of the strip, although it ran in such News-Tribune published comic books as *Popular Comics, Super Comics*, and so on, in the 1930s and 1940s. The strip folded, almost without notice, in the late 1950s, as did its accompanying Sunday anecdotal feature, *Jinglet*.

B.B.

SWINNERTON, JAMES GUILFORD (1875-1974)

James Guilford Swinnerton was one of the two grand old men of American comics (the other was Harry Hershfield, 1885-1975). Guilford was instrumental in the creation of the American comic strip, and he is noted as the author of *Little Bears and Tykes, Little Jimmy*, and *Canyon Kiddies*. He was born in Eureka, California, on November 13, 1875, the son of Judge J. W. Swinnerton, founder of the *Humboldt Star*, a Northern California weekly newspaper. Raised in Stockton, California, where the elder Swinnerton presided as a judge before going on to Republican Party politics, Jimmy took his cartooning talent to San Francisco and landed a job at age 16 on William Randolph Hearst's first newspaper, the *San Francisco Examiner*, in 1892.

Here, the young cartoonist's tiny caricatured bear cubs, derived from the full-grown emblem on the California state seal and flag, and featured in small weekly panel drawings on the children's page in the Sunday *Examiner*, were an immense public hit. Although minisculely reproduced, the drawing was witty and eye-catching, while the bears' weekly antics (in the schoolroom, camping out, flying kites, etc.) tickled adults as much as the kids for whom they were intended. The addition of kids themselves to the bears' weekly feature led to the caption *Little Bears and Tykes*, for a short period. But Hearst wanted more out of his young employee than comic bears (although he learned from the popularity of the feature that a regularly repeated graphic feature could sell a lot of papers and by 1896, Swinnerton, signing "Swin," had become the *Examiner*'s political cartoonist, turning out huge drawings that often filled the paper's front and inside pages. At 21, Jimmy Swinnerton was a widely admired, well-paid success, and he remained so for the rest of his life.

Well established on the San Francisco scene, he was already a member, from August 28, 1895, of the city's honored Bohemian Club, and spent his life on its famed list of Fifty. Swinnerton felt obliged to pack up and leave for New York when his boss invited him to join the strip staff of the Hearst *New York Journal* at the close of the century. Here he dropped the *Little Bears* strip after a few scattered episodes and began to work

on two new features (all like the last few *Little Bears*, in the new comic strip art form style Hearst and his artists had developed in New York). The earliest, which ran under a number of individual weekly captions, was the first strip to introduce the Noah's Ark theme, involving its landed boatload of animals in many exquisitely drawn escapades, and could be called *Mount Ararat* after the term most frequently used in the strip captions. (Swinnerton later revived this theme in a Sunday page, temporarily replacing his *Jimmy* in 1918, and called it *In The Good Old Days*.) The second, developed a little later, featured humanized orange-and-black-striped felines which Swinnerton called lynxes, but which the public widely termed tigers; a series which shortly became the long-lived strip called *Mr. Jack*. Mr. Jack, a feline like his fellow characters, was a merry bachelor who continually lost out with the chorus girls and bathing beauties he pursued. Both strips were well established when he introduced his best-known and longest-running strip, *Jimmy* (later *Little Jimmy*), early in 1904.

Swinnerton was an enormously prolific and inventive strip artist, and managed to undertake a number of imaginative but short-lived strips from the early 1900s on. With *Mount Ararat*, which faded from sight in 1906, he fielded such titles as *Bad Mans, Anatole, Poor Jones, Professor Knix, The Great Scientist, Sweet Little Katy, Sam and His Laugh, Mr. Batch*, and an odd daily or two, notably *Clarissa's Chances* and *Mr. Nutt* (which he bylined "Guilford," using his middle name), all between the turn of the century and 1920. After 1920, however, his creative orientation turned almost entirely toward the theme of American desert life, a subject that had come to interest Swinnerton after he was sent to Arizona in 1902 to recuperate from incipient tuberculosis. (In the 1920s he moved to Los Ange-

James Swinnerton, "The Little Bears."

les where he could reach the desert easily and frequently.) Using the colorful subjects of the Navaho Indians and the desert wildlife, Swinnerton began to draw his famed *Canyon Kiddies* series (not a strip) for *Good Housekeeping* in the early 1920s. He developed his landscape painting at the same time, becoming one of the most famed Southwestern oil painters in the world. In addition, Swinnerton wrote numerous travel articles for newspapers and magazines, reviewed books in his field, and illustrated several volumes, from Annie Laurie's *The Little Boy Who Lived on the Hill* in 1895, to his own *Hosteen Crotchety* in 1965.

Still painting until his hands became too shaky to do the sort of work he demanded of them in 1965, Swinnerton retained his broad interest in art and life until his death at the considerable age of 98 on September 5, 1974, in a Palm Springs hospital.

B.B.

TAD *see* Dorgan, Thomas Aloysius.

TAGISAN NG MGA AGIMAT (Philippines) *Tagisan Ng Mga Agimat* ("The Sharpening of the Talismans") made its debut during the first anniversary issue of *Redondo Komix* on May 5, 1964. It ran consecutively for 31 issues and had more than 150 pages after completion.

This long, sequential novel deals with the ambitions of three men, Mando, Lauro, and Crispin, who were able to acquire superpowers through different methods. Mando won his talisman by leaping into the heart of a cyclone. Lauro gained his by following prescribed, traditional steps. At exactly midnight he had to cut off the tip of the heart of a special fruit located in the gloomiest part of the forest. Then he had to combat the nonhuman forces of the woods to succeed in his goal. Lastly, Crispin got his anting-anting ("talisman") by killing and burying a black cat and fulfilling certain superstitious beliefs in his attempt to gain his prize.

Each individual got involved with a series of adventures dealing with a witch, deadly creatures, cave people, and ordinary bandits and crooks. The focal point of the novel is the rivalry of the three men using their powers (specifically speed, strength, and invisibility) to battle each other in a variety of situations. The power that was gained by each individual somehow led to greedy desires. When one of them is pursuing an evil goal, another of them somehow finds out about it and tries to stop him. The novel culminates when the three have a head-on collision that causes havoc and destruction in the vicinity. Eventually the great powers that they hold cancel each other out and they finally become normal human beings again.

The novel, besides being an interesting and entertaining adventure story, provides the reader with a unique look into regional beliefs and superstitions. The lifestyles and the customs of the provincial natives are realistically portrayed with an intimate knowledge of the ways and mores of its inhabitants.

Virgilio Redondo, though known primarily as a writer, is the excellent artist who illustrated the strip for both Philippine and American publications. He has written numerous novels that have been drawn by many of the finest artists in the Islands, including himself. He has also done short stories that appeared in American comic books.

Redondo is considered by experts in the field to be one of the great draftsmen in the medium. As an artist, he was the most imitated in his homeland. His influence went beyond artistic technique since he was also responsible for discovering and training a new generation of artists.

O.J.

TAILSPIN TOMMY (U.S.) Created by Hal Forrest (artist) and Glen Chaffin (writer) in April 1928, *Tailspin Tommy* was distributed by Bell Syndicate. Building up slowly, the new strip soon gained newspapers from coast to coast and the following year the syndicate felt secure enough to release a Sunday version (October 1929).

Tailspin Tommy was the classic daredevil aviator, boyish and eager, ready to undertake any crazy stunt on a bet; his friend Skeeter was more of a wise kid and he provided most of the comic relief. Finally there was Betty Lou Barnes, an engaging and spunky brunette with a crush on Tommy, and a full-fledged aviatrix in her own right. The three companions were the

"Tagisan Ng Mga Agimat," Virgilio Redondo. © Redondo Komiks.

"Tailspin Tommy," Hal Forrest. © Bell Syndicate.

founders of a shaky airline company appropriately named Three-Point Airlines.

The plots of *Tailspin Tommy* were the garden-variety adventure-cum-aviation stories. The artwork was awful and the dialogues (always too verbose) specialized in aviation lingo ("ready for a three-point landing?, get your nose on the beam, let's make a 6-40 and land on his tail"). Yet there was enough authenticity in Tommy's air acrobatics to make this into the most popular aviation strip of the early 1930s. (In the middle 1930s Glen Chaffin left the strip and Hal Forrest assumed sole authorship—with no perceptible improvement in the writing.)

As was the custom with aviation strips of the time, *Tailspin Tommy* thrived not only on accuracy but on didacticism as well. The Sunday page opened with a single panel called "The Progress of Flight," which related (in some detail) the early efforts of such obscure pioneers as Charles Spencer and Alphonse Penaud, along with more established figures like the Wright brothers and Bleriot. In 1935, as the readers got tired of so much history, "The Progress of Flight" was replaced by *The Four Aces*, a strip dealing with the postwar adventures of a quartet of World War I air heroes.

By the end of the 1930s, *Tailspin Tommy* was seriously faltering and Forrest (who owned the feature) decided in 1940 to change syndicates. This proved of no avail, however, and within two years, *Tommy* was swept clean out of the skies (by that time newspaper readers were getting more demanding as to standards of draftsmanship, and furthermore the U.S. involvement in World War II made the strip's acrobatics into something of an anachronism).

Tailspin Tommy was profusely reprinted in comic books and in Big Little Books. In 1934 it had the distinction of being the first adventure strip to be made into a movie serial (produced by Universal and directed by Lew Landers who signed Louis Friedlander; it starred Maurice Murphy and Noah Beery, Jr). The serial was so successful that a sequel was produced the next year (with Ray Taylor directing, and Clarke Williams playing Tommy). In 1939 Monogram produced four more *Tailspin Tommy* serials with John Trent as Tommy, Marjorie Reynolds as Betty Lou, and Milburn Stone as Skeeter.

Ushered in at the end of the 1920s, snuffed out by the early 1940s, *Tailspin Tommy*, more than any other aviation strip, symbolized the romance of flight so prevalent in the depression decade. Less skillful (or less cunning) than some of his colleagues, Hal Forrest could not adapt to the changing times, and his strip did not long survive the spirit that brought about its birth.

M.H.

TALBOT, BRYAN (1952-   ) Bryan Talbot is a British artist born February 24, 1952, in Wigan, England. While studying at Preston Polytechnic in 1972, Bryan Talbot produced a weekly comic strip for the college newspaper in collaboration with a fellow student. After graduating with a degree in graphic design he worked for four years for the underground Alchemy Press, writing and drawing *Brainstorm Comix*. This was followed in 1978 by a space opera spoof, *Frank Fazakerly, Space Ace of the Future*; that same year he began his long-running saga, *The Adventures of Luther Arkwright*. In 1982 he started to work for the comic magazine *2000 AD*, notably producing *Nemesis the Warlock*; at that time he also drew some *Judge Dredd* stories.

All this production attracted the notice of American publishers. In 1987 Valkyrie Press began the U.S publication of *Luther Arkwright* (it was later taken over by Dark Horse). Talbot's first original contribution to American comic books appeared in 1989 on DC Comics' *Hellblazer*; this in turn led to more work in the United States on such titles as *The Sandman, Batman*, and *The Nazz*. In 1994 to 1995 he produced *The Tale of One Bad Rat*, an original story that won him great acclaim. Then in 1995 to 1996 came his penciling of several issues of Neil Gaiman's *Teknophage*; he is currently at work on a new *Luther Arkwright* graphic novel.

Talbot has received a large number of comic book awards, has had several one-man shows of his works exhibited in London and New York, and is a frequent guest at comic festivals around the world.

M.H.

TALIAFERRO, CHARLES ALFRED (1905-1969) American comic strip artist born August 29, 1905, in Montrose, Colorado. His family later moved to Glendale, California, where he graduated as an art history major from Glendale High School and found work as a designer for a lighting fixture company. During his free hours, Taliaferro (who, by now, had assumed the nickname of "Al") pursued his art studies with correspondence courses, as well as attending lectures at the California Art Institute. On January 5, 1931, he joined the Walt Disney animation studio as an assistant artist.

One of Taliaferro's first jobs at Disney was inking some of the early *Mickey Mouse* newspaper strips, penciled by Floyd Gottfredson. In April 1932, Al began a seven-year run as penciler and inker of the *Silly Symphonies* Sunday comic strip. The strip, which adapted Disney shorts into panel form, occasionally featured Donald Duck and, when that character began his own strip, Taliaferro was chosen as the illustrator.

The *Donald Duck* newspaper strip began as a daily on February 7, 1938. A Sunday page was added (independent of the *Silly Symphonies* format) beginning December 10, 1939, by which time Taliaferro had abandoned the *Silly Symphonies* strip to Bob Grant. For most of its run, the *Donald Duck* strip was drawn completely by Taliaferro and written by Bob Karp.

The strip never attempted a continuity of the sort that appeared in the *Mickey Mouse* strip for a long time. Perhaps because of this, the *Donald Duck* strip soon became the most popular and widely circulated of all the Disney-based strips, reaching at one point a total of 322 newspapers or more than double the circulation of the *Mickey Mouse* strip. Along with Carl Barks's version in the comic books, Taliaferro's conception of Donald Duck became the standard version, especially after the studio ceased production of *Donald Duck* cartoons.

In 1965, Taliaferro relinquished the inking on the strip to other artists, although he carefully watched over their work to ensure its quality. He died on February 3, 1969.

During his 38-year career in comic art, the name Al Taliaferro appeared only once in a credit line when he did the drawings for a 1951 book, *Donald Duck and the Hidden Gold*.

M.E.

TANGUY ET LAVRDURE *see* Michel Tanguy.

TANK MCNAMARA (U.S.) In 1973 *Houston Chronicle*'s film critic and humor columnist Jeff Millar conceived the notion of a sports-based comic strip that would appeal equally to armchair athletes and to sport haters. For the drawing he turned to Bill Hinds, a 23-year-old freelance cartoonist, and the two men cobbled together six weeks of daily strips and three sample Sunday pages, which they sent to Universal Press Syndicate, which promptly accepted the project. The strip, christened *Tank McNamara* for its main protagonist, made its initial appearance on August 5, 1974.

Tank is a big, burly lug of a man, a former defensive tackle for the Houston Oilers, turned sports announcer. A master of misstatement and malapropism, he is only kept on because people keep betting on how many bloopers he will commit on any given broadcast (and because his lovable if bumbling personality proves appealing to the mother's instincts of the female viewers and to the killer instincts of the male audience). "St. Looie thirty, Cincinooti twoty," "And now ladies and gummelmen, here's the norts spews," and "Speaking from the women's shotput event, this is Mank Tanamara" are some of the tongue slips that earned him the affectionate nickname "Fumblemouth" and eventually got him canned (he was later reinstated due to public protest).

"Tank McNamara," Jeff Millar and Bill Hinds. © Millar/Hinds.

Around Tank there revolves a gallery of oddball characters: Sweatsox, the rabid sports fan who can name every player in the NFL but can't remember his kids' names; the psychopathic Dr. Tszap, professional therapist and demon inventor; Bush Bakert, the star NFL quarterback who spends more time in the television room pitching swimwear and dog food than on the gridiron playing ball; and Tank's airhead girlfriend, Barbi, are only a few of them.

The strip satirizes sports professionals, sports fans, and sports celebrities, and the culture from which they spring, but it is never biting or vicious. As Roger Staubach of the Dallas Cowboys stated in his foreword to the 1978 anthology, *The Tank McNamara Chronicles*, "It shows that all of us, professional players and fans alike, should take our games a bit less seriously."

M.H.

TANKU TANKURŌ (Japan) Created by Gajō, *Tanku Tankurō* made its first appearance in the September

"Tanku Tankurō," Gajō. © Yōnen Kurabu.

1934 issue of the monthly children's magazine *Yōnen Kurabu*.

Tanku Tankurō was a kind of superman. Ensconced in a gigantic iron ball with eight windows, Tanku could, when faced with danger, pull his head, hands, and legs into the ball, like a turtle. He was also able to produce a number of implements out of his shell, such as a pistol, a machine gun, a sword, money, among other things. He could change into a tank (his name was derived from the word "tank"), an airplane, or a submarine. He could also liberate his alter ego, Mame Tankus ("Little Tanku"), to fight out of the shell.

In the course of his exploits, Tanku met plenty of challengers: Bozu the shaven-headed monster; the gigantic sumo wrestler Tenguyama; and Tsujigiri, the chief of a band of highwaymen. One of his more formidable enemies was the black-helmeted Kurokubato against whose army Tanku, his monkey companion Kiku, and their allies, had to fight a titanic battle, in the course of which they used such weapons as a cannon ball loaded with troops, a cyclone-gun, and other far-out inventions.

Tanku Tankurō, who is regarded as the oldest superhero in Japanese comics, made his last appearance in the December 1936 issue of *Yōnen Kurabu*.

M.H.

TARDI, JACQUES (1946-   ) Jacques Tardi is a French comics artist born August 30, 1946, in Valence, in southeastern France. Studies at art schools in Lyons and Paris led Tardi to try his hand at cartooning with a number of short stories published in the weekly *Pilote* at the beginning of the 1970s. His early efforts did not yet reveal a strong personality, as he flitted from political fiction (*Rumeurs sur le Rouergue*, the first of the so-called Today's Legends on a script by Pierre Christin, 1972) to lyrical fantasy (*Adieu Brindavoine*, which he wrote, also 1972) even to Western tales (*Blue Jacket*, 1973).

Tardi came into his own in the mid-1970s with a series of strongly felt tales, starting with *Un Episode Banal de la Guerre des Tranchées* ("A Banal Episode of Trench Warfare"), a powerful indictment of war; con-

Jacques Tardi, "La Bascule à Charlot." © Casterman.

tinuing with *Knock-Out*, an apology of pacifism; and culminating with *La Bascule à Charlot* ("Charlie's Seesaw," a slang name for the guillotine), an impassioned denunciation of the death penalty. Those were followed by longer stories, *Polonius* (1976); *Adèle Blanc-Sec*, a political fantasy set in the Paris of *la belle époque* (also 1976); *Griffu*, a political thriller on a script by Jean-Patrick Manchette (1977); and *Ici Même*, yet another political fantasy on texts by Jean-Claude Forest this time (1977-1979).

The decade of the 1980s proved particularly prolific for Tardi. From 1981 on he unfolded his cycle of sociopolitical thrillers based on French mystery novelist Leo Malet's anarchistic private eye Nestor Burma. After *Brouillard au Pont de Tolbiac* ("Fog over Tolbiac Bridge") there came *120 Rue de la Gare* ("120 Station Street," 1986) and *Une Gueule de Bois en Plomb* ("A Lead Hangover," 1990). Each one of these stories is a suspenseful narrative in its own right, but taken together they present a disturbing view of French society. In addition the artist in this period turned out countless book and magazine illustrations, published several print portfolios, and held a gallery showing of his paintings.

Tardi's entire *oeuvre* has been dominated by his horror of war. On this theme he has written and/or illustrated an impressive number of stories, the most noteworthy being *Tueur de Cafards* ("Roach Killer," 1983), *Jeux pour Mourir* ("Games for Dying," 1992), and *C'était la Guerre des Tranchées* ("This Was Trench Warfare"), the definitive summing up of his thoughts on the subject, which he completed in 1993. His pacifist views have also led him to illustrate the novels of French writer (and convicted Nazi collaborator) Louis-Ferdinand Céline. It should be noted at this juncture that in his antiwar stories Tardi has almost exclusively dealt with World War I. He has carefully eschewed tackling the thornier issue of World War II in which pacifism (skillfully nurtured by Nazi propagandists such as Céline) was partly responsible for France's ignomini-

ous defeat in 1940 and the subsequent occupation of its territory by the Germans for four long years.

An author of undisputed power and intensity whose stories are more forcefully rendered in black and white (the artist is less persuasive in his use of color), Tardi is regarded as one of the foremost comics creators in his country. His almost exclusive devotion to French situations and concerns, to the detriment of more universal subjects, has largely prevented his fame from spreading beyond France's borders.

M.H.

TARÓ (Germany) *Taró* is one of the few adventure newspaper comic strips to come out of postwar Germany. *Taró* was created for *sternchen* ("starlet"), the children's supplement of *stern* ("star"), a weekly news magazine in the *Life* format, when the editors asked Fritz Raab, who had already written several novels for *sternchen*, to write a realistic adventure strip. In order to combine a contemporary setting with the romance of Indian stories, Raab picked a Latin American locale for his adventure strip. He also arrived at this decision because he had met the Swiss ethnologist Franz Caspar in the early 1950s and asked him about his experiences in living with an Indian tribe in the Mato Grosso area for six months.

Raab did extensive geographic and ethnographic research for *Taró*. Even Taró, the name of the hero, was carefully selected by Raab from a list of 50 possible names to ensure that the name was exotic and could be read and pronounced easily. *Taró* depicts the adventures of a highly trained, modern-day Latin American Indian working for the Brazilian Indian Protective Agency. Besides sheer adventure, Taró also had an occasional run-in with politics: in one episode the hero was pitted against a fascist organization. Raab's stories were aptly drawn by F. W. Richter-Johnsen, whose art (on textured paper), makes *Taró* into a highly satisfying strip. Writing and art blend into an outstanding example of modern-day comic strips. It comes as kind of a surprise therefore, that Raab and Richter-Johnsen met only four times during the nine years of *Taró*.

The first episode of *Taró* appeared on June 13, 1959; the last one on March 3, 1968. During that time, *Taró* lived through eight stories, the first one, "The Amulet," having 129 episodes published over a period of two years and six months. When *sternchen* was changed from a supplement to two normal pages in *stern* for technical and financial reasons, *Taró*'s reproduction size shrank considerably. Finally, the editors decided to end one of the comic strips. *Jimmy das Gummipferd,* having been included in *sternchen* from the very start, won out over *Taró*. Seventeen days after *Taró* ended, newspapers headlined atrocities of Brazilian Indian Protective Agencies, which would have been irreconcilable with the idealized comic strip activities. The end of the strip was therefore marked up to sheer luck.

Taró has never been reprinted in book or comic book form, but one of the stories, titled "Piranyas," was put on a long-playing record, a sign of the comic strip's success, a success made possible by excellent writing and art that make *Taró* one of the modern-day classics of the German comic strip.

W.F.

TARZAN (U.S.) 1—As a newspaper strip, *Tarzan* has known a long and complicated history. In 1928, Joseph H. Neebe, an executive of the Campbell-Ewald advertising agency, had acquired the comic strip rights to Edgar Rice Burroughs's creation and (after being turned down by *Tarzan* illustrator Allen St. John) had asked one of his staff artists, Harold Foster, to draw 60 daily strips to illustrate his condensation of Burroughs's *Tarzan of the Apes*. The Metropolitan Newspaper Service

then took over the syndication and sold the new feature on approval to a few newspapers. The first episode appeared from January 7 to March 16, 1929. This *Tarzan* version was enthusiastically received by the few readers who saw it and a sequel was decided upon. The second episode, "The Return of Tarzan" (also based on Burroughs's novel), debuted on June 17, 1929, drawn by Rex Maxon who had replaced Foster, and success continued unabated. (It should be noted at this juncture that British publication of Foster's *Tarzan* had anticipated American syndication by more than two months with the weekly magazine *Tit-Bits* starting serialization of the feature as early as October 20, 1928.)

In 1930, United Feature Syndicate absorbed Metropolitan Newspaper Service and immediately decided to launch a *Tarzan* Sunday page in addition to the daily strip. The first page appeared on March 15, 1931, drawn by Maxon who proved inadequate to the task. The syndicate then called back Foster, who took over the Sunday feature on September 27, 1931.

While Maxon ploddingly went on with the task of illustrating Burroughs's *Tarzan* novels (condensed by staff writers into a text running underneath the pictures—a definite throwback to the European picture story), Foster brilliantly developed his techniques in the Sunday page (where the narrative was enclosed within the frame of the picture, thus giving it more immediacy). Foster's style became more and more decisive and powerful, and was ultimately to achieve a graphic classicism which gave Tarzan his noblest and most serene incarnation. Foster's strip then became the most widely imitated of adventure strips.

In 1937, Foster went on to create *Prince Valiant*, and *Tarzan* passed into the hands of Burne Hogarth (his first signed page appeared on May 9). At first imitating his predecessor, Hogarth later developed his own style,

"Tarzan," Burne Hogarth. © ERB, Inc.

which made him into one of the most celebrated artists of the comics. Into *Tarzan* he poured all of his artistic knowledge, blending form and content into a single visual manifestation. *Tarzan* became a vast panorama of grandiose and jarring images, which stayed in the reader's mind long after Hogarth had abandoned the strip. Hogarth drew the Sunday adventures of the lord of the jungle until 1950, with a two-year interruption (1945-1947) during which the feature was done by Rubimor (Ruben Moreira).

The dailies, in the meantime, had remained in the hands of Maxon (except for a time in 1937-1938 when William Juhre had to take over the strip) until 1947. Then it was successively drawn by Hogarth (August-December 1947), Dan Barry (1947-1949), John Lehti (1949), Paul Reinman (1949-1950), Cardy (Nicholas Viskardy) later in 1950, Bob Lubbers (1950-1953), and John Celardo (1953-1967).

In 1967, Russ Manning (who had been doing the comic book version) was given the daily strip, and during the next year he took over the Sunday page as well, following Bob Lubbers (1950-1954) and John Celardo (1954-1968). Manning succeeded in restoring *Tarzan* to some of its erstwhile splendor. Unfortunately the daily strip was discontinued in 1973 (with old reprints being offered for syndication), while the Sunday page appeared in a pitifully small number of newspapers. After Manning left in 1979, the page was illustrated by Gil Kane and scripted by Archie Goodwin; in 1981 Mike Grell took over, succeeded in his turn by Gray Morrow (art) and Don Kraar (writing) in 1983.

The earlier *Tarzan* strips (notably those of Foster and Hogarth) have gone through a number of reprints in paperback and hardbound form, and in 1972 Watson-Guptill published an entirely new pictorial version of *Tarzan of the Apes* by Burne Hogarth followed in 1976 by *Jungle Tales of Tarzan*.

M.H.

2—When United Feature attempted to transfer *Tarzan* to the fast-growing comic book market, they began reproducing the comic strip version in their comic book titles. Reprints of the Hal Foster rendition appeared in *Tip Top* numbers 1 through 62 (April 1936-June 1941)

"Tarzan," Harold Foster. © ERB, Inc.

and in *Single Series* number 20 (1940). Rex Maxon's strips were reprinted in *Comics on Parade* numbers 1 through 29 (April 1938-August 1940). The second series of the *Sparkler* title carried reprints of Burne Hogarth material in issues 1 through 86 and 90 through 92 (July 1941—March 1950), while *Tip Top* numbers 171 through 188 carried reprints of Bob Lubbers material between November 1951 and September 1954.

3—In addition to the United Feature comic reprints, *Tarzan* was also appearing in books published by Dell, the first being *Black and White* number 5 (1938). That book carried reprints of Foster material, but two later Dell one-shots—*Color Comics* numbers 134 (1946) and 161 (1947)—contained original material. Dell also released *Tarzan* text stories with comic illustrations in *Famous Feature* number 1 (1938) and *Crackajack Funnies* numbers 15 through 36 (September 1939-June 1941).

Tarzan finally began appearing in its own original material comic book in January 1948, but writer Gaylord Dubois attempted to blend the Burroughs material with the currently popular motion picture version. What resulted was an unsatisfactory hybrid of Burroughs and movies: Tarzan's son was erroneously called Boy, Jane was a brunette, Tarzan lived in a treehouse, and covers sported photographs of Lex Barker or Gordon Scott from the movie *Tarzan*.

Jesse Mace Marsh's artwork was excellent, however. His renditions were uniquely angular, his layouts were clean and expressive, and he portrayed the jungle mood as well as any of the feature's more vaunted illustrators. He continued to draw *Tarzan* sporadically throughout the early 1960s, but his more frequent replacements were inferior and the book slipped sharply; by 1964, it was one of the poorest titles on the market.

Late that year, however, Charlton began issuing *Jungle Tales of Tarzan*, stories based on public domain Burroughs material. Although it lasted only four issues, it spurred Gold Key (the publisher had changed names in 1962) to upgrade their title. Russ Manning began illustrating *Tarzan* in November 1965, and he eventually became the best of the latter-day *Tarzan* artists. Manning eventually inherited the *Tarzan* newspaper strip in 1967 and dropped the comic book. After some inspired work by Doug Wildey, Paul Norris, and Mike Royer assumed the feature and the book collapsed into mediocrity.

Gold Key finally lost the rights to *Tarzan* and National began publishing the book in April 1972. Joe Kubert took over as artist, writer, and editor, and, relying on Burroughs adaptations and Foster's early *Tarzan* renditions, made the book solid once again. Already an accomplished jungle illustrator (he drew the *Tor* feature two decades before), Kubert will probably be ranked with the other great *Tarzan* artists.

National discontinued its *Tarzan* comic book in 1977. Marvel then took up the challenge and between 1977 and 1979 published a line of monthly *Tarzan* stories illustrated by such stalwarts as John Buscema and Rudy Nebres. The latest appearances of the apeman in comic books have happened in 1992, in a short-lived series issued by Malibu comics, and since 1996 in *Edgar Rice Burroughs's Tarzan* published by Dark Horse.

J.B.

TEDDY TAIL (G.B.) The Mouse that will make your children laugh. This was how *Teddy Tail* was trailered in the *Daily Mail* on Saturday, April 3, 1915, with a sketch initialed "C. F." C. F. was Charles Folkard, a children's book illustrator of considerable quality, and he fulfilled the paper's promise. On the following Monday, *Teddy Tail* appeared in not only the first British daily strip but the largest for many years to come—nine big panels, each with a five-line caption. Subtitled "The Diary of the Mouse in your House," Teddy's serial was swiftly under way, introducing the first of many regular characters, Dr. Beetle, in panel number 1.

By September 1915 Teddy was in his first book, a reprint of his daily strip with added tint in red ink; *The Adventures of Teddy Tail of the Daily Mail*, published by Adam and Charles Black, sold for a shilling. More collections followed: *T. T. in Nursery Rhyme Land* (1915), *T. T. in Fairyland* (1916); *T. T. in Historyland* (1917); *T. T.'s Fairy Tale* (1919); *T. T. at the Seaside* (1920); *T. T.'s Alphabet* (1921); *T. T. in Toyland* (1922); *T. T.'s Adventures in the A.B. Sea* (1926); and *T. T. Waddle Book* (1934).

The strip was taken over by Folkard's younger brother Harry, an artist of considerably less talent. Harry Folkard's Teddy decorated the original *Teddy Tail* League badge, and he also drew Teddy's full-page adventures for *Boys & Girls Daily Mail*, a colored comic supplement to the newspaper, starting April 8, 1933. By this time Teddy had become domesticated, and, instead of traveling into fantasies, he had homey adventures with his pals Piggy, Douglas the Duck, and Kittypuss the Cat, under the aegis of the widowed Mrs. Whisker (a large mouse).

A new turn in Teddy's tale came when Herbert Foxwell, the *Tiger Tim* artist, was brought over from Rainbow to redesign the strip. His first *Teddy* page was published on Saturday, November 4, 1933. An immediate success, the comic increased to three editions a week, then enlarged to full broadsheet format from September 14, 1935. A *Teddy Tail Annual* commenced Christmas publication from 1933 to 1941 (dated 1934 to 1942), the last two editions drawn by J. Michman and Ern Shaw.

From 1940 Teddy was dropped for the duration of the war but returned in about 1946. This time the artist was Spot (whose real name was Arthur Potts), and the style was slicker. All the old pals were present, including Dr. Beetle. The *Teddy Tail Annual* was revived and ran from 1948 to 1955, and some new reprints of the strip were issued in comic book form and printed in red and black as of yore: *T. T. and the Magic Drink*; *T. T. and the Pearl Thief*; *T. T. Goes West*; *Willow Pattern Story*; *T. T. and the Cave Men*; *T. T. and the Gnomes* (all 1950-1951). After the death of Potts, Edgar Spenceley took over, followed by Bill St. John Glenn, with Roland Davies in the *Annual*. The strip was finally discontinued on October 25, 1960, after an interrupted run of 46 years.

D.G.

TED TOWERS (U.S.) In 1934 King Features must have felt a need for another jungle strip besides the highly successful *Jungle Jim* (King's policy was to have at least two entries in every possible strip category) and they commissioned the noted explorer and animal trapper Frank Buck, author of the best-selling *Bring' em Back Alive* to create one for them. Thus on November 11, 1934, a new Sunday feature appeared under the heading: "Bring' em Back Alive Frank Buck Presents Ted Towers, Animal Master" (mercifully shortened to simple *Ted Towers* a short time later).

Glen Cravath was the first artist on this strip which he drew until February 1936; in the short span of four months (February to June) no fewer than three cartoonists tried for his succession: first an anonymous staff artist, then Joe King (probably a pseudonym), and later Paul Frehm. Finally the feature was taken over by Ed Stevenson, who carried on until its demise in May 1939. (For a few months in 1935 *Ted Towers* had a companion strip, *Animal Land*, about a young, Mowgli-like boy who consorted with jungle animals.)

Ted Towers was a wildlife trapper who worked for American zoos. Helped by his trusted Hindu assistant Ali and by his girl companion Catherine, he roamed the jungles of India in search of some rare or unusual specimen. Wild tigers and rogue elephants were not the only perils that Ted had to face: he also got to fight diamond smugglers and ivory hunters, and even, on one occasion, a villainous maharajah with a desire for Catherine.

Ted Towers's scripts were too often puerile (it is doubtful that Frank Buck ever wrote any of them), but the drawing was for the most part competent, and the jungle scenes convincingly handled. Today the strip has a period charm which makes it worth studying.

M.H.

TEENAGE MUTANT NINJA TURTLES (U.S.) One of the most meteoric—and most inexplicable—successes of the comics came about in 1984, when writer Kevin Eastman (then working as a short-order cook) and artist Peter Laird (then mostly unemployed) conceived a goofy parody of samurai and ninja comics, a faddish conceit in comic books of the time. Husbanding their talents they came up with the idea of a quartet of turtles living in the sewers who become mutated into humanoid beings and made superpowerful by radioactive waste floating in the waters. To add to their powers they later got training in the martial arts from Splinter, the pet rat of an assassinated ninja master. Thus were the Teenage Mutant Ninja Turtles born.

The four Turtles, facetiously named after celebrated Italian painters of the Renaissance and endowed with erect posture, three-fingered hands, and the ability to speak, are all differentiated by very human traits. Raphael is the wit of the foursome, coming up with quips and wisecracks in the teeth of danger; Michaelangelo is a fun-loving, laid-back character, fond of ice cream and pizza; while Donatello possesses the resourcefulness and cunning of a chess-player. The group is led by the swordmaster Leonardo, a cool customer who never loses his nerve or his purposefulness. In the course of the years the Turtles have battled a renegade ninja clan known as "the Foot," an international terrorist cell based in a tenement, and various other miscreants, human and animal.

Originally published by the creators in a print run of 3,000 black-and-white copies, *Teenage Mutant Ninja Turtles* would have died a quick death if by some fluke a United Press reporter hadn't written a piece about it. This twist of fate turned the mildly amusing spoof into a comic book version of the American Dream. Circulation by 1986 had skyrocketed to 130,000 copies per issue, and the title later received the full-color treatment as Archie Comics, and later Image, took over distribution. A successful animated version hit the television screen in 1988, and a theatrical film came out in 1990, quickly followed by a sequel in 1991. That same year a newspaper strip saw light of print under distribution by Creators Syndicate. The story continues. . . .

M.H.

TELESTRIP (G.B.) Trailed as The Craziest Cartoon in the business and Choor Goonory in black and white, *Telestrip* arrived in the *London Evening News* on May 28, 1956. A series of lampoons on current television programs, complete with commercials, it opened with a three-week satire on *Dragnet* entitled "Dragnut," wherein Sgt. Friday and Fred Smith set forth on Crunday the Blunge of Foon, 1956 a.m., in search of the dreaded Facts, accompanied by much Dum-de-Dum-Dum on the overlapping soundtrack.

"Ye Adventures of Robbin' Hood (Ye Dab of Sherbet Forest)" followed, after a short plug for Baff. Then came "The Groove Family"; Kenneth McComfy's "Closed-Up," a film profile of Alan Lead; "Goon Law" with James Harness as Mick Gallon (changed from the artist's original Mutt Dullard by a nervous editor); "Ze Count of Monty Cristo"; "Ask Chuckles" (a burlesque on Ask Pickles, again censored from the artist's original Ask Giggles); and the final series, which was never published: "The Strange World of Planet Fred." The *Telestrip* was canceled before its six-month contract was completed. It had created too many headaches for the editor, with its parodies of products, and was the first casualty in the satire revolution which ultimately led to *Private Eye* magazine.

Denis Gifford, writer and cartoonist, completely switched styles for his first (and last) daily strip, clearly inspired by Harvey Kurtzman's *MAD* comic book and the new look cartoon films of U.P.A. He continued the *Telestrip* technique as *Teletoons*, drawing Davy Crackpot, Charlie Chump, Sea Weed (i.e., Sea Hunt), and even Mumbleman in Marvelman, T.V. Heroes, etc. (1960), and as Tellytoon (with the added spice of a per-

missive society) in Rex (1971): Star Wrek; The Virgin 'Un; The F.I.B.; Public Eye; etc.

D.G.

TENPEI TENMA (Japan) *Tenpei Tenma* was created by Taku Horie and made its first appearance in the June 1957 issue of the Japanese monthly *Shōnen Gahō*.

Tenpei Tenma is a *ronin* (a kind of roving samurai popularized by Kurozawa's films) of the Edo era, a master of sword, whip, and pistol, and a medicine man to boot. With the help of his favorite white stallion Tsukikage ("Moonlight") he battles against countless villains such as Sasori-dojin, Kaitō Ryuikitai, chief of a gang of mysterious thieves, the warlord Akugarō, and others.

The stories are highly entertaining as well as wildly imaginative. A kind of primitive James Bond, Tenma, when in a pinch, does not hesitate to resort to all kinds of gadgetry, firing a volley of shots from his whip, or laying a smoke screen to cover his escape. His adversaries are hardly less ingenious: Kaitō Ryuikitai uses a movable bridge as his hiding place, stones fly out of a wall to meet the enemy, and so on.

Tenpei Tenma was Horie's first popular creation. It was particularly appreciated for its spectacular battle scenes pitching masses of armed warriors against one another in a manner reminiscent of *Prince Valiant*.

Tenpei Tenma made its last appearance in the March 1961 issue of *Shōnen Gahō*. Before then, however, it was made into a television series that lasted two years.

H.K.

TERRORS OF THE TINY TADS (U.S.) On October 15, 1905, the *New York Herald* came out with two brand new features: one was the celebrated *Little Nemo*

"Telestrip," Denis Gifford. © Denis Gifford.

"Tenpei Tenma," Taku Horie. © Shōnen Gahō.

"The Terrors of the Tiny Tads," Gustave Verbeck.

named creations such as the Trolleycaribou and the Hippopotamosquito, to the accompaniment of jingling verse reminiscent of Edward Lear, such as the following: His Falconductor takes the fare, five acorns a ride/ The Tiny Tads have paid for theirs, we see them all inside./And now they climb up mountains to the dizziest of heights/Then down again in valleys where they see most wondrous sights.

From 1910 on, the *Tads'* appearances in the *Herald* became more and more infrequent until they finally bowed out around 1915 to 1916.

M.H.

TERRY AND THE PIRATES (U.S.) Milton Caniff created *Terry and the Pirates* for the Tribune-News Syndicate, which wanted to add an exotic adventure strip to its feature lineup. The daily strip version appeared first on October 22, 1934; a Sunday page was later added on December 9.

The strip, which took place in China, was not startingly original at first: it involved the same combination of a tall, handsome adventurer (Pat Ryan) and his youthful companion (Terry) that Caniff had already used in *Dickie Dare*; these two were soon to be joined by a comic Chinese relief nicknamed Connie. But the narrative gradually increased in interest as the settings became more and more authentic, the dialogue wittier and pithier, and the characters matured accordingly. A colorful gallery of rogues were to cross Pat's and Terry's path: the infamous Captain Judas, the perverted Pyzon, the barbarous general Klang, the sinister baron de Plexus, and others, while in the background hovered the ever-present Japanese menace. It was the

in Slumberland, the other, less well-known but of more than passing interest, was *The Terrors of the Tiny Tads* by Gustave Verbeck (or Verbeek).

The four tiny tads of the title are lost in a fantastic world of monsters and freakish creatures (this is a constant theme running all through Verbeck's not inconsiderable body of work). The animal, vegetal, and artificial meet and clash in such oddly shaped and oddly

"Terry and the Pirates," Milton Caniff. © Chicago Tribune-New York News Syndicate.

women however who made the fortune of the strip: the voluptuous and deadly Dragon-Lady, the golden-haired, golden-hearted Burma, and the headstrong Normandie Sandhurst (nee Drake) vied for Pat's affections; while Terry was soon to acquire his own girl in the person of piquant, capricious April Kane.

When America entered World War II, Terry changed character. Terry, having finally passed the adolescent stage, became a pilot with the air forces in China, and his commanding officer, Colonel Flip Corkin, replaced Pat Ryan as the strip's father figure. Terry had finally become the star of the feature that bore his name, and the situation did not change after the war.

On December 29, 1946, following a contractual dispute with the syndicate, Caniff signed his last *Terry* page, and George Wunder took over the following week. Under Wunder's pen, *Terry* became obvious and heavy-handed. Most of the humor had gone, and the characters lost all personality. Terry himself became a major in the U.S. Air Force and a fierce upholder of the cold war philosphy (with none of Steve Canyon's redeeming graces). Wunder's Terry, to everyone's amazement, lasted for more than 25 years, until it was finally done in by a combination of bad plotting, poor characterization, stiff drawing, and a changed political atmosphere; it disappeared on February 25, 1973.

What everyone remembers is, of course, Caniff's *Terry*. It can be said that no other strip (not even Foster's *Tarzan*) was so widely imitated by so many people; its techniques of lighting, framing, and editing were assiduously studied not only by cartoonists but by moviemakers as well (the opening sequence and many of the shots, as well as the atmosphere of Lewis Milestone's *The General Died at Dawn* are clearly inspired by *Terry*).

Terry's popularity built up slowly and reached its peak during the war years. It had its own comic book version and was adapted to radio. In 1940 James W. Horne directed a movie serial of *Terry and the Pirates*, and in the 1950s the strip was also made into a television series.

Terry and the Pirates is one adventure strip that would not stay dead, however. Bucking the trend, it resurfaced in March 1995, distributed by Tribune Media Services, the successor to the News-Tribune Syndicate. The new version was set in a futuristic late-twentieth century, with Terry and Pat battling pirates, hijackers, and extortionists from their base in Hong Kong. Comic book writer Michael Uslan was in charge of the scripts, while the drawings were initially done by the brothers Tim and Greg Hildebrandt, who were replaced in 1966 by Dan Spiegle, a veteran of comic books and comic strips.

M.H.

TETSUJIN 28GŌ (Japan) *Tetsujin 28gō* was created by Mitsuteru Yokoyama in the April 1958 issue of the monthly magazine *Shōnen*, where it ran for approximately 10 years until 1966. Growing rapidly in public favor, *Tetsujin 28gō* for a long time competed with Tezuka's *Tetsuwan-Atom* for first position among adventure strips.

Tetsujin 28gō ("Iron Man no. 28") was a robot that had been created by Dr. Kaneda and Dr. Shikishima. These robots had been planned by the Japanese Secret Weapon Institute during the Pacific War (as the Japanese call World War II), but they were destroyed by the bombers of the U.S. Air Force. Dr. Kaneda and Dr.

"Tetsujin 28gō," Mitsuteru Yokoyama. © *Shōnen*.

Shikishima did not give up their plans, however, and succeeded in producing *Tetsujin 28gō* in 1955. The robot was created not for war this time, but for peace, and was to assist the Japanese police in their fight against crime.

Tetsujin had a helmet-covered head, a rocket engine on its back, and a gigantic metallic body. The son of Dr. Kaneda, Shōtarō, manned the controls that directed Tetsujin. Tetsujin and Shōtarō battled criminals, other robots (evil ones), and monsters. Their arch-enemy was Dr. Franken, a mad scientist creator of a multiplicity of monsters and robots with which he was forever trying to smash in Tetsujin. At one point the control machine was stolen by a gang of criminals, and Tetsujin turned against Shōtarō and the police in an epic battle during which the controls were finally wrested from the evildoers.

Tetsujin 28gō has inspired a radio program and a series of television animated cartoons (in the United States it was released as "Gigantor"). The strip also gave rise to a spate of giant robot strips (*The Dai Machine, Giant Robot, King Robot*, and others).

H.K.

TETSUWAN-ATOM (Japan) Atom-Taishi ("Ambassador Atom") later called *Tetsuwan-Atom* ("Mighty Atom") was created by Osamu Tezuka in April 1951 for the Japanese comic monthly *Shōnen*. *Tetsuwan-Atom* soon developed into the most popular boy's strip of all time as well as one of the best of science-fiction strips.

Atom was a robot created by Dr. Tenma as a surrogate to Tenma's son who had been killed in a traffic accident. At first Dr. Tenma loved Atom as if he were his own son but came little by little to hate him, because Atom was a robot and as such could not grow up or mature. After being sold to a circus, Atom was adopted by kind, understanding Dr. Ochanomizu who infused him with a sense of purpose. Since then Atom has been fighting one enemy after another: the black-hearted robot Atlas; the Ice Men; the Hot-dog soldiers (cyborgs with the brains of dogs); and Satan, the giant monster robot.

From the first, Atom has been extraordinarily popular in Japan. Despite the fact that he is a robot, he displays human feelings, he can laugh, he can cry, he can

"Tetsuwan-Atom," Osamu Tezuka. © Shōnen.

get angry. But what has made him so beloved is that he is a friend of humanity, which he is able to protect from all kinds of dark menaces.

Tetsuwan-Atom was the longest-running strip in Japanese comic history up to that time (it lasted from April 1951 to March 1968). It is also one of the greatest and most famous creations of post-World War II Japanese comic books. *Tetsuwan-Atom* has inspired a series of animated cartoons (the first one was released in January 1963) which have been shown in more than 20 countries. (In the United States they were aired by NBC-TV under the title of *Astroboy*.)

H.K.

TEXAS SLIM AND DIRTY DALTON (U.S.) Easily the funniest of the Western strips before *Lucky Luke* was Ferd Johnson's little-seen but long-lived *Texas Slim and Dirty Dalton*, which began as a Sunday page titled simply *Texas Slim* in the *Chicago Tribune* on August 30, 1925. Launched in the midst of a group of already famed Sunday pages in the *Tribune* (*The Gumps, Gasoline Alley, Moon Mullins, Winnie Winkle,* etc.) at a time when most American Sunday papers ran only four pages a week, *Texas Slim* was not given a wide publication in the 1920s, but was enormously relished in Chicago and those few other areas where Johnson's broadly slapstick narrative of two cowboys in a big city (clearly Chicago) could be read. Johnson, an aide to Frank Williard on *Moon Mullins*, was given Sunday space by the *Tribune* so long as he felt he had time to draw the strip, but it was, sadly, not a priority item for the paper.

Texas Slim, and a boldly moustachioed, rather scurvy buddy named Dirty Dalton, veered from their boss, Mr. Akers's cattle spread in Texas to the Akers mansion in Chicago, where Texas was hamhandedly courting Jessie Akers during most of the early period of the strip. Dropped by the *Tribune* early in 1928, *Texas Slim* next surfaced as a short gag strip appearing Sunday at the bottom of Johnson's half-page *Lovey Dovey*, a new feature involving a typical married strip couple which ran for a few months in the middle of 1932 in the *Tribune*. Submerged again for half a decade, *Texas Slim* made its final, longest, and most successful

appearance as one of a number of strips included in a half-tabloid size Comic Book Sunday section issued by the *Tribune* together with its regular Sunday comic section on March 31, 1940.

The *Tribune* Comic Book utilized several of the *Texas Slim* pages from the 1920s, together with two weekly pages of new material by Johnson. It was here that the *Texas Slim and Dirty Dalton* title was used for the first time, on August 18, 1940. Also for the first time, Johnson began serious week-to-week continuity, developing some excellent cliff-hanging comic suspense narrative, focusing initially on the grim doings of a cave-dwelling, hideously aged Joaquin Murrieta, then turning to other often hilariously inventive subjects. The 1940s were inarguably the high point of the *Texas Slim* strip, and it was clear that the public agreed: when the *Tribune* folded its Comic Book section due to paper shortages in April 1943, *Texas Slim and Dirty Dalton* continued as a generally distributed half-page feature for many years after, disappearing from sight only when Johnson took over the *Moon Mullins* strip upon Frank Willard's death in 1958.

B.B.

TEX WILLER (Italy) *Per tutti i diavoli, che mi siamo ancore alle costole?* ("By all the demons in Hell, are they still on my tail?"); thus did the protagonist of *Tex Willer* introduce himself to readers in the second panel of the first weekly comic book (September 30, 1948).

It proved to be the start of a phenomenal climb which, to this day, had suffered no setbacks. Twenty-six years went by since that time, but our hero, the only survivor among the multitudes of adventurous characters born in the postwar period, still rides into the sunset in 15 different editions published here and abroad. Tex has become a byname for two generations of readers because of its thematic and graphic qualities.

Credit for *Tex Willer*'s success should go to scriptwriter Giovanni Bonelli, who has authored some genuinely original stories built upon a meticulous historical and geographical documentation, and the artist Aurelio Galleppini, a master of the chiaroscuro and the photographic style. Bonelli and Galep (as the authors sign their pages) are as well known as their creatures.

"Tex Willer," Aurelio Galleppini and Giovanni Bonelli. © Edizioni Araldo.

Tex, a Texas Ranger, is friend of the Navajo Indians, who call him Night Eagle. He is a champion of justice and a righter of wrongs with very unorthodox methods; he resorts to blows quite often, uses his Colts almost ceaselessly, and speaks in racy language. In his missions he is accompanied by Kit Carson (a very personal interpretation of the famous frontier scout), and by his own son Kit who has learned much from his dynamic and eternally youthful-looking father. (Tex, left a widower while still young, has stubbornly refused to remarry and has consistently shown his misogyny.)

While Bonelli still writes all the stories, the growing *Tex Willer* production has compelled Galleppini to seek help from a number of assistants (Mario Uggeri and Francesco Gamba in the beginning, now also Virgilio Muzzi, Erio Nicolo, Guglielmo Letteri, Giovanni Ticci, and Ferdinando Fusco).

Published initially by Edizioni Araldo, *Tex Willer* was later distributed by Daim Press in Milan. In 1985 Claudio Nizzi took over most of the scripting chores, while a long succession of artists, including Jesus Blasco, Fernando Fusco, Virgilio Muzzi, and Carlo Marcello, have also worked on *Tex Willer*, which is now being published by Sergio Bonelli, the creator's son.

G.B.

TEZUKA, OSAMU (1926-1989) Japanese comic book and comic strip artist born November 3, 1926, in Osaka, Osamu Tezuka created his first comic strip, *Māchan no Nikkichō* ("Machan's Diary") in 1946 for the children's magazine *Mainichi Shogakusei Shinbun*, while he was a student at Osaka University. In 1947 he produced his first best-selling comic book, *Shin Takarajima* ("New Treasure Island"), followed by a host of other

successes: *Lost World* (a science-fiction feature, 1948); *Metropolis* (also science fiction, 1949); *Jungle Tatei* (an animal strip, 1950); *Atom Taishi* (later changed to *Tetsuwan-Atom*, Tezuka's most famous creation, 1951); *Ribon no Kishi* ("Ribon the Knight," a girl strip, 1953); *Lemon Kid* (a Western, 1953); *Ogon no Trunk* ("The Golden Trunk," 1957); *Majin Garon* (science fiction, 1959); *O-Man* (1959); *Captain Ken* (1960); *Big X* (1963); *W 3* (1965); all of them science-fiction stories; then came *Vampire* (a tale of horror, 1966); *Hinotori* ("Phoenix," 1967); *Dororo* (an historical strip, 1967); *Buddha* (the life of Buddha adapted to strip form in 1972); *Black Jack* (a medical strip, 1973); and many others. Among his latter creations special mention should be given to *Adolf ni Tsugu* (1983-1985), an epic tale of World War II and beyond, and to *Hidamari no Ki* ("A Tree in the Sun," 1981), another medieval strip.

In 1961 Tezuka founded Mushi Productions which contributed a number of firsts to the Japanese animation field: the first television series of animated cartoons (*Tetsuwan-Atom*, 1963, known in the United States as "Astroboy") and the first color television series (*Jungle Tatei*, 1965). Tezuka also adapted *Ribon no Kishi* for television in 1967 and produced a number of movie cartoons from 1969 on.

Osamu Tezuka is the artist most directly responsible for bringing cinematic techniques to the Japanese comic strip. Before the war, Japanese comics were flat and cramped: Tezuka brought to them a sense of space and depth, a dynamic, pulsating rhythm, and an exciting story line. His strips are imaginative, fresh, and of

Osamu Tezuka, "Tetsuwan-Atom." © Shōnen.

epic proportions (especially his science-fiction stories). He has created hundreds of popular characters in all genres (science fiction, horror, fantasy, Western, animal, etc.) demonstrating his tremendous versatility and artistic range. Consequently his death from stomach cancer on February 9, 1989, at the relatively young age of 62 sent shock waves through the manga community.

Influenced in large part by Walt Disney (particularly in his animated films) and by old movies, Tezuka has in turn influenced countless numbers of Japanese cartoonists (Reiji Matsumoto, Shōtarō Ishimori, Fujio Fujiko, Hideko Mizuno, Shinji Nagashima, to name only his more famous disciples). Tezuka's works are being reprinted again and again, earning him the undisputed title of King of Japanese Comics. It can be said without exaggeration that Tezuka's career constitutes the capsule history of Japanese comic art since the end of World War II. After his death the National Museum of Modern Art in Tokyo organized a retrospective exhibition of his works in 1990; and in 1994 the city of Takarazuka, where he grew up, inaugurated the Osamu Tezuka Museum of Comic Art.

H.K.

THEIR ONLY CHILD   see Newlyweds, The.

THEY'LL DO IT EVERY TIME (U.S.)   Jimmy Hatlo's sports page gag-panel series, *They'll Do It Every Time*, first appeared on the daily comic page of Hearst's *San Francisco Call* on February 5, 1929. Uncopyrighted and unsyndicated, the weekday feature was used as a routine staff artist filler, Hatlo then being on the *Call* payroll. Hatlo's idea of making a satiric comment on the repeated bad habits and manners of people in general caught a ready response among the *Call* readers, however, and they began to send Hatlo suggestions. When Hatlo used these the first time was September 14, 1929, with "thanx to E. C. Thomas" he thanked the donor in print. These thanks later became the famed tip of the Hatlo hat to which millions of readers vied to obtain (especially since the original of the published drawing often went to the donor).

The paper's editors, watching its popularity grow, moved the small panel in a larger size to the *Call* sports page, and on May 4, 1936, *They'll Do It Every Time* went into national syndication via King Features. In the 1930s, Hatlo began to develop recurring characters in a family called the Tremblechins, with emphasis on their devilish daughter, Iodine. These characters were moved into Hatlo's first Sunday half-page called *Little Iodine*, which was released on July 4, 1943. Later, a second half-page, a weekly panel collection of gags with the same name as the daily panel, was syndicated by King Features on May 8, 1949. A noted subfeature of the Sunday *They'll Do It Every Time*, with an independent title and popularity, was Hatlo's *Inferno*, dealing with the desirable future torments of various obnoxious types. Large numbers of these daily and Sunday panels were collected into books from the late 1930s on, many in paperback format. On Hatlo's death, Bob Dunn carried on the daily and Sunday strips and features, with the aid of Al Scaduto and Hy Eisman. Since Dunn's death in 1989, Scaduto has been carrying the feature solo.

B.B.

"Thimble Theater," E. C. Segar. © King Features Syndicate.

THIMBLE THEATER (U.S.)   1—In 1919 W. R. Hearst noted with interest the work of one of his recent acquisitions, a cartoonist named Elzie Crisler Segar, and brought him to Manhattan to start work on a daily strip for the national Hearst chain. The new strip, to be called *Thimble Theater*, appeared to be a Hearst bid to maintain the format and content of Ed Wheelan's popular *Midget Movies*, which Hearst had just lost, along with Wheelan, to another syndicate.

The first *Thimble Theater* episode ran in the *New York Journal* on Friday, December 19, 1919, and appeared in other Hearst afternoon papers a few days later. Reader response was favorable, and Segar developed the interplay between his enlarged cast of characters, including a top-hatted villain called Willy Wormwood; the comic hero Harold Ham Gravy; his girlfriend, the ungracious Olive Oyl; and her irascible brother Castor Oyl.

Thimble Theater appeared in full Sunday color for the first time on the front page of the Saturday *Journal* on April 18, 1925. By then Segar had moved his daily *Thimble Theater* into the area of fantastic adventure *Continuity* with increasing audience interest. In the later 1920s he introduced *Continuity* into his Sunday pages, initiating one of the longest Sunday-page adventures in strip history with the desert trek that lasted from 1928 to 1930.

On January 17, 1929, the addition of the fabled Popeye figure to the strip made *Thimble Theater* into one of the most successful comic features of the 1930s. Popeye devastated readers everywhere: nothing like the fighting, wise-cracking, omnipotent sailor had ever been seen in the comics before. Then Segar created J. Wellington Wimpy the moocher who further delighted the public. A speedy succession of memorable characters followed: the Jeep, Toar, the Sea Hag, Alice the Goon, Swee'pea, and many others. Segar's ship had come in, laden with riches and fame: in a short time, artifacts based on the Popeye characters and his associates were on sale everywhere; a dozen books based on the *Thimble Theater* strip appeared and were sold out; Max Fleischer of Paramount Studios picked Popeye as the figure on which to move his animated film career to the greatest worldwide success this side of Disney (the Fleischer *Popeye* films began in 1932, and are still being made by other hands with continuing success). Popeye's famed spinach-eating for strength increased sales of spinach in the Depression era and earned Segar an enormous statue of Popeye in Crystal

City, Texas. In the midst of all this acclaim, Segar died on October 13, 1938.

So powerful, however, were the impressions his principal characters had made on the public imagination in less than a decade of brilliant narrative and inspired comedy that they managed to prosper in the lesser, ineptly imitative hands of Tom Sims, Bela Zaboly, and Bud Sagendorf for almost a generation after his death. Only in our time (so badly has the Segar heritage been mismanaged), have we seen *Popeye* disappear from most comic sections, vanish from theater and television screens, and continue to limp along only in a low-selling, infrequent comic book. But the fundamental genius of Segar remains as implicit in his totally unaged original strip work as that of Charles Dickens in his novels.

B.B.

2—*Thimble Theatre* (as it is most commonly spelled) or *Popeye* (as it was later renamed) was carried on by Bud Sagendorf, Segar's son-in-law and sometime assistant, from 1959 to the time of his death in 1994. From 1986 to 1992, however, he had to relinquish the dailies for former underground comix artist Bob London, who did a creditable job of revamping the venerable feature. His updating proved too radical for his antediluvian syndicate editors; and when he tried to present a pregnant Olive Oyl he was promptly fired for his pains. Since 1994 the Sunday page has been done by Hy Eisman, while the dailies have gone into reprints.

M.H.

THOMAS, ROY (1940-   ) 1—Roy Thomas is an American comic book writer and editor born November 22, 1940, in Missouri. Besides being one of the best writers and editors in the field today, Thomas is the most celebrated of the comic book fans who later became a professional in the field. Along with Dr. Jerry Bails, a Wayne State professor who is credited with beginning comic fandom, Thomas founded *Alter-Ego* in 1961. It was the first fanzine (fan magazine) devoted solely to the superhero comic (it had been preceded by some E. C. fanzines, but they were short lived) and is still considered one of the finest amateur magazines ever produced.

In it Thomas began to recount the careers of famous comic book features. In 1965 his proximity to the field brought him his first writing assignment, and he wrote several lacklustre superhero stories for the Charlton Publishing Company. Thomas deserted Missouri and his teaching career in 1965, moved to New York, and started working for National Comics, the home of Julius Schwartz, a man Thomas constantly touted as one of the greats in the field.

But his tour at National lasted only two weeks and he promptly moved to Marvel Comics, home of Stan Lee and the superhero-with-problems concept. After a stint writing non-superhero material, Thomas began to produce work on a broad range of superheroic titles, and it became quickly apparent that he was a talented writer. He had his most consistent success as the scripter of the *Avengers*, an ever-shifting conglomeration of Marvel heroes. Most of this *Avengers* work, and his other material as well, was well above the standard comic book fare. Thomas seemed to have an empathy for the superhero, and comic book critic Gary Brown once commented that Thomas understood the superhero psyche better than any other writer. On the other hand, however, he was also consistently attacked for the plastic stereotypes of his women characters. Paty, a critic who later became a Marvel artist, once wrote that he does not know the workings of a woman's heart . . . and was often in terrible error.

His editing career also began to progress. He was made Marvel's associate editor shortly after his arrival and was soon their most valuable asset. When editor Stan Lee became publisher in 1972, it was Thomas who became the group's editor-in-chief. (The title was more symbolic than actual, however, since Thomas had been doing the bulk of the job for several years anyway.) Throughout his tenure as editor, the fan press constantly reported he had little impact on the corporate decisions or editorial directions of the company. And, although he angrily lashed out against anyone who reported this, he admitted that his abrupt resignation in 1974 stemmed mostly from an incapacity to affect high-level decisions. He remained with Marvel as a writer and editor of his own titles after he left the editorship.

In recent years, Thomas's best writing has come on the *Conan* feature and its many spin-offs. Adapting scripts from creator Robert E. Howard and later from other sword-and-sorcery sources, Thomas almost single-handedly made barbarian strips a force in the comic book industry. His writing and editing talents have won him many fan and industry awards.

J.B.

2—In the late 1970s Thomas moved to southern California where he unsuccessfully tried to write for television. He came back to DC in the early 1980s, scripting, among other titles, *All-Star Squadron, Infinity Inc., Plastic Man,* and the mini-series *The Ring of the Nibelung* (1989-1990). His work in the 1990s has been mainly for Topps Comics. After more than three decades writing for comic books (his efforts in other fields have all been failures), Thomas is now showing his age in the repetitiveness and predictability of his stories and the triteness of his dialogues.

M.H.

THOR (U.S.) There were few who could have predicted Marvel's dizzying rise to prominence after the 1961 debut of the *Fantastic Four*, least of all editor Stan Lee. Consequently, Marvel expanded not in a burst, but one feature at a time. After *The Hulk* and *Spider-Man, Thor* finally premiered in *Journey Into Mystery* number 83 (August 1962).

Originally plotted by Lee, written by brother Larry Lieber, and drawn by Jack Kirby, *Thor* was freely adapted from ancient Norse mythology. Feeble and frail Dr. Don Blake became the legendary god of thunder when he pounded a magical walking stick on the ground. The cane would instantly convert into an uru hammer, Blake's body would turn from Kirby-emaciated to Kirby-super-muscular, and thus meteorological. Most of the other old Norse gods eventually popped up, too: Odin, the god of gods and ruler of Asgard; Heimdall, guardian of the rainbow bridge; Balder, the brave; and later, Lady Sif, Thor's beloved. Also in attendance were a troupe of Norse villains, most notably Loki, Thor's half-brother and god of mischief.

Lee almost immediately assumed total script control, and they usually involved epic battles: Asgard would invade earth on occasion, with Thor fighting one side or the other half-heartedly; and Asgard seemed always to be under siege by some menace dug out of the

"Thor," © Marvel Comics Group.

Norse legends. Several times, Lee managed to write death itself into the script. But perhaps most unique in Lee's material was the patchwork grammar he supplied for the gods. Thor was always mangling some conjugation of "hath" or "thine" and phrases like: "if thou wilt permit me to charge yon frothy drink" were not uncommon. Lee also introduced another of his super-races, The Inhumans here, and for several years, they appeared in a back-up feature along with the *Tales of Asgard* strip.

Kirby, already recognized as comic book's definitive artist, literally went wild in *Thor*. Epic battles were his forte and every god and goddess was drawn extravagantly. Many feel Kirby's best fantasy art appeared here because he was given free reign to draw not only earth, but heaven, hell, several netherworlds, and any-place in-between. Whereas his *Fantastic Four* was enmeshed in machinery, *Thor* became a picture book of men in armor, well-endowed women, brandished swords, and super-fantasy worlds.

Given the monumental proportions of both script and art, *Thor* may have once been Marvel's finest feature. But Kirby (1970) and then Lee (1971) left the feature, and writer Gerry Conway and artists Neal Adams, John Buscema, and others could not stop the strip from becoming a shadow of its former self. It now runs in *Thor* comics, which replaced *Journey Into Mystery* in 1966. Among later illustrators of the series John Buscema, Gil Kane, and Walt Simonson have been the most prominent.

J.B.

THORNE, FRANK (1930-   ) American cartoonist and illustrator born in Rahway, New Jersey, on June 16, 1930, Thorne picked up his first comic book assignments in 1948 while in his freshman year at the Art Career School in New York City. At that time Standard Comics gave him several romance stories to pencil.

After graduation he was tapped by King Features to draw the *Perry Mason* newspaper strip (1951-1952), a stint that was followed by more comic book work, for Dell this time; he turned out a multitude of stories for *Flash Gordon, Jungle Jim, The Green Hornet, Tom Corbett,* and other of the company's titles in the 1950s alone.

Thorne returned to the newspaper field with *Dr. Guy Bennett,* a medical strip he produced for the Arthur Lafave Syndicate from 1957 to 1964. Shuttling back to comic books, he then contributed his talents to a number of titles for Gold Key (*Mighty Samson*), DC Comics (*Tomahawk, Enemy Ace, Tarzan, Korak*), and the ephemeral Atlas/Seaboard Company (*Sherlock Holmes, Son of Dracula, Lawrence of Arabia*).

His breakthrough came in 1975 when he was asked to draw the *Red Sonja* comic book for Marvel. Thorne perfected his mastery at the sword-and-sorcery genre with erotic undertones (soon to become overtones) in these tales spun off from Robert E. Howard's *Conan.* Under his expert guidance the red-haired Amazon (dubbed the "she-devil with a sword") attained heights of popular and critical acclaim that were hard to duplicate by his successors.

In 1978 the artist left *Sonja* to create his own barbarian woman warrior, Ghita of Alizzar, an indestructible blonde of unprecedented ferocity and unquenchable sexual drive. Set in an unspecified, long-forgotten past, the action was fast, the dialogue snappy; and the obligatory scenes of violence seemed to float in a fluid, almost balletic mise-en-scène. Best of all, the sexual shenanigans were liberally sprinkled with the salt of bawdy humor.

Since then there has been no stopping Thorne's vein of erotic fantasy. In the 1980s he produced *Lann* for *Heavy Metal, Moonshine McJuggs* for *Playboy,* and *Ribit!* for the Comico Company, all of these creations starring generously endowed females. They were followed in the 1990s by *The Iron Devil* and *The Devil's Angel,*

Frank Thorne, "The Devil's Angel." © Frank Thorne.

which continued to mine the erotic lode for which the artist had become famous.

In addition to his work in comics, Thorne has contributed numerous gag cartoons to *Playboy*, has done *The Illustrated History of Union County* (in New Jersey, where he was born), and has starred in touring humor and magic shows based on his comic book creations. As he recently declared, "I'm still having the best fun!"

M.H.

THUNDER AGENTS (U.S.) *THUNDER Agents* was the creation of Wallace Wood, Larry Ivie, and Leonard Brown, debuting in the first issue of the comic book of the same name, published by Tower in November 1965. The publication and its companion titles were never great successes, owing in large part to their 25-cent price at a time when most comic books sold for 12 cents. Although Tower offered twice as many pages in their books, they were unable to attract any sizable readership.

T.H.U.N.D.E.R. stood for The Higher United Nations Defense Enforcement Reserves, a secret espionage agency that employed men, equipped with superpower devices, to combat possible world dictators. Three agents were introduced in the first issue: Dynamo, a desk worker entrusted with a belt that bestowed super strength on its wearer; NoMan, an aging scientist who could transport his mind to a squad

"Tibor," Hansrudi Wäscher. © Hansrudi Wäscher.

of android bodies and hide in a cloak of invisibility; and Menthor, gifted with a mind-reading helmet. Also introduced in the first issue was the THUNDER Squad, a team of commando specialists. They, and each of the super-agents, had a strip in the *THUNDER Agents* comic book, usually all joining together for the finale of the issue.

The THUNDER Agents battled various organizations of evil and, during their brief run, gained and lost several agents. In the fourth issue, the *THUNDER Squad* feature was replaced by Lightning as one of that team's members received a costume that granted its wearer super-speed, à la Flash. In the seventh issue, Menthor was killed, to be replaced the following issue by Raven, a flying agent.

Although the comic failed to achieve great success, two spin-off magazines were tried. *Dynamo* got its own book, starting in August 1966, but it only lasted through four issues. There were two issues of *NoMan*, the first in November 1966. In addition, the book division of Tower issued several paperbacks reprinting early *THUNDER Agents* stories.

Many comic book fans highly prize their collections of *THUNDER Agents* because of the usually high standards of artwork, due mainly to the talents of main artist Wally Wood. Among the men who either wrote or drew (often both) for the series were Gil Kane, Reed Crandall, Steve Ditko, Mike Sekowsky, Dan Adkins, Steve Skeates, George Tuska, John Giunta, Manny Stallman, Ogden Whitney, Len Brown, Larry Ivie, Chic Stone, and Paul Reinman. The standards fell somewhat in the later issues which were published on an erratic schedule, once with an entire year between issues. The final issue of *THUNDER Agents*, number 20, was dated November 1969. The title was revived briefly by Archie Publications in 1983 to 1984.

M.E.

TIBET *see* Gascard, Gilbert.

TIBOR (Germany) Tibor is Germany's entry in the jungle hero field. He is a relative of Tarzan, if a distant one. The relation to the Italian vine-swinger, Akim, is a rather close one as the feature did evolve from the

Akim saga. *Akim Sohn des Dschungels* ("Akim Son of the Jungle") came to Germany in July 1953 in the oblong piccolo format of $2^7/8 \times 6^5/8$ inches, which is somewhat like the format of the 1947 *Cheerio Premiums*. This first *Akim* was replaced in 1954 by *Herr des Dschungels* ("Lord of the Jungle"), written by Rasmus Jagelitz and drawn by Hansrudi Wäscher. Five issues later the feature reappeared as *Akim, New Adventures* after a second run-in with the Federal Office for Supervision of Literature Harmful to Young People. This run-in resulted in a blacklisting of the feature because of alleged excessive violence. The same office recently blacklisted a German edition of Warren's *Vampirella* and it is no longer in existence.

The *New Adventures of Akim*, drawn by Wäscher, lasted until 1959, with earlier stories reprinted in more regular-sized comic books. In September 1959 *Akim* was replaced by *Tibor, Sohn des Dschungels*. This piccolo-sized comic ceased publication after 187 issues in 1963 but continued in large-sized reprints until April 1968 when the publishers closed shop. The feature had a short comeback in 1971.

It is complicated enough to keep track of all the various editions of this particular jungle hero. To further complicate matters there actually are two origins for the *Tibor* character because some of the *Tibor* books of regular format are reprints of *Akim* tales, in which only the names have been changed. The *Tibor* piccolo comic book that replaced *Akim* in 1959 started with a new tale to make Tibor an original jungle hero. Instead of having a hero who has grown up in the jungle, now there is a young millionaire, Gary Swanson, who has crashlanded in the jungle and lost his memory. He is taught in the ways of the jungle by Kerak, a Great Ape, who he freed from a death trap. When Swanson-Tibor finally regains his memory, he learns that his cousin Chuck has spent the Swanson fortune and committed suicide. Finally, he learns that his fiancée has married another man. He decides to remain in the jungle to help protect his animal friends.

Like other comic books done by the prolific Hansrudi Wäscher, *Tibor* has gained a large following despite its somewhat wooden, relatively simple graphic style. The second *Tibor*, in order to differ from both

Tarzan and *Akim*, bends over backward to reverse all of its elements of origin. If it had not been played as a straight adventure series, this might have made quite a nice parody of the jungle genre with all of its standard elements of action. It is doubtful, however, that a parody would have had a comparable success. Reprints of the entire *Tibor* series were started in 1985 as a companion venture to reprints of *Sigurd, Akim, Nick, Tarzan*, and others.

W.F.

TIFFANY JONES (G.B.) Age: 19. Outlook: sunny. Heart: warm. A real switched-on, with-it girl of the sixties. Men will like her because she is the sort of girl every man dreams of meeting. Girls will like her because she is the sort of girl they can all identify with themselves. . . .

With these words Tiffany Jones was introduced to the readers of the *Daily Sketch* on Wednesday, November 11, 1964. Her daily strip began the following Monday. In an unprecedented plug for a cartoon, the *Sketch* trailered *Tiffany* in its full two-page centerspread, introducing not only her, but artist Pat Tourret and writer Jenny Butterworth, proudly presented as the first all-girl comic strip team in history. She's pert, lively, the bachelor girl, "every young man in a bed-sit will recognise at once," wrote Neville Randall. Jenny Butterworth commented, "She is the synthesis of all sixties girls, an all-systems-go girl. She has something of pop girl Marianne Faithfull. Something of an entrancing model girl whose career I have followed closely. And an appeal and character entirely of her own."

Tiffany Jones was conceived by Julian Phipps, a strip editor of the Associated Newspapers group, and he brought her artist and writer together for the first time. Jenny Butterworth, wife of comic page editor and writer Mike Butterworth and mother of three children, had a London University Bachelor of Arts degree in English. She had written stories for comics and pieces for her husband's weeklies for teenage girls. Pat Tourret, one of four artist sisters, also worked on strips and colored covers for the teenage weeklies. Together the two created a strip that quickly rose to the top in the British field. In May 1967 *Tiffany* reached her century: the *Chicago Sun Times* became the hundredth newspaper to acquire her syndicated adventures. She had

"Tiffany Jones," Pat Tourret and Jenny Butterworth. © Associated Newspapers Ltd.

reached 23 countries on five continents, with 55 newspaper outlets in America and Canada. When the *Daily Sketch* was discontinued, Tiffany moved to the *Daily Mail*, where she moved from the swinging 1960s into the 1970s, but was dropped in the 1980s.

Anouska Hempel played Tiffany in the 1973 film *Tiffany Jones*, directed by Peter Walker.

D.G.

"Tiger," Bud Blake. © King Features Syndicate.

TIGER (U.S.) *Tiger* was created by Bud Blake in May 1965 for King Features Syndicate, as one of King's perennial attempts to infuse new blood into the kid strip lineup. In this respect *Tiger*, while not outstanding by today's standards, was more successful than such doomed enterprises as *Nubbin* or *Dudley D.*

Tiger, with his cap falling over his eyes, his oversized sweater, and his idiot dog Strip, is a conventional comic strip kid, as is his younger brother Punkinhead, whose name evokes memories of *Reg'lar Fellers*. Tiger's best friend Hugo, the gluttonous dullard, also harks back to comic strip tradition—as far back as Feininger's *Kinder Kids*. The two girls in the strip, Bonnie and Suzy, are less well-defined, perhaps because Blake could not find any suitable comic strip model for them.

In the course of the strip's history, Blake has made a few timid forays into the field of social relevance, although *Tiger* is a far cry from *Peanuts* or even *Miss Peach*. Usually the daily and weekly gags revolve around the kids' innocent pranks, their musings, and their dreams. Not revolutionary, to be sure, not even mildly innovative, but a valiant and craftsmanlike effort at refurbishing an ancient and somewhat run-down genre. Relaxed, agreeable, and unassuming, *Tiger* (which won the NCS award for best humor strip in 1970) is proof that even the most worn-out comic strip formula can still work if it is done with integrity and skill. In 1995 it passed the 30-year mark and it is now published in more than 400 newspapers.

M.H.

TIGER TIM (G.B.) "Hooray! Mrs. Hippo has left the schoolroom! Now is our time to peep into that treacle jar!" cried Tiger Tim in his very first caption, thus setting the style of merry mischief that has been his code of behavior for 71 years. The oldest and longest-lived British comic hero, Tim is the ringleader of Mrs. Hippo's kindergarten, a strip of three oblong panels that also made history by being the first newspaper strip in England. It appeared on April 16, 1904, in the *Daily*

"Tiger Tim," H. S. Foxwell. © Rainbow and Fleetway Publications.

Mirror, and was drawn by Julius Stafford Baker, who modeled his funny animals on the well-established style of American artist James Swinnerton. Unfortunately for history, the strip was not a continuing one at first, but was one of several, one-shot strips that appeared in the *Mirror* children's corner around that time. However, never one to lose sight of a good thing, Baker revived his kindergarten for *The Playbox*, one of the first British comic supplements. This children's section appeared as a color pullout to the monthly magazine, *The World and his Wife*, and *Tiger Tim* was its star from the start (November 1904). Upon the demise of the magazine in 1910, he was transferred, still in color, to *The Playhour* (later renamed *Playbox*), a supplement similar to another monthly magazine, *The New Children's Encyclopedia* (February 1910). With another change of title to *My Magazine*, Tim and his pals ran well into the 1930s.

The original Hippo Boys were Willy Giraffe, Peter Pelican, Billy Bruin, Jumbo Jim, Jacko the Monkey, and some unnamed animals: a fox, a leopard, a parrot (undoubtedly Joey), and a female goat. The cast changed slightly (as did the giraffe's name, to Georgie) when they all moved to page one of the new colored comic *Rainbow* (February 14, 1914). They found themselves at a new school, Mrs. Bruin's Boarding School, thus winning a new subtitle, "The Bruin Boys." An ostrich called Willie came in and the only girl went out. By mid-1914 a new artist had taken over, Herbert Foxwell, who remolded Baker's characters in his own superb style, making them the most popular in nursery comics. A second weekly began on June 1, 1919, called *Tiger Tim's Tales*, which soon converted itself into another colored comic, *Tiger Tim's Weekly* (January 31, 1920).

Meanwhile the good Mrs. Hippo had reopened her school. Her pupils were Tiger Tim's sister, Tiger Tilly, and the sisters of all the rest of the Bruin Boys, known collectively as the Hippo Girls. This strip appeared on the front page of yet another colored comic weekly, *The Playbox* (a revival of the old title), beginning on February 14, 1925. *Tiger Tilly* lasted until the paper merged with *Jack & Jill* (June 11, 1925), but *Tiger Tim* survived *Rainbow*'s merger with *Tiny Tots* (April 23, 1956). He continued in that nursery comic and after its demise reappeared in *Jack & Jill*, where he has been from 1966 to the present. Currently drawn in a revamped animated cartoon style by Peter Woolcock, the *Tiger Tim Annual*, published yearly from 1922 to 1957, was revived in 1973 as the *Tiger Tim Fun Book*. The strip was again dropped in the 1980s, but a revival is rumored.

D.G.

TILLIE THE TOILER (U.S.) Russ Westover created *Tillie the Toiler* for King Features Syndicate in January of 1921. As the title indicates, Tillie Jones was a working girl who labored (but not too hard) as secretary and part-time model in the fashion salon of Mr. Simpkins, alongside her sad-faced, pint-sized, gape-mouthed suitor Clarence MacDougall ("Mac") and under the watchful eye of Wally Whipple, her supervisor and Mac's hated rival.

Tillie was a dark-haired, wide-eyed, slender beauty whose brains were not on a par with her looks. She managed to get into all sorts of trouble of her own making, forever falling for handsome strangers with fast cars and faster schemes, only to be rescued in the nick of time by faithful, sober-headed Mac. Her relations to other men were flirtatious but innocent (in the

"Tillie the Toiler," Russ Westover. © King Features Syndicate.

convention of the times) and were aimed, more often than not, at triggering Mac's burning jealousy (although Tillie came close to getting married on a couple of occasions).

Tillie the Toiler's style was sketchy and almost crude, despite the fact that Westover employed some of the best ghost artists in the business (including a youthful Alex Raymond) once the strip had become established. One of the reasons for the strip's popularity was neither the writing nor the drawing but the fashions (to keep up to date Westover subscribed to every fashion magazine in the western world). When this aspect of the strip began to falter in the 1950s, Westover turned *Tillie* over to Bob Gustafson who prettied it up considerably, but to no avail. *Tillie* disappeared from the comic pages after marrying the long-suffering Mac, in April of 1959. (The syndicate listed Westover's retirement as their reason for killing the strip, but in fact the theme had gone out of style, and few readers at this point cared about Tillie's inane misadventures.)

In 1927 a movie of *Tillie the Toiler* was directed by Sidney Salkow, with Marion Davies as the heroine and William Tracy as Mac.

M.H.

TILLIEUX, MAURICE (1922-1978) A Belgian novelist, scriptwriter, cartoonist, and father of *Gil Jourdan*

César, Marc Lebut, and a natural daughter, Anne, Maurice Tillieux was born in Huy, in 1922. Tillieux's first job was with *Spirou,* where he illustrated the Fureteur column. Inspired by true events, Tillieux wrote the novels *Le Navire que tue ses capitaines* ("The Ship That Kills Its Captains") and *L'homme qui assassine* ("The Man Who's Killing"). In 1944 he started drawing 20 pages a month of the series, *Jeep,* for the journal, *Bimbo.* He also worked for *Heroïc Albums,* where he created a new feature, *Felix.*

Tillieux's *Gil Jourdan* appeared for the first time on September 20, 1956, in *Spirou* magazine; he had over a dozen of *Gil Jourdan*'s albums published. In the police adventures of Jourdan, his assistant, Libellule, and Inspector Crouton, Tillieux proved himself a top-flight scriptwriter and a good cartoonist. He became the most popular scriptwriter in the group of *Spirou* magazine of the time and collaborated with Roba on his comic strip, *La Ribambelle,* with Will on *Tif et Tondu,* with Francis on *Ford T,* and with some other cartoonists.

Tillieux's vocabulary was very original, brisk, and colorful; his sense of humor great. His drawing style, which would show his characters in surroundings typical of Atlantic France (the harbors, big cities, etc.), presented the adventures in often rainy and mysterious atmospheres, lending a mystic note to the police stories.

In order to stay closer to home, Tillieux produced the *César* strip for *Spirou,* giving complete freedom to his sarcastic humor. *César* is a brilliant caricature of a bachelor who is occupied with domestic problems. *Marc Lebut,* drawn by Francis, was also Tillieux's idea. The strip tells about two neighbors with different characters who experience hilarious adventures in the company of an old Ford Model T. Tillieux was a master of surprise, sarcasm, and nonsense. He died in a car crash in February 1978, but the characters he created live on.

E.R.

THE TIMID SOUL (U.S.) H. T. Webster's first drawing of Caspar Milquetoast, the titular hero of his *The Timid Soul* daily panel and Sunday page, appeared on several dates early in May 1924, in various papers subscribing to Webster's *New York World* gag panel series. Like a similar series of daily panels by Clare Briggs, on which Webster's strip was based, the *World* artist carried a number of continuing titles, used irregularly on various days, such as *Life's Darkest Moment, How to Torture Your Wife (Husband), The Thrill that Comes Once in a Lifetime,* and *The Events Leading Up to the Tragedy.* The new *Timid Soul* occasional title was the first Webster daily series to feature a recurrent character, however, and readers proved to be enthusiastic about the new, if infrequent, visitor to the comic page. Caspar Milquetoast, with his drooping white moustache, pince-nez, stooped shoulders, and lean, tired frame, was a new kind of comic figure among the rough and tough figures that generally populated the comics of the time (although a Milquetoast prototype, not followed up, appeared a few times in an earlier Webster series circa 1919 called *Are You One of these Spineless Creatures?*).

By the late 1920s, *The Timid Soul* had become so popular that it was appearing once a week in Webster's daily panels, and Caspar Milquetoast had been featured in a large volume of his own (published by Simon & Schuster in 1931, called *The Timid Soul,* and introduced by Ring Lardner). On Sunday, May 3, 1931, the first

"The Timid Soul," H. T. Webster. © New York Tribune.

concluded some time after Webster's death in April 1953, but were immediately pressed into a reprint series, together with his other daily panel features, for several years longer.

B.B.

Timid Soul Sunday page appeared, replacing Webster's preceding page dating from 1923, called The Man in the Brown Derby (which featured a considerably more aggressive and irascible hero than Caspar).

Timid Soul daily panels were reprinted everywhere and were featured in two more Webster collections, Webster Unabridged (1945) and The Best of H. T. Webster (1953). The generally accepted favorite seemed to be the 1928 drawing showing Caspar waiting in the pouring rain on a busy downtown street corner, his hat collapsed damply about his face, water puddling around his shoes, and saying firmly: Well, I'll wait one more hour for him, and if he doesn't come then he can go and borrow that $100 from someone else. The Timid Soul Sunday page and weekly black-and-white panel

TIM TYLER'S LUCK (U.S.) Lyman Young started Tim Tyler's Luck for King Features Syndicate as a daily strip on August 13, 1928, which was followed by a Sunday page in July 1931 (with Young's earlier creation The Kid Sister as its top piece).

Lyman Young grew up reading Horatio Alger stories and he was strongly influenced by them. The early Tim Tyler was drawn in silhouette and had a sentimental story line combined with a pseudo-Victorian atmosphere. Tim was an orphan who loved airplanes and the free life, and along with his pal Spud Slavins, this led him into some unlikely scrapes culminating in 1932 with their getting stranded in darkest Africa. In the course of their wanderings Tim and Spud came across the Ivory Patrol, a paramilitary organization set up to keep law and order in this part of Africa (1934). Tim and Spud soon joined the crack outfit and before long aviation was forgotten. Under the leadership of dark, handsome sergeant Paul Clark (later promoted to captain) and with the help of their pet black panther Fang, Tim and Spud performed their duties with creditable spirit.

In May of 1940 the two young heroes left the Ivory Patrol and went back to the United States where they eventually joined the Coast Guard. They did their best during the war in their fights against assorted groups of foreign spies and saboteurs. Soon after the war ended they went back to Africa and the Ivory Patrol (which had proved to be the strip's most popular attraction).

Tim Tyler's Luck is famed in comic strip circles for the number and quality of the ghosts who worked on the strip under the titular leadership of Lyman Young. Alex Raymond practically drew the daily strip and the Sunday page all by himself in 1932 and 1933 and he was followed by a number of others, including Charles Flanders and Burne Hogarth. Ever since 1952 the daily strip is officially credited to Lyman Young and his son Bob, while the Sunday page bears the signature of Tom Massey.

Be it as it may, Tim Tyler's Luck occupies an honorable position among adventure strips. The drawing is always competent and the story line very imaginative and sometimes inspired, which accounts for the tremendous success of the feature in Europe before World

"Tim Tylers's Luck," Lyman Young. © King Features Syndicate.

War II. In the United States the strip never reached such a high pinnacle but it was fairly popular. A series of *Tim Tyler* comic books were issued by Standard in the 1940s; in 1938 Ford Beebe directed a memorable movie serial of *Tim Tyler's Luck*, with Frankie Thomas in the starring role. The Sunday page was discontinued in July 1972. The daily strip continues, however, despite the death of its creator in 1984, and it is now the oldest adventure strip in existence.

M.H.

TINTIN (Belgium) Created by Hergé (Georges Rémi) in 1929, *Tintin* first appeared in *Le Petit Vingtième*, the weekly supplement of the Belgian daily *Le Vingtième Siècle*. It was a success from the first, and each of Tintin's adventures was later reprinted in book form, starting in 1930.

As with all original creations, Tintin's is a self-contained coherent fantasy world. The hero is a teenager and a reporter. In the conventions of the genre this means he does everything from detective work to space exploration, all assignments that Tintin carries out with characteristic aplomb and suitable humility. He is always flanked by his faithful fox terrior Milou (Snowy in the English version) already present in the first adventure ("Tintin in the Land of the Soviets"). Other unforgettable characters came to join Tintin and Milou in latter years. These included the twin detectives Dupont and Dupond (Thomson and Thompson) similarly black-attired and equally dimwitted, and the evil genius Rastapopoulos (they first appeared in 1934); in 1937 the incurable conspirator General Alcazar, and in 1939 the overbearing opera singer Bianca Castafiore. Captain Haddock, the irascible and rum-guzzling sailor,

made his appearance in 1941, followed in 1945 by the absentminded (and deaf to boot) Professor Calculus. These and dozens of others form an ever-changing gallery amidst whom our hero moves.

At the time of Hergé's death in 1983 there were 23 *Tintin* albums in print (the twenty-fourth, *Tintin and l'Alph Art*, was left unfinished): in the United States they are published by Little, Brown. *Tintin* has been brought to the screen numerous times (there have been two live features and countless animated cartoons) and has also appeared in a stage play. There have been many scholarly studies devoted to *Tintin* from the 1950s on, along with a flood of merchandising that reached a crescendo in the 1990s with the opening of a number of *Tintin* stores across Europe and even in the United States.

M.H.

TIRAMOLLA (Italy) Tiramolla, son of rubber and glue, is the creation of Roberto Renzi and Giorgio Rebuffi. He appeared first in the *Cucciolo* comic book of August 1952. Due to the success encountered by the character, a *Tiramolla* comic book was finally issued in July 1959. By then the character had been taken over with excellent results by Umberto Manfrin, while the texts continued to be scripted by Renzi.

Thanks to his particulate structure he is able to distend himself and assume all kinds of shapes, not unlike Plastic Man. *Tiramolla* is capable of performing the most extraordinary, impossible, and outlandish feats. To make up for his abilities, he is also extremely lazy. As his assistant he retains Saetta ("Lightning"), the butler. Tiramolla has overwhelmed a whole array of

"Tintin," Hergé (Georges Rémi). © Editions Casterman.

adversaries, the most outstanding being a science-fiction character named Mister Magic.

In the pages of the monthly *Tiramolla* have been featured many other series, such as *Ullao* by Umberto Manfrin, *Zeffy & Cerry* by Egidio Gherlizza, the long-lasting *Teddy Sberla* drawn by A. Terenghi, and *Robotman* by Franco Aloisi. *Whisky & Gogo* and *Pepito* have also been published in *Tiramolla*. The *Tiramolla* strip has had many scriptwriters and illustrators in addition to those already mentioned: Alfredo and Andrea Saio, Tiberio Colantuoni, M. L. Uggetti, Franco Frescura, Attilio Ortolani, and Carlo Chendi. The *Tiramolla* magazine was published up to the mid-1980s; an attempt to revive it was made in 1990 until 1993.

Tiramolla has also been published with great success in France, where it is known as *Elastoc*.

G.B.

TOBIAS SEICHERL (Austria) Created in 1930 by Ludwig Kmoch (actual name Ladislaus Kmochk) *Tobias Seicherl* was the first comic strip of Austrian origin. Kmoch (1897-1971) was a self-educated cartoonist who started working for the press after World War I. He worked for the satirical magazines *Muskete* and *Simplizissimus*, finally joining *Das kleine Blatt*, a social democrat newspaper, in 1929. For this paper he created the characters of Tobias Seicherl and his dog Struppi.

Tobias Seicherl first appeared on October 5, 1930. While the hero of the strip was a kind of typical loser, his dog was his better self, offsetting and commenting on his mistakes and prejudices. The most interesting thing about this strip is that it was always written in Viennese dialect which, apart from the strip content, made it a genuine Austrian strip. *Tobias Seicherl* presented readers with contemporary political satire commenting on current events of the day. The strip was obviously social democrat in outlook and propaganda. It criticized the Nazi movement, which also started cropping up in Austria. Kmoch achieved this by having the somewhat dense hero of his strip pick up Nazi

"Tobias Seicherl," Ludwig Kmoch. © Ludwig Kmoch.

ideas as his own and having the dog setting things straight. However, this was not the safest thing to do.

So when Kmoch felt he might get into hot water, he simply sent his hero on a number of world tours to avoid politics back home. In 1938, after the Austrian "anschluss," Tobias Seicherl changed fronts and henceforth propagated Nazi ideas. While Kmoch had visibly joined his former political enemies—whether of his free will or forcibly is open to debate—he seems not to have been too happy about this development. So he once more sent his hero on a world tour in 1939, afterward phasing out the series.

"Tiramolla," Giorgio Rebuffi. © Edizioni Alpe.

"Tobias Seicherl," Ludwig Kmoch. © Ludwig Kmoch.

After World War II the character of Tobias Seicherl was revived occasionally. Finally Kmoch was coaxed into doing new strips, which appeared from 1958 to December 23, 1961. Some of the early material has been reprinted, the historic background of the 1930 to 1933 strips has been commented and explained in a book publication which, however, did not explain Kmoch's collaboration. It is probable that he was exonerated fully or partially after the war or else his series might not have been revived.

Mention of *Tobias Seicherl* in an encyclopedia seems to be warranted only as the feature is of historic relevance as the first Austrian comic strip of note. However, its role in politics is so ambiguous that one would prefer the feature not to have had any historic relevance at all.

W.F.

TODANO BONJI (Japan) *Todano Bonji* ("Average Boy") was created by Yutaka Asō and made its first appearance in the evening newspaper *Asahi* in May 1933.

At the time the Great Depression was at its peak in Japan as well as in the United States, and there was a great deal of unemployment among college graduates, causing a great social problem. Todano Bonji was a mediocre boy who lived up (or down) to his name: he was faint-hearted, superficial, and conforming. After graduation from the university, Todano was unable to find a job. The story followed him as he sent out hundreds of résumés to no avail (he was so destitute at one point that he used the rejection notices to light his bamboo pipe). Finally Todano received a favorable answer, and he went to a nightclub in order to celebrate, got drunk, unknowingly insulted the president of the company that had just hired him, and got himself fired before he had even started on the job.

Other misadventures dogged Todano in search of the elusive job. Asō was able to express in very graphic terms the plight of the intelligentsia, and he won a great deal of sympathy for his luckless anti-hero. The popularity of *Todano Bonji* never reached, however, the heights of its creator's more famous work, *Nonkina Tousan*, and was discontinued in July 1934.

H.K.

TOKAI (Bangladesh) Bangladesh's most popular comic strip, *Tokai* was conceptualized in the late 1960s when the area was still part of Pakistan. The idea had to be shelved during the bloody civil war at the dawn of the 1970s and while its creator, Rafiqun Nabi (Ranabi), studied in Greece from 1973 to 1976. It finally saw print in the weekly *Bicitra*, beginning in 1977.

The exploits of a downtrodden street boy much in the tradition of *San Mao* in China, *Tokai* has had impacts throughout Bangladeshi society: Adults look to it for political messages and children view Tokai as the ideal character. Tokai was even introduced to the Bengali lexicon about 1990, when dictionaries included the word to describe the desperately poor.

The strip is purposively drawn in a very simple manner, a "bit illustrative, a bit realistic for our general readers who do not have an aesthetic richness," in the words of Ranabi. Attuned to the public's wants, Ranabi inserts messages into *Tokai*—"not direct political ones, but mixed with social commentary"—and occasionally allows readers to participate in the strip. For example, although Tokai is a Dhaka character, Ranabi has moved him to the countryside for short periods at the demands of readers. He said the strip for years has depicted current events and acted like a history of Bangladesh.

Ranabi started drawing cartoons on a regular basis in 1961, while an art student at the University of Dhaka. Throughout the decade, he joined other cartoonists in propaganda campaigns to liberate the territory from Pakistan, his works appearing in the *Weekly Forum* and as posters and leaflets. Besides drawing *Tokai*, Ranabi teaches full-time at the Institute of Fine Art, University of Dhaka, where he is also a painter.

J.A.L.

TOM AND JERRY (U.S.) The cartoon industry's most famous cat-and-mouse team was created by producer Fred Quimby and directors William Hanna and Joseph Barbera in 1939. The first *Tom and Jerry* short, *Puss Gets the Boot*, proved successful in theaters and began a series that lasted for well over a hundred films produced by M.G.M. in the next 25 years. The cartoons were characterized by an almost total dependence on slapstick sight gags, often bordering on the very violent, as the spunky mouse, Jerry, eluded Tom the cat. In 1942, Tom and Jerry and other M.G.M. properties were combined into a Dell/Western Publishing Company comic book named *Our Gang*. It was in this magazine that the format from the cartoons was expanded and modified into what became a highly successful comic book series for over 30 years.

"Tom Poes," Marten Toonder. © Marten Toonder.

The lead feature of the *Our Gang* comic book was a series, drawn by Walt Kelly, based on the Hal Roach *Our Gang* kid comedies. The popularity of *Tom and Jerry* soon eclipsed the lead feature and, as of issue 40, the cat and mouse received special cover billing. When a 1948 one-shot Dell Color Comic (number 193) starring Tom and Jerry sold extremely well, the feature took over the *Our Gang* comic completely, beginning with number 60 (1949).

For the comic books, Jerry the mouse was equipped with a cohort in the form of a small, gray, diapered mouse named Tuffy. Jerry and Tuffy lived in a mousehole in a home ostensibly guarded from mice by Tom. Some stories involved Tom's continuing efforts to evict the unwanted tenants; others concerned Tom's constant get-rich schemes which invariably failed. The best stories were usually those illustrated by Harvey Eisenberg, although many other artists rendered the feature from time to time.

In addition to the *Tom and Jerry* comic, the characters appeared in a number of Dell and Gold Key specials, published by Western, including comics such as *Tom and Jerry Summer Fun, Tom and Jerry Winter Carnival, Golden Comics Digest* and a promotional giveaway comic, *March of Comics*. Most of the specials also featured stories of other M.G.M. cartoon characters such as Barney Bear, Droopy, Wuff the Prairie Dog, and Spike and Tyke.

In 1961, the *Tom and Jerry* comic suspended publication for one year, resuming in 1962 and continuing until 1974 when it ceased publication with number 291. The title was picked up by Harvey Comics, which has been publishing it since September 1991 (mostly in the form of reprints of old episodes).

M.E.

TOM POES (Netherlands) Tom Poes ("Tom Puss") is the chef d'oeuvre of Dutch writer and artist Marten Toonder. Created in 1938, the strip was published in foreign newspapers until it was picked up by the Dutch newspaper *De Telegraaf* on March 16, 1941. This first run of the daily strip ended on November 20, 1944, and Toonder closed up shop for the rest of World War II. Finally, on March 10, 1947, the strip was reinstated in the newspaper *N.R.C.* The strip for quite some time has also been included in *Volkskrant* and, since story number 109, in daily newspapers like *Het Vaderland, Tijd-Maasbode,* et al. Thus far there have been more than 150 stories published in the daily strip version, which consists of pictures with narrative below them. The weekly version, with speech ballons and all the other comics trimmings, was started in *Ons Vrije Nederland* in 1945. New and reprint stories have since appeared in a number of weeklies including *Wereldkroniek, AVRO-bode, De kleine Zondagsvriend,* and *Revue.* Since 1955 the *Tom Poes* weekly version has been a welcome addition to the Dutch *Donald Duck* comic. Tom Poes also starred in his own weekly comics magazine, *Tom Poes Weekblad,* from November 1947 to June 1951. This magazine for children included various features, puzzles, and games. Many of the stories were also published in book form, others were originally created for books or in connection with advertising campaigns.

Tom Poes started out as a rather plump, cuddly cat. He got streamlined over the decades, walking upright into one comic adventure after another. The introduction of Heer ("Mr.") Olivier B. Bommel, a bear, in the third story of the series, provided a comrade and antagonist for Tom Poes. Bommel's popularity soon overshadowed that of Tom Poes.

The stories, originally written for a young audience, started changing when the strip returned to the newspapers after the war. Although plots and dialogue were still aimed at children, the humor of the strip was becoming more and more refined and establishment figures were being parodied. In the 1950s the stories became more intellectual, with an undertone of satire throughout the strip. The level was heightened even more in the 1960s and 1970s so that now the strip may very well be regarded as one of predominantly adult appeal. *Tom Poes* has grown up over the decades, along with the strip's readership. This, in part, explains its tremendous success in the Netherlands. The strip's intrinsic artistic and literary qualities have also helped to make it an international success. Hundreds of dailies and weeklies reprint the adventures of Mr. Bommel and Tom Poes. Some of the stories have also been produced as cartoons for television showing and for theatrical release.

W.F.

"Tony Falco," Andrea Lavezzolo and Andrea Bresciani. © Editoriale per Ragazzi.

TONY FALCO (Italy) *Tony Falco* appeared for the first time on December 11, 1948, as a weekly comic book published by Editoriale per Ragazzi. It unfolded over 48 issues (evenly divided in two parts), ending on November 5, 1949.

Tony Falco is doubtless Andrea Lavezzolo's masterpiece. It is a genuine novel in comic strip form and is of a literary value superior to that of most of Salgari's novels. The historical and costume details are always accurate. A dictionary, which did not limit itself to translating foreign dialogue but gave all necessary explanations concerning the ambience in which each story took place, was cleverly inserted within the panels of the strip.

As in a novel, the protagonist is surrounded by highly individualized characters: Babirousse represents shrewdness; Mohamed el Chelifa, generous strength; Haydee, delicate love, blindly loyal and mysterious. The drawings, meticulously rendered and artfully composed, were by Andrea Bresciani, a talented cartoonist who inexplicably and unfortunately disappeared from the Italian scene after the *Geky Dor* strip. (He is now reported to be living in Australia.)

G.B.

TOONDER, MARTEN (1912-   ) Marten Toonder, Dutch cartoonist, writer, and animator, was born May 2, 1912, in Rotterdam, Netherlands, where he grew up and went to high school and to the Rotterdam Academy of Art. There he learned the techniques of comic strips and of animated cartoons from a former Disney staffer, Dante Quinterno, from Buenos Aires.

During that time he made his debut as strip artist with Tobias (1931) and Bram Ibrahim (1932). From 1934 his strip *Uk en Puk* appeared in the weekly *Unicum*. In 1938 he started *Tom Poes*, a strip starring a cuddly pussycat that became more streamlined over the years. From 1938 to 1941 *Tom Poes* was published in Czechoslovakia and Argentina only, before being picked up by a Dutch newspaper. Over the years Toonder's creative genius came up with many more strips like *Japie Makreel* (1940), *Kappie* (1946), *Panda* (1946), *Koning Hollewijn* (1954), and many others. On the side he also produced comics for advertising.

At first, Toonder was assisted by his wife, Phiny Dick, his brother Jan Gerhard Toonder, by Piet Gertenaar, and Wim Lensen. The number of assistants grew with the number of strips created. This meant that, in the long run, roughly 80 percent of the Dutch comic artists have done work, at some time or other, for the Marten Toonder Studios that were founded in June 1942, originally to produce animated cartoons but soon including and branching out into comic strips. The Toonder strips' format ranges from strips of pictures with running narrative underneath them to full-blooded comic strips with balloons, and so on. At first, most work at the Toonder Studios was done by staff artists, then the studio relied more and more on freelancers.

Most of the Toonder animated cartoons and comic strips were financial successes. The comic strips are published in 15 countries. Marten Toonder isn't only a brilliant artist but also an excellent writer; he has added colorful expressions to the Dutch language. The Toonder style of doing funny comics has long influenced many comic artists in the Netherlands either directly through work for the studio or indirectly to stab at success through emulation.

For his eightieth birthday in 1992, Toonder was awarded the Tollens Prize, one of the most important literary awards of the Netherlands. Toonder commented that this showed that his work was definitively recognized as literary work. In the same year the first volume of his autobiography, *Toch is de aarde plat* ("But of course the earth is flat") was published.

W.F.

TOONERVILLE FOLKS (U.S.) Fontaine Fox's classic comic satire of rural life, *Toonerville Folks*, began as a daily gag panel distributed by the Wheeler Syndicate in early 1915 without running title or any thematic link beyond a vaguely country-suburban setting for most of the jokes. Many of the later famous characters emerged in these early panels (the Terrible-Tempered Mr. Bang, the Powerful Katrinka, Aunt Eppie Hogg, etc.), but they did not live in a specifically designated location, while other figures developed at this time (Thomas Edison, Jr., Uncle Peleg, etc.) were later dropped. The early occasional titles for the daily gags ("Pathetic Figures," "Pleasures of Light Housekeeping," etc.) included no reference to Toonerville, nor did the panel captions and dialogue.

"Toonerville Folks," Fontaine Fox. © McNaught Syndicate.

The famous Toonerville Trolley, name, skipper, twisted antenna and all, did not appear in the panel until 1916, while the other recurring characters were not linked in residence to the trolley's skipper until later. (The first authoritative unification of the Fox figures in one community came with the launching of Fox's Sunday page, *Toonerville Folks*, by the Bell Syndicate in 1920, at which time some papers gave the daily panel the running *Toonerville Folks* title, while others continued to use differing daily titles, as well as an earlier running title, *Life*.)

Virtually all of Fox's inimitable cast of characters: Mickey (Himself) McGuire, Tomboy Taylor, Wise-Cracker Wortle, Little Stanley, Willie Smith, the Dwarf, Old Man Flint, Stinky Davis, Suitcase Simpson, George Washington Smith, plus Katrinka, Mr. Bang, Eppie Hogg, and numerous others, were individually followed in the daily panel and Sunday page by the strip's millions of readers as if they were actual people. They were so recognizable that Fox could drop them in and out of the strip for weeks or months without using their names, with the full assurance that the readers would know who they were when they reappeared.

Most famed and admired of all Fox's inventions, however, was a trolley car and its living adjunct, the trolley skipper (never given a further name). This tall, angular, four-wheeled trolley with its interior stove and smokestack and its twisting miles of rural track was the delight of newspaper readers throughout the 1920s and 1930s; toys in its image were sold everywhere; and Educational Pictures' live-action *Toonerville Comedies* by Fontaine Fox of the early 1920s featured a replica of the trolley and its capped, bespectacled, and bearded skipper in every film. Various localities vied to lay claim to the original Toonerville trolley, and for decades every trolley line laid to rest across the country was called a Toonerville by local news writers.

Fox supplied little information about the line and its stops (although some were named from time to time in the strip: East Scurvee, etc.), although he did name its

founder occasionally, variously titled Captain and Colonel Silas Tooner, for whom the town was also named. But what happened on the line was hilariously documented in detail for 40 years including the grim period after World War II when the trolley was replaced by a bus, still jauntily and haphazardly operated by the old skipper.

Later in the 1920s, another Fox character, Mickey McGuire, was featured in a series of short live-action film comedies starring Mickey Rooney (who took his first name from the strip character). Several Toonerville strip collections by Fox were published in the late 1910s and early 1920s: Fontaine Fox's *Funny Folk*; *Cartoons*; and *Toonerville Trolley and Other Cartoons*, while a recent collection called *Toonerville Folks* was published by Scribner's in 1973. Fox himself folded the daily and Sunday strip in 1955 and retired to Greenwich, Connecticut, where he died in 1964.

B.B.

TOOTS AND CASPER (U.S.) Jimmy Murphy's gentle strip of family life and comic soap opera, *Toots and Casper*, first appeared in the *New York American* as a daily strip on July 8, 1919. It was launched as a Sunday strip on January 2, 1922. Syndicated by King Features, *Toots and Casper* began as a simple, domestic gag strip about a young middle-class couple with a baby in a big city. Never given a last name by Murphy (the point is routinely evaded in the strip by such statements as "A Mr. Casper to see you, Miss Jones."), the two reflect the mores of the postwar era with comic conflicts over Toots's daring clothes ("She's wearing a slit skirt and men's socks!") and Casper's interest in the good-looking baby-sitters hired to stay with their son, Buttercup.

The Sunday page continued the daily gags, and for some time the strip was a second-string filler feature for the Hearst daily and Sunday papers. In the mid-1920s, however, Murphy switched to a semi-serious continued story line on the order of that in *The Gumps*, complete with a rich bachelor uncle named Everett J. Chuckle, who drops in from money-making activities abroad long enough to get romantically involved and even married (just like Uncle Bim Gump), threatening the couple's hope of a plush inheritance. Other characters who emerged solidly in the developing narrative were Colonel Hoofer, a neighbor; Elsie Ferguson, Everett's long-lost love; Lemuel Plunkett, Casper's boss; Sophie Hoofer, the Colonel's wife; Danny Hoofer, the Colonel's son; Stella Klinker, a Mae West-type golddigger; Roger Kailerton; and Uncle Abner Chuckle, a second uncle (presumably poor, but actually rich also). A standby figure in the earlier gag episodes, a huge, bow-tied yellow dog companion for Buttercup named Spareribs, receded into the wings in later years.

Alternately half- and full-page, as advertising space dictated, the Sunday *Toots and Casper* page finally gained permanent full-page status once the continuing narrative became established and reader interest mounted. A single row of four panels was added as a weekly gag strip to the Sunday page and named *Hotsy-Totsy* on January 10, 1926; it featured an unnamed boy and girl couple romancing a la *Rosie's Beau*. On April 25, 1926, the permanent second Sunday strip, a third-page named *It's Papa Who Pays*, was added and focused on a middle-aged couple, simply called Mama and Papa, with four children of varying ages. A competent gag strip, this feature was routine filler material. (Later it was reduced in size to accommodate a highly popular series of cutouts featuring most of the Murphy characters in the early 1930s.)

Avidly read through the 1930s, *Toots and Casper* suffered a reduction in size and narrative complication during World War II, thus diminishing public interest. By the time the daily strip was discontinued on November 12, 1951, and the Sunday half-page on December 30, 1956, circulation of the strip had dropped radically. Attractively drawn and engagingly written, *Toots and Casper* was, with the daily *Gumps*, the best of the humorous, soap opera strips, and, in fact, of all soap opera strips.

B.B.

Sergio Toppi, illustration for the magazine Corto Maltese. © Milano Libri Edizione.

Rodolphe Töpffer, "M. Crépin."

TÖPFFER, RODOLPHE (1799-1846) French-speaking Swiss artist and writer born in Geneva in 1799, Rodolphe Töpffer was the son of well-known artist Wolfgang Adam Töpffer. Although he intended to be a painter like his father, Töpffer had to renounce his ambition because of poor eyesight. After studies in Paris he taught in several schools in Geneva, and was titular professor of rhetoric at the Geneva Academy of Belles-Lettres.

Töpffer Junior made a name for himself as a writer with charming and fanciful works such as *La Bibliothèque de mon oncle* ("My Uncle's Library," 1832), *Le Presbytère* ("The Presbytery," 1839-1846), both whimsical reminiscences about his childhood and youth; and *Voyages en Zigzag* ("Zigzagging Journeys," 1845), a description, with illustrations by himself, of his trips to the Swiss mountainside. His short stories, collected in 1841 in an anthology titled *Nouvelles Genevoises* ("Genevan Short Stories") also won him high praise.

But Töpffer's best-known and best-remembered works remain the more than half-dozen picture-stories, full of wit and mordancy, which he wrote in the course of his later years. These stories (much admired by Goethe) which anticipated the modern comic strip by some 50 years, were posthumously anthologized in the series of volumes published in 1846 to 1847 under the title *Histoires en Estampes* ("Stories in Etchings").

Rodolphe Töpffer who, along with Wilhelm Busch and Christophe, is regarded as one of the foremost precursors of the comic form, died in Geneva in 1846.

M.H.

TOPPI, SERGIO (1932-   ) Sergio Toppi is an Italian cartoonist and illustrator born October 11, 1932, in Milan. After high school Toppi decided to devote himself to illustration, and his first works were published in 1954 in the *Enciclopedia dei Ragazzi Mondadori*. From 1957 to 1966 he worked for the Studios Pagot contributing to the realization of animated television spots. During the 1950s and the 1960s he illustrated several children's books and in 1960 he began contributing to the weekly *Corriere dei Piccoli* with illustrations, funny anecdotes, and war comics stories. For the new magazine *Corriere dei Ragazzi* (1972) Toppi drew many episodes of the series *Fumetti verità* and *I grandi del giallo*, both based on Mino Milani's scripts.

In 1974 he started drawing for the magazine *Messaggero dei Ragazzi* biographies of historical figures based on Milani's scripts and later collected in the volume *Uomini che non ebbero paura* ("Men who were not afraid," 1980). In these stories Toppi began to change his graphic style, breaking the traditional division of the page in regular panels and working on the whole page as a single unit. Here the size of the panels, and consequently of the characters, changed according to their narrative importance. Over the years this technique has been accentuated and has turned into Toppi's distinctive graphic mark, also characterized by strong cross-hatchings.

In the mid-1970s Toppi contributed to the magazine *Sgt. Kirk* with covers and a set of his own stories later collected in the volume *Cronache d'armi, di giullari, di briganti e militari* (1976). In 1976 Toppi started an ongoing collaboration with the weekly *Il Giornalino* for which he has drawn for stories by himself *I racconti della vita*, *Un giorno per caso* (both also collected in book form, the first in 1977 and the second in 1980), *Viso nascosto*, *Storie d'oro e di frontiera*, *I racconti del vento della sera*; for stories by G. Ramello the series *Il Vangelo sconosciuto*, and *La città*, a long sci-fi tale written by Gino D'Antonio.

During the 1970s Toppi also worked for Bonelli publishing house by drawing covers and the adventures *L'uomo del Nilo* (1976) and *L'uomo del Messico* (1977), based on Decio Canzio's scripts, and *L'uomo delle paludi* (1978), based on his own script. In the 1980s he wrote and drew for the monthly *Orient Express* the series *Il collezionista* ("The Collector") and these adventures have been collected in three volumes: *Il calumet di pietra rossa* (1984), *L'obelisco della terra di Punt* (1985), *La lacrima di Timur Leng* (1986) printed by L'Isola Trovata.

In the same period Toppi contributed to the magazine *Alter Alter* and then to *Corto Maltese* with his own stories, which later on have been partially reprinted by Milano Libri in the volumes *Sacsahuaman* (1980) and *Sharaz-De* (1984). Toppi's collaboration with the monthly *Comic Art* has produced a collection of stories reprinted in the volume *Myetzko e altre storie* (1992). Many of the comics created by Toppi, though drawn in perfect realistic style, are embued with a magical atmosphere that makes the reader wonder about the objective reality of things. Toppi has also collaborated with some foreign publishers. He drew some episodes of *L'histoire de France en B.D.* (1976) and of *La découverte du monde en B.D.* (1978). He also wrote and drew two long stories on the Spanish conquest of America published in book form in Spain (1992): *El Cerro de la Plata* and *Las fabulosas ciudades de Arizona*.

Toppi's artwork devoted to illustration consists of covers for the magazine *Tempo Medico* illustrations for E. Sotsass's volume *Ukiyo è Haiku & Suspençe*; for he has also worked the magazine *Corto Maltese*, for the nationwide daily *Corriere della Sera*, for the Italian edition of the *Reader's Digest* condensed books, and he did two packs of tarot cards. Toppi has been awarded in Lucca a Yellow Kid in 1975 and a Caran D'Ache for illustration in 1992.

G.C.C.

TORPEDO 1936 (Spain) In the early 1980s the Barcelona publisher Josep Toutain conceived the idea of a hero similar to those characters played by James Cagney, George Raft, or Humphrey Bogart in the classic American gangster movies of the 1930s that he had loved in his youth; thus was *Torpedo* born. Toutain entrusted the writing to Enrique Sanchez Abuli and for the art he turned to American Alex Toth. In February 1982, in the pages of the Spanish edition of *Creepy* magazine, the series, baptized *Torpedo 1936* (the vintage year was appended to situate the timeframe in a nutshell), finally saw light of print.

Luca Torelli was an orphan born in southern Italy in 1904 (as his police record indicated); immigrating to the United States as a child he grew up in the mean streets of an unnamed American city. Starting with petty theft and extortion, he progressively graduated to bank robbery and eventually attained the status of a hitman, which earned him the nickname *Torpedo* for his lethal efficiency. Tall and gaunt (the artist had playfully modeled him after his publisher), Torpedo showed no weakness or mercy in his errands of death, dispatching his victims with knife, gun, and bomb.

After only two episodes Toth quit, protesting the senseless violence.

He was replaced by Catalan artist Jordi Bernet who endowed these brutal tales with a stylized choreography of violence and an almost documentary sense of time and place. "One is struck, first of all and especially in Jordi Bernet's work, by the precise re-creation of period details," David H. Rosenthal wrote in his introduction to the first American edition of the series. "In this respect, *Torpedo 1936* recalls not the Thirties but films like Roman Polanski's *Chinatown*."

At first rendered exclusively in black-and-white, the series later received the full-color treatment. While color somewhat distracted from the pervasive atmosphere of blackness prevalent in the strip, it did not appreciably tone down the overall mood of nihilism, cynicism, and despair of the tales. An international hit (pun not intended) almost from the outset, *Torpedo 1936* has been extensively reprinted in this country by Catalan Communications.

M.H.

TORRES, DANIEL (1958-   ) Spanish cartoonist and illustrator born August 20, 1958, in Valencia, Spain, Daniel Torres started making himself known as a comics practitioner the same year he was getting his B.F.A. from the Valencia School of Fine Arts, in 1980. Since then his career has experienced a meteoric rise, first in Spain whence his fame spread rapidly to France, Belgium, Denmark, Italy, and the United States. A professional through and through, he could trace his roots to the so-called "Valencia School" of Spanish comics and to the international movement known as "the clear line" derived from Hergé, the creator of *Tintin*. Taking a post-modernist stance the "clear line" cartoonists prefer heavily black, hard-edged contours to the softer line, halftones, and shaded areas favored by most modern graphic artists.

At any rate Torres shows in his work a firm determination to assimilate a variety of concepts currently in fashion in a vast compilation of influences culled from the visual history of the twentieth century. In this he displays a highly personal and creative spirit, and he embellishes his experiments with stylistic flourishes that show he is an artist who enjoys his own creative discoveries. His vitality, at once adventurous and ironic, and the exquisiteness of his line succeed in bringing to life a very personal universe of characters, clothes, objects, places, and incidents.

Torres first made a name for himself in the pages of the magazine *El Vibora* in which the cult of the underground comix was nurtured along with an interest in the latest modes of graphic expression. There in 1980 he created his comic strip character Claudio Cueco and, with or without him, successively published from 1980 to 1983 *Asesinato a 64 imagenes por segundo* ("Murder at 64 Frames per Second"), *Alas y azar* ("Wings and Chance"), *El angel caido* ("The Fallen Angel"), and other stories. In the meantime he had started with *Opium* his long collaboration with *Cairo*, a monthly whose esthetic ideology was more in accordance with his own tastes.

After completing an original story, *Sabotage!*, for a Belgian publisher in 1982, he began the first of the adventures of his new hero, Rocco Vargas, *Triton*, later followed by *El misterio de Susurro* (1984), *Saxxon* (1985), and other titles. The saga of Rocco Vargas represents a trend currently much in fashion, a version (halfway

Daniel Torres, "Rocco Vargas," © Daniel Torres.

between parody and homage) of the space-opera genre, and it is replete with quotes, visual and textual, from works that have influenced the artist's personal mythos. As Armando Mistral, the protagonist is the owner of a nightclub, and a science-fiction writer to boot; as Rocco Vargas he doubles as a space hero. Humor is a fundamental element of the graphic line, the narrative, and the dialogues; joined to a deliberate blurring of the lines between different realities, the psychological instability of the characters, and the constant shifting of the situations, it adds depth and distancing to the ostensibly escapist plot. In 1984 *Heavy Metal* started serializing the Rocco Vargas stories in the United States.

While continuing to draw and write "the astral adventures of Rocco Vargas," Torres has also in recent years turned out several shorter tales, later anthologized in *El octavo dia* ("The Eighth Day," 1993). In 1997, in the pages of *Penthouse Comix*, he started *Aphrodite*, about the investigative and sexual exploits of a scantily clad female private eye.

J.C.

TORRES, ELPIDIO (1925-1973) A Filipino artist born September 2, 1925, in San Juan del Monte, Quezon City, Elpidio Torres came from a family of artists: his father was a sculptor; his brother, Jess, is a painter; and his younger brother, Menny, is a cartoonist. Four of his eight children are also involved with art. Despite all the art influence in the family, Elpidio did not start drawing until the age of 20. He attended the University of the Philippines and took up fine arts. While there he met Larry Alcala, who had been doing comic books since he was a youngster.

In 1946 Torres landed his first art job with *Bulaklak*. Within a year he was promoted to art director for *Bulaklak* and for Philippine *Movieland* magazine. After he had been working for many years for these publications, a long strike occurred and Elpidio decided to transfer to Ace Publications. While at Ace he was teamed up with Mars Ravelo, who is considered by many to be the foremost writer in the Tagalog vernacular. Their first comic collaboration was *Roberta* for *Pilipino Komiks*. It was a success so the two continued to work together on many popular comic book series for various publications. Among their most famous strips were *Booma*, a jungle fantasy; *Dyesebel*, a dramtic novel about a beautiful mermaid and her relationship with people; *Bondying*, a humorous story about a mature male who retains his infantile behavior due to his unusual upbringing; *Gog*, a tongue-in-cheek comedy-horror story about a many-eyed, blob-type, monster; and *Dobol Trobol*, a situation comedy dealing with twins. Many of these were also made into motion pictures.

Toward the latter part of his career Torres wrote many of his own scripts. He did *Robina*, a jungle series for Craft Publications' *Redondo Komix*. *Planeta X*, which he did for PSG Publications, was a moody, science fantasy series dealing with aliens and supernatural beings. For Ares Publications he produced *Planet Eye*. *Planet Eye* was a very unusual strip in that it had an old pulp-type feeling to it, combined with a surrealistic approach in its storytelling.

Torres was one of the most popular of all the comic artists in the Philippines. He was respected and admired by his peers. His work has influenced many of the younger artists, particularly Abe Ocampo, who is now illustrating for National Periodicals (U.S.).

Of all the comic illustrators in the Philippines, Torres's artwork reflects the classical style typified by Fernando Amorsolo, the master of Philippine art. While many of his compatriots patterned their works after the popular American strips, he preferred to draw and create art that conveyed the spirit of his country. His pastoral scenes capture the lyrical imagery of the *barrio* ("countryside"), and his sensitive renderings of the typical *provinciana* ("country lass") illustrate his strong attachment to the traditional concepts of romanticism and chivalry that is lacking in today's comics. Elpidio Torres died in 1973.

O.J.

TOTH, ALEXANDER (1928-) American comic book artist born June 25, 1928, in New York City, Alexander Toth studied at the School of Industrial Arts in New York. In 1944, Toth began freelancing after school for Eastman Color/Famous Funnies Company. When that firm folded several titles in 1946, Toth was laid off. He completed his schooling and secured work under editor Sheldon Mayer at Superman-DC (later National) in 1947, commencing with *Dr. Mid-Nite* and *Atom*, then progressing on to *Green Lantern*. To each of these and other strips, Toth lent a powerful and graphic style, highly influenced by various illustrators, especially Noel Sickles. Toth's approach gained him considerable respect in the field and his style was frequently imitated in other National books, even after his departure.

In 1950, he moved to California to assist Warren Tufts on the *Casey Ruggles* newspaper strip for United Feature Syndicate. He left DC in 1952 to join Standard Comics for two years, also working on crime comics for Lev Gleason Publications and war comics for EC. In 1954, Toth was drafted into the army where he labored on the base newspaper and created his own adventure comic strip, *Jon Fury* in Japan.

Upon discharge in 1956, he joined Western Publishing Company (Dell) and worked on comic book versions of motion pictures and television shows (*The Land Unknown*, *The FBI Story*, *Zorro*, and others). In 1960, he began directing art on the *Space Angel* television series. This was followed by freelance work for

Alex Toth, "Thunderjet." © William M. Gaines, Agent, Inc.

National's romance and mystery books until he joined Hanna-Barbera studios in 1964 to do layout and character designs for Saturday morning animated shows. Toth and Joe Barbera designed superhero-oriented programs including *Space Ghost*, *The Mighty Mightor*, and *The Herculoids*. Designing model sheets for cartoon shows could not keep Toth away from comics; throughout the 1960s, he freelanced for National (on *Hot Wheels* and *The Witching Hour*, among other titles), Warren, and for black-and-white hot rod comic magazines such as *Big Daddy Roth* and *Drag CARtoons*.

In later years, Toth simplified his art style, concentrating on an economy of line and an emphasis on panel composition. His sense of layout and story continuity is generally considered to be among the finest in the field. Toth continued to work for Warren until the late 1970s. In the early 1980s he drew the first two episodes of *Torpedo 1936* for the Spanish publisher Toutain and *Bravo for Adventure* for an independent American publisher. He was reprinted in the 1986 *True Love* comic book that reproduced some of his old stories for Standard. Since the late 1980s he has devoted most of his talents to television animation (*Batman*, *Thunderbolts*, etc.).

M.E.

TRIPJE EN LIEZEBERTHA (Netherlands) *Tripje en Liezebertha* ("Tripje and Liezebertha"), while not the first comic strip to be created by Dutch cartoonist Henk Backer, remains his most successful creation. It appeared in the *Rotterdamsch Nieuwsblad* ("Rotterdam News") from 1923 to 1963, when Backer retired.

On April 1, 1921, Backer had started *Yoebje en Achmed* ("Yoebje and Achmed"), the daily newspaper strip considered by most experts to be the first of its kind to originate in the Netherlands. *Yoebje en Achmed* had also appeared in *Rotterdamsch Nieuwsblad*, the newspaper Backer had turned to after *De Telegraaf* had rejected him because they were already reprinting an English strip.

Like *Voorwaarts* ("Forward"), the Social Democratic party's newspaper that published Backer's second strip, *Hansje Teddybeer en Mimie Poezekat* ("Johnny Teddybear and Mimi Pussycat") in 1922, the *Rotterdamsch*

"Tripje en Liezebertha," Henk Backer. © Henk Backer.

"Les Trois Mousquetaires du Maquis," Marijac (Jacques Dumas). © Coq Hardi.

Nieuwsblad never regretted welcoming the young artist into its fold. Only one year (1924) after the start of *Tripje en Liezebertha*, a first book of *Tripje* was published and people had to stand in line to get a copy. *Tripje en Liezebertha*, because of its growing popularity, also sparked its own Buster Brown effect by endorsing a number of products from lollipops to chocolates to mouth organs.

Tripje en Liezebertha was so enthusiastically received by the public for a reason. For one thing, the stories offered a chance for an innocent escape into the realm of fantasy which appealed both to children and the young at heart. For another, the art was exquisitely simple-looking yet superbly animated. Reading the strip was like watching marionettes coming to life, acting out their whimsical, fairy-tale adventures in the never-never land of fantasy.

Backer's strip is proof of the fact that most early European comic strips were aimed at children, in the tradition of the Bilderbogen of the nineteenth century. Backer's work also proves that, while appealing to children, it is also possible to charm adults by allowing them fleeting glimpses at their own childhood fantasies.

W.F.

TROIS MOUSQUETAIRES DU MAQUIS, LES (France) During the German occupation, the prolific Marijac (Jacques Dumas) created his famous strip, *Les Trois Mousquetaires du Maquis* ("The Three Musketeers of the Maquis") in the Resistance newspaper *Le Corbeau Déchainé* as a humorous release from the extreme tensions of underground resistance and as a defiant satire on the occupation forces and their French collaborators. After France's liberation, *Les Trois Mousquetaires* was featured on the front page of *Coq Hardi*, a new illustrated newspaper published and edited by Marijac (October 1944).

The mechanics of the plot were very simple: three Resistance fighters (drawn from real life) and known as l'Avocat ("the Attorney"), Pinceau ("Paintbrush"), and la Torpille ("Torpedo") wage an unrelenting private war against the German occupation forces. The action, however bloody it may appear on paper, is more slapstick than mayhem. A typical instance shows one of the three musketeers getting hired as chef in a hotel serving as headquarters for the Germans, and blowing up the entire staff by means of a bomb concealed in a birthday cake. On another occasion, one of the friends, disguised as a farm girl, leads a whole German company into a booby-trapped barn. In spirit the musketeers are first cousins to another famous trio of French rogues, the *PiedsNickeles*, whom they emulate in cunning, deviousness, and sheer effrontery.

The strip was drawn in Marijac's usual nondescript style, but in this particular case the draftsmanship was less important than the merry absurdities of the plot. Early in 1949, *Les Trois Mousquetaires du Maquis* underwent a radical transformation in outlook. By then anti-German feelings had somewhat abated and the three friends decided to devote their energies to fighting gangsters, racketeers, and black-market profiteers. These, however, proved less diverting enemies than the hated Germans and, on November 23, 1950, the strip was finally dropped.

Les Trois Mousquetaires du Maquis is not a highly remarkable strip. The drawings are atrocious and the continuity slapdash at best. Yet it immediately caught the French spirit of the postwar period. Nor was the strip trying to capitalize (as so many others of the time) on the French Resistance's real or imagined exploits. Marijac was a former underground fighter and never hesitated to depict the faults of the resisters as well as their virtues. When some of the episodes of *Les Trois Mousquetaires* were reprinted in book form 25 years later by Editions Albatros, they received a warm reception, not only from former *Coq Hardi* readers but also from many young people curious about a time and a state of mind which must have seemed very remote.

M.H.

TRUDEAU, GARRY (1948-) American cartoonist born 1948 in New York City, Garry Trudeau graduated from Yale University and the Yale School of Art and Architecture. According to the rather tongue-in-cheek biography released by his syndicate, Trudeau had, at one time or another, participated in the archaeological excavation of a small, but significant medieval village, cofounded and edited a trilingual magazine for the diplomatic corps in Washington, D.C., designed and constructed light murals for Mayor Lindsay's Ping-Pong room in Gracie Mansion, worked as a photographic researcher for *Time-Life*, acted as assistant to the original producer of the off-Broadway hit *Futz* , contributed to *New York Magazine*, and wrote and illustrated a well-received series of columns on the 1972 Conventions for the *Miami Herald*!

In addition to quoting verbatim from this biography to researchers looking into his professional career, Trudeau is also fond of another self-deprecating quote from his editor: "Garry Trudeau is a thoughtful, concerned, and highly creative young man who is out to make a fast buck." Any objective assessment of Garry Trudeau's position, however, is not so simple.

Of course, Trudeau is best known for *Doonesbury,* which he created (as *Bull Tales*) in the pages of the *Yale Record* when Trudeau was an undergraduate. In 1969 the strip moved up to the *Yale Daily News* where it attracted wide notice. Universal Press Syndicate gave the feature its new title and started distributing it nationally the following year. Since then, Trudeau's renown has soared: his work is often quoted and analyzed in the news media (the *Washington Post* once proclaimed him "the youngest and most successful of the new wave of comic strip artists appearing in today's newspapers"), his strip appears in more than 400 newspapers around the country, and the book he coauthored with Nicholas von Hoffman, *The Fireside Watergate* (Sheed and Ward, 1974), has become a best-seller. Garry Trudeau remains a basically shy and private individual, however; his interest in the art of the comics is genuine (he once wrote a somewhat fanciful, but entertaining, history of comic art in *New York Magazine*) and there can be no doubt that he is more concerned with recognition than with money.

Garry Trudeau's draftsmanship (or lack of it) has been duly noted in many quarters. It should be mentioned, however, that his drawing style, consisting of a line reduced to its simplest expression, perfectly suits the purpose of the strip which is literary and not visual. The analogy between Trudeau and Feiffer is obvious, but only on the surface. Trudeau's idea of political sophistication is to make jokes, half anti-Left, half anti-Right, without regard to more universal relevance. Unlike such otherwise divergent comic strip satirists as Al Capp and the aforementioned Feiffer, he lacks conviction. When Garry Trudeau finally saw fit to express a strong viewpoint (whether political, moral, aesthetic, or whatever else he might choose) he was able to take his place in the ranks of the foremost comic artists.

In his already long career Trudeau has fought in favor of many political and humanitarian causes, and he has been a strong advocate of cartoonists' rights. He was the first newspaper strip artist in modern times to take a prolonged sabbatical from his work (in 1983-1984). He received the Pulitzer Prize in 1975, and (after 16 unsuccessful nominations) he finally won the National Cartoonists Society's Reuben Award in 1996.

M.H.

TSUGE, YOSHIHARU (1937-) Japanese comic book artist born October 31, 1937, in Oshima, Tokyo, Yoshiharu Tsuge quit elementary school while in the fifth grade and worked at a variety of odd jobs. He made his comic book debut in 1953. Among his very prolific production some works stand out prominently: *Yottsu no Hanzai* ("Four Crimes") in 1956; *Koroshiya* ("A Killer") in 1958; *Fukuwajutsushi* (a fantastic story about a ventriloquist) in 1960; *Nazo* (a mystery strip) in 1961; *Mishiranu Hitobito* ("The Strangers") in 1964; *Nezumi* ("The Rats") in 1965; *Unmei* ("Fate") in 1965; *Akai Hana* ("The Red Flower") and *Sanshōuo* ("The Salamander"), both in 1967.

In his early strips Tsuge came under the influence (as did so many other comic book artists) of the masters Osamu Tezuka and Sanpei Shirato. He created a great many strips in many genres (mystery, thriller, horror, etc.) but these strips were only for entertainment and Tsuge did not feel satisfied with his commercial production; so in 1966 he created the short comic story *Numa* ("The Shallow Man"), which really shocked readers. In it Tsuge revolutionized the concept of the strip: he went from entertainment to total self-expression, using psychodramatic techniques. This strip and the following, also thoughtful and brooding, disconcerted the majority of readers, but aroused the enthusiasm of a small group of devotees of comic art. Yoshiharu Tsuge's later production, if small in output, is highly significant in style and concept. It may yet prove a landmark in the history of Japanese comic art. Prolonged bouts of depression have prevented Tsuge from producing many comics in the 1980s and 1990s, although he has illustrated records of his trips around Japan and of his dreams.

Yoshiharu's younger brother, Tadao Tsuge, is also a comic book artist.

H.K.

TSUKIOKA, YOSHITOSHI (1839-1892) Yoshitoshi Tsukioka was a Japanese Ukiyo-e artist born March 17, 1839, in Tokyo into a powerful samurai family. In 1850 Tsukioka became a pupil of the famous master Kuniyoshi Utagawa, and in 1853 he made his debut, illustrating a famous Heike story. In 1866 Tsukioka and his rival in fame, Yoshiiku Ochiai, created the *Eimei Nijuhasshuku* ("The Sadistic Collection of Blood") series. In 1866 Tsukioka worked on another Ukiyo-e series, *Kaidai Hyakusensō* ("The Collection of Death Art"), and in 1872 started *Ikkai Zuihitsu* ("The Collection of Monster Art"). After completing only a few etchings of the latter series, Tsukioka suffered a nervous breakdown which temporarily incapacitated him.

Tsukioka recovered his health in 1873 and resumed work, using the pen name "Taiso" (meaning "great revival" in Japanese). Many important works were to come out of Tsukioka's pen in the following years: *Ii Tairō Sōnanzu* ("Prime Minister Ii Met With Disaster," 1874); his series on the Seinan Sensō (the Japanese southwestern war) in 1877, which became a best-seller and made his name famous; *Dainihon Meishō Kagami* (a series of traditional Japanese art) in 1878, another best-selling work. In 1885 Tsukioka started on his life work *Tsuki Hyakusha* ("Collection of Tsuki's Masterpieces"), which seriously taxed his mental faculties. In 1891 he was committed to a mental institution where he died on June 9, 1892.

Yoshitoshi Tsukioka was the foremost Ukiyo-e artist and the last great one in the Meiji era. His style was influenced by his master Kuniyoshi Utagawa, but he was also influenced by the European copperplate etchings in his later works. He was very good at depicting monsters and fantastic and grotesque creatures. In turn Tsukioka influenced a number of Ukiyo-e artists who later became the leading practitioners of the art (Kiyokata Kaburaki, Shinsui Ito).

In the last days of the Meiji era (toward the end of the nineteenth century) there were no cartoonists in the real sense of the word. Rakuten Kitazawa was to be the first Japanese cartoonist; but Yoshitoshi Tsukioka, along with his colleagues Gyōsai Kawanabe, Kiyochika Kobayashi, and Yoshiiku Ochiai, played an important role in the prehistory of Japanese comic art, until Kitazawa definitively established the form.

H.K.

TUFTS, WARREN (1925-1982) An American cartoonist born in Fresno, California, on December 12, 1925, Warren Tufts started to take an art course in his first year of high school, but locked horns with the instructor and at his invitation transferred to something else. When about 12, shortly after joining the Boy Scouts, Tufts was cast in a weekly radio program series about scouting and later developed his own dramatic mystery program series, writing the scripts and enacting all the roles. Tufts joined the navy in 1943 following high school graduation; first he drew survival adventure strips, then he was involved briefly in war bond promotions, then functioned as an artist and writer and finally an editor of Naval Air Station newspapers.

From the navy Tufts returned to radio and then, suddenly in 1948, he resigned from the field completely to devote three months to the development of the *Casey Ruggles* strip, which was syndicated following the strong recommendation of the *San Francisco Chronicle*. Five years later, as an outgrowth of disagreements with United Feature Syndicate over the handling of *Ruggles*, Tufts's new comic satire titled *The Lone Spaceman* was born. He wanted to syndicate it himself, and his father and brother joined him in the enterprise as his sales force. *Spaceman* was sold to some 30 papers in the United States, but was discontinued after four to six months.

Then *Lance* was created. *Lance* underwent development as a full-page art feature, weekly only, incorporating color treatment not attempted before or since in this country in comic strip regular production. The father/brother sales team again did well, placing *Lance* in three out of five cities contacted. The feature enjoyed premium rates, many noteworthy cover placements, and numbered select newspapers among its approximately 100 clients. However, the enterprise made arrangements with two Eastern U.S. syndicates for handling the feature. They did not perform well and argued that the addition of a daily strip was necessary. Tufts compromised his goals and added the daily strip. Then the two syndicates suffered internal problems and went out of business and Tufts was left without the representation he required and was overcommitted.

Since the conclusion of *Lance* in 1960 Tufts dabbled in several things as a freelancer: television and motion pictures as an actor, writer, and story director; television series design and development, film titles design, comic book production, magazine feature writing and illustration; and light aircraft design and development.

It was while flying an airplane of his own design that he died in a crash on July 6, 1982.

E.R.

"Tumbleweeds," T. K. Ryan. © King Features Syndicate.

TUMBLEWEEDS (U.S.) Tom K. Ryan's hilarious anti-Western *Tumbleweeds* made its appearance in 1965 distributed by the Register and Tribune Syndicate.

In the village of Grimy Gulch, on the farthest reaches of civilization, there lives the slow-witted, slow-moving Tumbleweeds, the most inept cowboy that ever plied the West, mounted on his equally anemic and faint-hearted hag grandiosely named Epic. Tumbleweeds would live happy, basking in the obscurity of his talents, were it not for the persistent Hildegard Hamhocker, the town spinster, who constantly tries to force her slobbering affections on him; and Hildegard's endless rounds of pursuing counteracted by Tumbleweeds's no less determined dodging are among the highlights of the strip.

Among Grimy Gulch's other denizens, there is Sopwell the town drunk, the irascible judge Frump and his gambling partner Ace, and Claude Clay the undertaker ("You plug'em, we plant'em"). The somnolence of the town is only disturbed by the periodic raids of Snake Eye, the resident outlaw, followed by the epic (but harmless) gunfights with the sheriff and his benumbed deputy Knuckles. There is also a neighboring tribe of hostile(¿) Indians whose feckleness and ineptitude are only matched by the incompetence of their adversary, Colonel Fluster, commander of the hapless garrison of Fort Ridiculous.

More than 20 *Tumbleweeds* books have been published since 1968. In the late 1970s the strip was adapted into a Saturday-morning television cartoon series. A stage production premiered in 1983, and a live musical show called *Tumbleweeds Gulch* has played at the MGM Grand in Las Vegas since 1993.

Tumbleweeds is a good representative of the modern humor strip, fast, witty, and irreverent. Several collections of reprints have been published in pocket book form. (The strip is now being distributed by King Features Syndicate.)

M.H.

TURNER, LESLIE (1899-1988) Leslie Turner, the talented sustainer of a classic comic strip cast of charac-

Leslie Turner, "Captain Easy." © NEA Service.

ters in his daily and Sunday *Captain Easy* strips for three decades, was born in Texas (like Roy Crane, whose work he carried on) in December, 1899: in the last week of the nineteenth century, as he puts it. A boyhood cartoonist and a four-year student at Southern Methodist University, Turner (again like Crane) hit the rails and high roads of foot-sore adventure in his early 20s, managing to sandwich in six weeks of intensive study at the Chicago Academy of Fine Arts. Returning to Dallas to marry and freelance (during which he sold a number of gag cartoons to the old *Judge* magazine), Turner went on to New York, and hit the big slick popular magazine illustration market with repeated sales of story art in the late 1920s to such typical titles as *Redbook, The Ladies' Home Journal, The Saturday Evening Post*, and others. Then he went to Colorado in 1929 to freelance again, while raising sheep.

A long admirer of Crane's work in the comics, Turner eventually met the creator of *Wash Tubbs*, and commenced working for him in 1937, at a time when Crane felt his work was slipping a bit, and took a long trip to Europe to recuperate from a too-long-sustained stint at the drawingboard. Crane was highly pleased with Turner's deft work on the strip, and worked closely with him from that date until he (Crane) left the daily and Sunday strips in June of 1943 to tackle his own original idea for King Features: a strip to be called *Buz Sawyer*.

Turner, continuing only with the daily *Tubbs*, published his first episode on June 1, 1943. The Sunday page, ghosted by other inept artists after Crane left (among whom was the ordinarily competent Walt Scott), was finally taken over by Turner on October 26, 1952, and drawn by him until January 31, 1960, when it was placed in the accomplished hands of Mel Graff. (Turner returned to the Sunday page once between February 19 and March 26, 1961; otherwise the page was carried on with fair competence, but with little of the Crane and Turner style or wit, by Graff.) Later the

Tubbs daily changed its title permanently to *Captain Easy* (not surprisingly in view of the small part the married Wash was taking in the strip) in the late 1940s, the date varying from paper to paper. By the late 1960s, Turner tired of the daily routine, and retired, his last strip appearing on January 17, 1970. He died on February 28, 1988, in Orlando, Florida.

Turner is one of the great masters of the comic strip medium. His humorous suspense stories rank among the finest sustained strip comedies of all time: as fine in its frequent peaks as anything Frank Willard, Billy De Beck, Cliff Sterrett, or Crane himself ever did.

B.B.

TURNER, MORRIE (1923-   ) American cartoonist born December 11, 1923, in Oakland, California, Morrie Turner learned to draw in high school and he graduated just in time to be inducted in World War II. Upon his return to civilian life, Turner joined the Oakland police department as a civilian clerk, freelancing all the while as a cartoonist for various magazines. In 1964 he quit the force to devote himself fully to cartooning. With the help and encouragement of fellow cartoonist Charles Schulz and comedian Dick Gregory, he created *Wee Pals*, an engaging kid strip featuring a merry band of youngsters of varied races and backgrounds. The strip, first syndicated by the Lew Little Syndicate in 1965, is now being distributed by the Register and Tribune Syndicate.

Morrie Turner has an easygoing, pleasing style, with few surprises but a neat line and a lively sense of composition that are deceptively simple. His dialogues are down-to-earth and fairly radiate genuine warmth and sympathy. Since the inception of the strip, Morrie Turner has received a wide variety of humanitarian awards, including the Brotherhood Award of the B'nai Brith Anti-Defamation League. He animated his little band of urchins in a television show called *Kid Power* (1973-1976) and has also published a series of pamphlets on antidrug, anti-gang, and child safety themes.

Morrie Turner is not, as many believe, the first successful black cartoonist (E. Simms Campbell preceded him by some 20 years with his *Cuties*), but he is certainly the first black cartoonist to find success with a strip featuring black characters. His efforts have paved the way for other black cartoonists (Brumsic Brandon with *Luther* in 1968, Ted Shearer with *Quincy* in 1970, and others).

M.H.

TURNER, RON (193?-   ) Although for millions who were subscribers to *The Eagle* (1950) Dan Dare is the great hero of the British science-fiction strip and Frank Hampson the finest artist of this comic century, for many others who were boys in the 1950s and who still collect and appreciate space art of the smaller, independent comics, no artist can touch the comic work of Ron Turner. However, due to the man's shy personality and refusal to come out of the artistic shadows, his name remains unknown to many. His age, background, and life is equally unknown, and will, it seems, remain so. Even his name, when it did emerge after some years of unsigned artwork, was originally believed to be Rowland Turner, according to his editor and his agent, through whom Ron supplied all his work.

Ron's artwork emerged in the independent comic books of 1949, published by the minor Scion Ltd. His first character, Scoop Grainger, was a newspaper reporter who appeared on the first three pages of *Big Scoop*, a one-shot. Inside was a two-page episode of "The Atomic Mole," the beginning of a four-part sci-fi serial. Although this adventure of Rip Rivers and Co. and their voyage under the earth embraced a terrible flying lizard and other prehistoric monsters, it would be in the worlds of outer space that Ron would find his true forte. He soon abandoned earthbound adventures like *Big Mounty* (1949) for *Captain Sciento* and *Space Pirates* in *Star Rocket* (1950), then took a giant leap in mankind's or boykind's publishing world from the cheapo indies to George Newnes's superb series of paperback "library" comic books, published in harness with their adult magazine, *Tit-Bits*. This was the well collected and quite rare series, *Tit-Bits Science Fiction Comics* (six issues,1953), which also carried Ron's first color work. He supplied the striking full-color covers as well as the main interior stories, including "Giants of the Second World" and "Terror of Titan."

In 1954 he began a series and sometimes serial, *Space Age* for *Lone Star Magazine*, which was so successful that the character won his own title from 1960 *Space Ace*. When the *Tit-Bits* series closed, Ron moved to the even more prestigious Amalgamated Press and began drawing for their pocketbook comic series, *Super Detective Library* (1954-1961), illustrating the 64-page adventures of Rick Random in *Kidnappers from Space*, *The Man Who Owned the Moon*, and many more. John Steele was another hero, this time more earthbound, which Ron started with *Gateway to Glory* (1960). Other "library" series followed, including *Times Five* for *Thriller Picture Library* (1962), *Claws of the Cat* for *Air Ace Picture Library* (1963), and entries for both *Battle* and *War Libraries* (1974).

Scoop Donovan, an echo of his earliest strip, began a long run of two-page strips in *Film Fun* (1961), and two fabled television sci-fi series were illustrated by him for T.V.: *Century 21*, *Stringray*, Anderson's underwater series, and *The Daleks*, a spin-off from *Doctor Who*

(1965-1966). Later came *Star Trek* for the same comic (1970). More junior serials were *Whizzer & Chips* from 1969, *The Space Accident*, and *Wonder Car* being the best remembered. Then he was back among more adult strips, drawing *Judge Dredd* for *2000 A.D.* and *Spinball Slaves* for *Action* (both 1977), and when the classic *Dan Dare* was revived for the new series of *Eagle* (1985), Ron took on his fabled rival.

D.G.

TUROK, SON OF STONE (U.S.) In 1954, tired of paying hefty fees for the licensed properties they were then publishing (*The Lone Ranger*, *Steve Canyon*, *Tarzan*, etc.), Western Publishing and its associates decided to put out some original titles of their own. Their first venture was *Turok, Son of Stone*, created by Western editor Matthew H. Murphy, which made its appearance in two stand-alone comic books in 1954 and 1955, before making it to its own title (starting with number 3) in March 1956.

Turok was an Indian warrior who, together with his youthful companion Andar, got lost in one of the limestone caverns that are so common in the American Southwest. That particular cavern happened to be the entrance to the Lost Valley, home of prehistoric tribesmen, legendary animals, and dinosaurs. The saga took off in earnest in 1957 with the arrival of Paul S. Newman as the main writer of the series. Under his guidance Turok and Andar fought fires and braved rapids, hunted dinosaurs and confronted hostile cavemen in their unending quest for an egress to the outside world. In their wanderings they also crossed paths with prehistoric pygmies, a lost Aztec tribe, and even had a close encounter of the third type with a flying saucer and its extraterrestrial occupants. The author was ably aided and abetted in his epic undertakings by Alberto Giolitti, an Italian-born artist whose vision of this lost world matched Newman's own in his sure delineation of even secondary characters and his depiction of relentless action.

The series ended in 1982; at that time the two protagonists were no closer to getting out of the Lost Valley than they had been after entering it. Exactly ten years later Valiant (now Acclaim) Comics acquired the rights to the character. After a dry run in *Magnus, Robot Fighter* number 12, he won his own comic book in June 1993. Since sales reports from Western had indicated that circulation had surged with those issues that happened to feature dinosaurs, the new publishers took note of the fact and altered the title to *Turok, Dinosaur Hunter*. They also gave the hero a disheveled look and brutish appearance that were clearly derived from *Conan the Barbarian*. This metamorphosis didn't quite meet with Newman's approval: In a letter to the trade magazine *Wizard* in 1995 he commented that the artist "was a graduate of the Blown-Hair-Across-Face School of Art;" later amplifying this statement (in a letter to this writer) by adding that he "would gladly drive a #2 pencil through the insensitive heart of this fly-by-night revampire of our comic heritage."

M.H.

TUTHILL, HARRY J. (1886-1957) Born in the slums of Chicago in 1886, the gifted, independently creative and personally reticent Harry J. Tuthill, who was to gain national fame with the wryly cynical but hilarious domestic fantasy strip, *The Bungle Family*, did not come naturally by such technical artistry as he developed.

Basically a storyteller and creator of characters, the young Tuthill strove to develop his gritty, grubby style of drawing sufficiently to carry his ideas into print.

Selling newspapers by the age of eight on the streets of Chicago, he went on the road in his early teens to sell picture frames, baking powder, soap, anything he could get into a pair of valises. Then he traveled with a medicine show from Oklahoma, a street carnival, and a larcenous corn doctor, finally winding up in St. Louis, Missouri, at 19. Here, working in a paint store, reading dime novels, and trying to perfect his dismal drawing style, he went on to toil in an ice house and a dairy before he landed a job on the *St. Louis Post-Dispatch* in 1910, where he worked as staff artist and went to art school nights on his new salary. From the *Post-Dispatch* he went to the *St. Louis Star*, continuing the political cartooning he had started on the *Post-Dispatch*.

Deciding to tackle the big city, he went to New York toward the close of World War I and was hired by the *New York Evening Mail* to begin a group of daily strips with varying titles and subjects, to be published on alternate days; one was called *Home, Sweet Home* and featured the characters and situations on which he was to build his later, famed strip about the Bungles.

When publisher Frank Munsey sold the *Evening Mail* to the *New York Telegram* in January 1925, Tuthill decided to try major syndication and launched *The Bungle Family* daily and Sunday through the McNaught Syndicate. Doing continuous narration here for the first time, Tuthill found his real talent and his long-deserved audience. Within a few years, he was earning an average of $150,000 a year, owned a vast estate in the Ozarks, a city house on Portland Place in St. Louis, and a nearby mansion in Ferguson, Missouri. He worked in the latter place, in a dark study surrounded by shelves and stacks of books, among which were the science-fiction pulp magazines on which he doted, and from which many of the fantastic themes of *The Bungle Family* were derived.

Tired of shaping much of his strip's content to syndicate demands, he folded *The Bungle Family* (which he owned) in mid-1942, then revived it eight months later to aid the war effort, doing the distribution on his own and writing the strip as he saw fit. Weary even of that by the close of the war, Tuthill once more folded his strip in June 1945, and lived out the remainder of his life quietly in Missouri, doing nothing more with the strip masterpiece which had won him the ardent devotion of millions of readers for 25 years. He died in St. Louis on January 25, 1957, one of the half-dozen finest narrative strip talents the comic strip has ever produced.

B.B.

UDERZO, ALBERT (1927-   ) A French cartoonist born in Italy in 1927, Albert Uderzo was taken to France by his parents while still a child. He grew up and received his schooling in the southeastern part of France, showing a drawing ability early in his childhood. In 1945 he moved to Paris and, the next year, became one of the first cartoonists on the newly created comic weekly *O.K.* His creations there include *Arys Buck*, the tale of an invincible Gaul, the forerunner of *Astérix*; *Prince Rollin*; and *Belloy l'Invulnérable* (1948).

After the demise of *O.K.* in the early 1950s, Uderzo became an advertising artist, though he never abandoned the hope of creating a successful comic feature. In 1955 he tried to revive *Belloy* without success, first in the Belgian daily *La Libre Belgique*, then in the short-lived *Pistolin* magazine. In 1956 he created *Tom et Nelly* in the weekly *Risquetout*, and in 1957 he teamed up for the first time with René Goscinny to produce *Benjamin et Benjamine* (a kid adventure strip featuring a brother and sister) for *Top-Magazine*. Neither of these ventures did too well, but the next year (1958) the Uderzo-Goscinny tandem proved luckier with *Oumpah Pah le Peau-Rouge* (Oumpah Pah the Redskin).

In 1959 the French comic weekly *Pilote* was founded by Goscinny and others. Uderzo started his collaboration in the first issue, drawing two features: the aviation strip *Michel Tanguy* (written by Jean-Michel Charlier), and *Astérix*, on texts by Goscinny. *Astérix* became extraordinarily successful, and in 1966 Uderzo left *Michel Tanguy* to devote his time to the feisty little Gaul. In the meantime he had tried (for the third time) to revive *Belloy* in *Pilote*, with Charlier as his scriptwriter. The strip lasted from 1962 to 1964 (in 1968-69 Uderzo made still another try at re-creating *Belloy*, this time in *L'Echo de la Mode*, a woman's magazine).

Unlike the egotistical and publicity-hungry Goscinny, Uderzo did not seem to have his head turned by *Astérix*'s success. He shuns interviews and devotes his time to what he likes best: drawing. Following Goscinny's death in 1977, he has assumed the writing of *Astérix* while continuing to draw the series, both with great success.

M.H.

ULYSSE (France) One of the most successful and enjoyable comic strips of the last 30 years is based on one of the oldest adventure tales known to man. In 1966 the Club Français du Livre—the French equivalent of the Book-of-the-Month Club—asked illustrator Georges Pichard and writer Jacques Lob for a comic strip adaptation of Homer's *Odyssey*. Pichard and Lob set to work, but the club turned down their version of the Homeric legend, judging it too farfetched. From that moment on *Ulysse* was to know almost as many vicissitudes as the legendary king of Ithaca. The first episode appeared in the Italian magazine *Linus* in July 1968; after an eight-month silence, the next seven

sequences were published in the French monthly *Charlie* (February-November 1969); the final episodes saw the light of print only in October 1973 (until June 1974) in the magazine *Phénix*.

The first liberty that the authors took with the *Odyssey* was to restrict the narrative to the central songs of the epic, those which relate Ulysses' wanderings. Accordingly, the story opens with the Greek warriors embarking aboard ships bound for their homeland (among the returnees is Homer himself, former war correspondent on the Trojan front) and ends with Ulysses regaining his wife Penelope and his kingdom over the pretenders. Furthermore, Lob and Pichard supplied a new interpretation to the ancient legend, treating it as a science-fiction story: the gods are extraterrestrial beings, technologically more advanced

"Ulysse," Jacques Lob and Georges Pichard. © Lob and Pichard.

than the humans, and they dream up all of Ulysses' ordeals for their private amusement. Within this framework, Lob and Pichard gave free rein to their imaginations and infused new life into the old Achaean myths: thus Polyphemos the Cyclops is nothing more than an android with a deadly laser gun for his only eye; the mermaids are abducted maidens on whom Poseidon has grafted a fish tail; and the shadows that Ulysses and his companions see on their journey to Hades are pictures from the filmed archives of the history of the world.

Lob's dialogue and texts are at once respectful and whimsical, blending slang expressions with Homeric vocabulary. But it is Pichard's illustrations that best convey the sense of awe and wonder that these old legends still conjure in the hearts of modern readers. In a time when every comic book scribe claims to be a new Homer, Lob and Pichard masterfully demonstrate that there can be no greater weaver of tales than the blind poet of Hellas.

M.H.

UP FRONT (U.S.) Bill Mauldin's famed and beloved World War II panel cartoon series, *Up Front*, began with a series of cartoons about army life and routine that he drew for the *45th Division News* in 1940 while a trainee. Like the formally titled *Up Front* that followed, this early series was reprinted and paid for by the civilian press, namely the *Daily Oklahoman* (then owned by the colonel who published the *45th Division News*). Mauldin's first panel for his divisional newspaper featured the two draftees who became famous as Willie and Joe of *Up Front*. (Undated, this panel appears in Mauldin's autobiographical *The Brass Ring* on page 92.) A collection of these drawings then appeared in Mauldin's first book, published when he was 19: *Star Spangled Banter* (1941).

Continuing the *News* and *Oklahoman* work into 1942 and early 1943, and submitting other panel gags to *Yank*, Mauldin continued to develop the content and style of the later *Up Front*. Following his participation in the invasion of Sicily in his unit's first overseas action, Mauldin began to draw his powerful combat cartoons, still for the *45th Division News*, which was the first U.S. Army newspaper to be published on European soil during World War II. In the summer of 1943 a second Mauldin collection was printed in Palermo for G.I. sales: *Sicily Sketchbook*. By Christmas 1943, with Mauldin headquartered in Naples and his *News* cartoons beginning to appear in the official army newspaper, *Stars and Stripes*, he published a third book collection of cartoons: *Mud, Mules, and Mountains*.

Also in late 1943, Mauldin was transferred to the staff of *Stars and Stripes*; at about the same time, his cartoon work attracted the attention of United Feature Syndicate. Now his work could be printed daily, and the *Up Front* title came to the fore, together with the growing emphasis on the Willie and Joe characters as regulars in the panel. A final European collection of this work was published by *Stars and Stripes* in Italy in 1945; it was called *This Damn Tree Leaks*. His first professional stateside book, based on the United Feature releases, was printed by Henry Holt and Company, and called, simply, *Up Front*. (The best extant collection of all Mauldin's wartime work is found in a large volume titled *Bill Mauldin's Army*, published by William Sloane Associates in 1951.)

The end of the war led Mauldin to change the name of his popular daily panel from *Up Front* to *Sweatin' It Out* (June 11, 1945), referring to Willie and Joe awaiting their discharges. After their discharges, the panel title switched to *Willie and Joe* (July 30, 1945). When Mauldin decided to broaden his scope of comment, the title was altered once more, to *Bill Mauldin's Cartoon*, on November 19, 1945. The last few Willie and Joe gags ran here, then the two were seen no more until the Korean War led Mauldin to resurrect them briefly in another context. Effectively, *Up Front* ran in various forms and titles from late 1940 until early 1951, at least as far as the continuing Willie and Joe characters, which made the panel a comic strip feature, were concerned.

B.B.

UPSIDE DOWNS OF LITTLE LADY LOVEKINS AND OLD MAN MUFFAROO, THE (U.S.) From October 1903 to January 1905 the Dutch-American artist Gustave Verbeck (or Verbeek) produced in the Sunday supplement of the *New York Herald* one of the weirdest comic strips ever conceived, *The Upside Downs*

"The Upside Downs," Gustave Verbeck.

of *Little Lady Lovekins and Old Man Muffaroo* (the title alone is characteristic of the whole enterprise).

The Upside Downs gave its readers two comic strips for the price of one; instead of ending with the last panel, the action of each weekly episode proceeded backwards, once the page had been turned upside down. The plot was very simple: Lady Lovekins and her mentor Muffaroo ventured forth into a fantastic universe inhabited by wild beasts, freaks, and monsters, where perils abounded and where the unusual became commonplace.

The Upside Downs was the product of an inventive but bizarre mind. Its innovative narrative technique was never emulated, and no wonder (as one critic pointed out: How Verbeek managed to work all this out without going mad passeth all understanding). Twenty-five of *The Upside Downs* weekly episodes were published in book form in 1905 by G. W. Dillingham, and 20 more were reprinted in a paperback edition by the Rajah Press in 1963.

M.H.

UTAGAWA, KUNIYOSHI (1797-1861) Japanese Ukiyo-e artist, born November 15, 1797, in Nihonbashi, Tokyo. Around 1811 Kuniyoshi Utagawa became a pupil of Tokuni Utagawa (no relation). In 1815 he illustrated his first book for Gobuji Chūshingura. All through the Bunsei era (1818-29) Kuniyoshi Utagawa labored in obscurity and often in want, until his Ukiyo-e series (Ukiyo-e refers to a series of traditional Japanese prints grouped around a central theme) *Suikoden Nishikie* (a collection of 108 pictures of illustrious heroes) made him famous as a master of Musha-e (warrior pictures).

After that time things went smoothly for Utagawa; other series followed: *Tōtō Meisho* (a group of famous landscapes) from 1832 or 1833 is probably the best known. Utagawa reached his height during the Kouka and Kaei eras (1844 to 1853), when he created *Miyamoto Musashino Kujirataiji* (a Musha-e), *Sōma no Furudairi* ("The Old Imperial Palace of Sōma"), *Myoukai Kou Goju Sanbiki* (a wordplay on the 53 coach stops along the Tokaido highway), as well as series depicting famous actors and battle scenes. Utagawa's *kyogas* (a kind of cartoon) also enjoyed great popularity in his time. Kuniyoshi Utagawa died on March 5, 1861.

Utagawa studied and mastered Western techniques along with the traditional techniques of Ukiyo-e art. He showed his versatility and inventiveness not only in his more celebrated print series, but also in his simple cartoons and many book illustrations. All of the next generation of Ukiyo-e artists (Tsukioka, Ochiai, Kawanabe, and other less famous ones) were greatly influenced by Utagawa's innovations, which directly led to the comic strip.

H.K.

VALENTINA (Italy) Valentina Rosselli made her appearance in the second issue of the Italian monthly *Linus* (May 1965) in a story called *La Curva de Lesmo* ("The Lesmo Curve"), drawn and written by Guido Crepax. Valentina was a sophisticated Milanese photographer, girlfriend of the enigmatic American art critic and criminologist Philip Rembrandt. Actually Rembrandt was none other than Neutron, a mutant endowed with superhuman powers, such as the ability to paralyze his enemies with a glance or to stop an engine from running. Valentina at first followed Neutron in his various adventures against the subterraneans, a race of extremely intelligent but sightless superhumans who tried at different intervals to subjugate the humans of the surface.

"Valentina," Guido Crepax. © Crepax/Milano Libri.

Little by little, however, Neutron disappeared from the story, and in 1968, in the short-lived magazine *Ali Baba*, Valentina appeared alone for the first time. The next year the strip was officially named *Valentina* in belated recognition of the heroine's dominant presence, and it soon veered away from primarily science-fiction themes toward pure fantasy, half oneiric, half hallucinatory.

In her dreams (nightmares? divagations?) of a troubling sadomasochistic nature, Valentina travels through space and time in a universe unbounded by rules or rationality. She meets, in turn, monocled Nazis, 17th-century pirates, and Czarist Cossacks, whose plaything she invariably becomes. Amidst a splendid and baroque background reeking of sensuality and decadence, Valentina is usually the victim of the most barbarous treatment: raped, whipped, quartered, impaled, hung by the thumbs, she always emerges phoenixlike from her ordeals, unmarked and apparently untouched. The author once stated that *Valentina* was an allegory of purity in the modern world. The resemblance to the Marquis de Sade's *Justine* is certainly striking and has been widely commented upon.

Valentina's remarkable story line is matched by an equally original and inventive graphic style. Crepax's compositions are greatly inspired by the author's incredibly catholic culture: side by side can be found flashes from Bergman's or Antonioni's movies, pointed reminiscences of famous paintings (Gericault's *The Raft of the Medusa*, Botticelli's *Primavera*), and tongue-in-cheek allusions to American strips (*Mandrake, Dick Tracy*). The images they conjure are also baroque in their profusion and intricacy, and the space is filled with architectonic devices and geometric precision which constantly remind the reader that this is a theatrical universe and that the protagonists are only a representation.

Valentina has been reprinted in a number of books published by Milano Libri in Italy and translated all over Europe and in the United States. In 1989-90 RAI-TV in Italy broadcast a series of *Valentina* telefilms.

M.H.

VALENTINA MELAVERDE (Italy) *Valentina Melaverde* ("Valentina Greenapple"), created by Grazia Nidasio in 1968 and one of the few Italian strips produced by a female cartoonist, was also one of the most popular features published by *Il Corriere dei Ragazzi*.

Valentina appeared as either protagonist or narrator of the adventures woven around her. She was surrounded by her family: her self-effacing parents, her brother Caesar (an automobile nut), her gossipy sister Steffi (a keen observer of Valentina's psychological and physical development), and her friends, neighbors, and people she met in everyday life. Grazia Nidasio is a sharp depicter of youth, and particularly of the world of adolescence, with its restlessness and easy enthusiasms. Valentina's vicissitudes resembled incidents in

"Valentina Melaverde," Grazia Nidasio. © Corriere dei Ragazzi.

feminine without being coy, she was warm and genuine and represented good qualities that exist in all of us. Nidasio's very original graphic style is ambiguous enough to leave many things to the reader's imagination. Nidasio received the award for best Italian cartoonist at the Lucca Comics Conference in 1972.

G.B.

VALÉRIAN (France) *Valérian, Agent Spatio-Temporel* ("Valérian, Spatio-Temporal Agent") appeared in issue 420 of the French comic magazine *Pilote* (November 1967). The strip was the product of the collaboration between cartoonist Jean-Claude Mézières and scriptwriter Pierre Christin (a professor of journalism at the University of Bordeaux who uses the pseudonym Linus).

The action takes place in 2720 A.D., at a time when the peoples of Earth have extended their power over the entire galaxy; Valérian and his lovely female assistant, Laureline, are crack operatives for the Terran Empire. Unlike the contemporary *Philémon* (which also runs in *Pilote*), *Valérian* is much more of a space-opera, with countless rocket flights, breathless escapes, and hair-raising chase and battle scenes. Linus's dialogues and scripts are inventive and entertaining, and Mézières's artwork displays a whimsical undertone (especially in the depiction of secondary characters and costumes) without being outré. There are no memorable protagonists in *Valérian* (aside from the two leading characters), but this in no way detracts from the solid construction of this fast strip.

A success almost from the start, *Valérian* has been reprinted in book form by Editions Dargaud. Still written by Christin and drawn by Mézières, it celebrated 30 years of uninterrupted publication in 1997.

M.H.

VALHALLA (Denmark) Valhalla, the home of the Norse gods, is the setting of *Valhalla*, a comic series that has been termed "the Astérix of the North." The series was created in 1979 by Danish comic artist Peter Madsen (born 1958) upon the initiative of Henning Kure. Along with writers Kure, Hans Rancke-Madsen, and Per Vadmand, Madsen has come up with record-

everybody's life and were made interesting enough to capture the reader's attention. She later grew up; and when she entered college she was succeeded by her kid sister Steffi in a new series of adventures starting in the 1980s in the *Corriere dei Piccoli*.

Valentina was a nice young girl with green eyes, red hair, and a freckled face. Loyal, honest, trusting, and

"Valérian," J. C. Mézières and Linus (Pierre Christin). © Editions Dargaud.

breaking, best-selling comic albums. The semi-humorous artwork ideally complements the well-thought-out ironic allegorical stories, which depict conflicts between very human gods and humans themselves.

The humorous epic has been exported to many European countries and even to Indonesia. From 1982 to 1986 an animated feature film based on Madsen's comics was produced. It was to become the most expensive animated feature ever produced in Denmark, costing some 30 million Danish kroner (about 7 million U.S. dollars). The film was judged the best animated feature at Cannes.

Both the albums and the movie produced spin-offs using the supporting character of Quark, a kind of troll. The comic strip *Quark* is produced by humorist Torben Osted. Swan Films, the producers of the feature film, spun off a slightly different series of animated *Quark* shorts for television. The latter were in turn spun off into a short-lived comic book version in Germany. However, the gods did not smile on the animated cartoon series. This had nothing to do with the visual quality of the shorts—the animation was impeccable—but involved content and, more important, copyright ownership of the character of Quark. The cartoon series was discontinued, though the *Quark* comic strip, which occasionally displayed a style reminiscent of Walt Kelly's *Pogo*, continued to be published.

Valhalla artist Peter Madsen was also successful with other types of comic albums, such as *Grönlandsk dagbog* ("Greenland Diary") and a realistic adaptation of the New Testament for the Danish Bible Society in 1994.

W.F.

VAMPIRELLA (U.S.) When Warren Publications decided to add a third black-and-white magazine, they broke away from the mold of their earlier *Creepy* and *Eerie* books and made the new entry a hero title of sorts. *Vampirella* number one premiered in September 1969 and introduced a character by the same name, a wench who just happened to be a beautiful vampiress. *Vampirella*'s creation was a group affair: publisher

"Vampirella," José Gonzales. © Warren Publications.

James Warren developed the character along the lines of French artist Jean-Claude Forest's *Barbarella*; writer Forrest Ackerman plotted the series' early direction; and artists Frank Frazetta (design), Trina Robbins (costume), and Tom Sutton (pencils and inks) brought the character to life.

Ackerman's origin story explained that the black-tressed Vampirella was a native of Drakulon, a dying planet where blood replaced water as a life-sustaining element. Vampirella took refuge on Earth to prey on human blood for survival, and most of her subsequent adventures have centered on her constant search for plasma or a suitable substitute. Artistically, the Frazetta-Robbins-Sutton team produced a lithe, raven-haired beauty of considerable proportions. She wore a skimpy red costume, a serpentine bracelet, black boots, and a gold bat insignia about her pubic area. A live bat, perilously perched atop her outstretched finger, was an occasional companion.

The early Ackerman scripts were heavily tongue-in-cheek, but Archie Goodwin later abruptly reversed the mood. He emphasized intrigue and human interaction over humor, his Vampirella always conscience-wracked whenever she took a life to survive. Goodwin also introduced Conrad and Adam Van Helsing, described as descendants of the Van Helsing in Bram Stoker's *Dracula*. Like their ancestor, the Van Helsings were vampire hunters, but Adam eventually fell in love with his quarry. After Goodwin's departure, John Cochran, T. Casey Brennan, and others handled the stories.

Tom Sutton handled most of the early *Vampirella* artwork in a crisp, fast-paced style that emphasized continuity before sex appeal. But when José Gonzales replaced him, the strip became more overtly sexual, an obvious attempt to entice Warren's considerable teen-aged male readership. Though he was a more accomplished illustrator than Sutton, Gonzales's work suffered because he was a poor storyteller and his ornate panels rarely helped the story's continuity.

J.B.

The last issue (number 112) of Warren's *Vampirella Magazine* appeared in March 1983. The title was then acquired by Harris Publications, which released issue number 113 in 1988; this turned out to be the last issue of the magazine. Since 1991 Vampirella has appeared in a number of miniseries published by Harris. Among the contributors have been artists Louis Small Jr., Joe Quesada, Rudy Nebres, and Jimmy Palmiotti, and writers Warren Ellis and James Robinson.

M.H.

VAN BUREN, RAEBURN (1891-1987) American artist, born January 12, 1891, in Pueblo, Colorado, the son of George Lincoln and Luella la Mar van Buren. The young van Buren, showing an early talent for drawing, joined the art staff of the *Kansas City Star* immediately after graduation from Central High School in Kansas City, Missouri, where the family had moved.

Van Buren called the *Star* the best school for pen-and-ink illustrators in the country at that time (1909) because its owner, Colonel Nelson, eschewed photographs and half-tone drawings. After four years as a sketch artist, van Buren traveled to New York to take courses at the Art Students League and do freelance illustrations.

The former endeavor ended after a few frustrating weeks; classes with Thomas Fogarty's father and oth-

Raeburn van Buren, magazine illustration.

ers seemed to be too slow-paced and rudimentary for the talented van Buren. Freelancing was more fertile and rewarding, however. Van Buren became a frequent contributor to *Life* (for which he had been drawing for several years already), *Puck, Judge,* and Street and Smith publications. The pulp publication *Smith's Magazine* was the first national periodical to use a van Buren illustration (his work for the humorous journals consisted of captioned cartoons).

Van Buren, whose early work betrayed no sign of his youth or relative lack of training, soon became one of the country's leading illustrators. His credits include 368 stories for the *Saturday Evening Post*, 127 for *Collier's*, and numerous others for *Redbook, Cosmopolitan, Green Book, Esquire, The New Yorker,* and *McCalls*, along with newspaper illustrations for King Features Syndicate and the McClure Syndicate.

In the mid-1930s, cartoonist Al Capp offered van Buren the drawing duties on a comic strip creation, and van Buren accepted on the strength of Capp's prediction that radio would kill the big magazines. Thus *Abbie an' Slats* was born in 1937, and van Buren added splendidly to the unfortunately small list of accomplished illustrators in the comics; Alex Raymond and Frank Godwin were brothers in this small band.

Van Buren's art was always distinctive, individualistic, and at home with the strictures and conventions of the comic strip. His adaptability was attributable in part to his professionalism and in part to the guidance of Capp, but mostly it reflected his overwhelming talent and genuine concern for *Abbie an' Slats*. His heroes were handsome and dashing; his heroines racy and winsome; and incidental characters were humorous or villainous to the extreme as the situation demanded.

Van Buren's long work in illustration gave the comic strip a constantly fresh, breezy, and narrative feel. Although some of his magazine work was in crayon, his medium was pen and ink, and he was a master of blocking, shading, vignettes, and close-ups.

He spent his last years in retirement, dividing his time between his homes in Florida and Great Neck, Long Island, where he died on December 29, 1987.

R.M.

VANCE, WILLIAM (1935-   ) Belgian cartoonist, born September 8, 1935, at Anderlecht, near Brussels. After three years of study at the Royal Academy of Fine Arts in Brussels, from which he graduated in 1956 with a first prize in drawing, William Vance started his career as a commercial artist for an advertising agency. In 1962 he began his collaboration with the comic weekly *Tintin*, to which he contributed a number of illustrations before creating his first comic strip, *Howard Flynn* (a sea-adventure story with a script by Yves Duval), in 1964. The next year, again for *Tintin*, Vance produced a Western, *Ray Ringo*, which met with only small success.

In spite of these false starts, William Vance had established himself as one of the more intriguing adventure strip artists, and in 1967 he started on the two series that he is most noted for: *Bruno Brazil* and *Bob Morane*. *Bruno Brazil* (written by Michel Regnier, alias Greg, under his pseudonym of Louis Albert) recounts the hair-raising exploits of a small group of dedicated crime-fighters, the "Cayman Commando"; *Bob Morane*, the comic strip adaptation of a popular series of adventure novels written by Henri Vernes, was first published in the woman's weekly *Femmes d'Aujourd'hui* before going over to the comic magazine *Pilote*. In 1984 he started doing, on texts by Jean Van Hamme, the spy thriller *XIII*, which is still ongoing; and in 1991 he took up the drawing of Gir's *Marshal Blueberry*.

William Vance's style is virile and vigorous, and his compositions, always to the point, make up in energy what they lack in subtlety. *Bruno Brazil*, particularly, has shown a marked improvement in recent times and can now be considered one of the top strips in its category.

M.H.

VANDERSTEEN, WILLY (1913-   ) Willy Vandersteen (full name: Willibrord Jan Frans Maria Vandersteen), Flemish-Belgian comic artist, writer, and producer, was born in 1913 in Antwerp, in the Flemish part of Belgium. He grew up in Antwerp and entertained his friends by drawing comics on the sidewalk, but they were always washed away by the rain, as they were drawn with chalk. He got his ideas from reading many books and comics of the time, like *Kindervriend* ("Children's Friend"), a kids' magazine that included reprints of English comic strips. In 1923 he was impressed by *Totor, chef de la patrouille des Hannetons*, Hergé's first comic strip. While still in school and dreaming of adventure, he started taking evening courses at the Antwerp Academy of Art at the age of 15 and continued until he was 24. (Some sources state that he started taking the courses at 13.) While working as decorator for the department store Innovation, he was doing a ladies' coats showcase when he read an American fashion magazine and there found an article titled "Comics in Your Life." This put him on the road toward creating comics, but before anything could come of it, he found himself in the role of ministerial statistician.

A chance meeting with an editor of the weekly *Bravo* led to his contributing comic strips to that magazine. He wrote and drew comics like *Sindbad de Zeerover* ("Sindbad the Pirate") and *Piwo* starting in 1943. In 1944 he added *Lancelot* and *Tori* to the comics published in *Bravo*. Early in 1945 he created another series, this time for newspaper publication. It did not begin until after the war had ended, however. Thus, *De Avonturen van Rikki en Wiske* ("The Adventures of Rikki and Wiske") started in late 1945 in the newspaper *De Nieuwe Gids*, which was later retitled *De Nieuwe Standaard* and still later, simply *De Standaard*. Despite the strip's success, it was felt that Rikki looked too much like Tintin and was therefore replaced by the orphan boy Suske. This also helped eliminate the age difference that had existed between Rikki and the girl Wiske. *Suske and Wiske* laid the groundwork for Vandersteen's success, which led to the Vandersteen studios and a number of comic strips, including *De familie Snoek* (1946), *Tijl Uilenspiegel* (1951), *Bessy* (1951), *Prinske* (1953), *De rode Ridder* (1959), *Karl May* (1961), *Jerom* (1963), *Biggles* (1964), and *Safari* (1969).

Vandersteen's style was largely influenced by Hergé, but over the years may have been hurt by over-industrialization. In part this may have been caused by foreign sales of his comics. Some of his features—for example, *Bessy*—have had more episodes printed in Germany than in his own country. It is understandable that putting out a comic book like *Bessy* week after week starts wearing both plots and art thin. On the whole, however, Vandersteen's work is a significant contribution to the history of European comic strips.

W.F.

"Vanilla and the Villains," Darrell McClure. © King Features Syndicate.

VANILLA AND THE VILLAINS (U.S.)

The last of the major variants on the theme of top-hatted stage villainy in the comic strip, Darrell McClure's daily *Vanilla and the Villains* began in several Hearst newspapers on September 10, 1928. Unlike the relatively sober, almost straight *Hairbreadth Harry* and *Minute Movies* melodramas of the 1920s (Kahles had abandoned his earlier fantasy for *Cat and the Canary*-style antics, while Wheelan was only slightly exaggerating the content of current film shockers), McClure's *Vanilla and the Villains* was wild, all-out, farcical nonsense, in a Marx Brothers–*Mad* magazine vein. Introduced in the first panel, Vanilla Graingerfield is shown riding a white horse amid a throng of worshipful plantation darkies in an Old South setting. (They are, as we shortly see, regularly horsewhipped into worshipfulness by Vanil-

la's wicked stepfather, Bourbon Mash.) A villain, Lambert Leer, tempts the stepfather into selling Vanilla's plantation and darkies for a sack of gold, only to be thwarted by Vanilla's poetry-reading but heroic boyfriend, Stonewall, and a bit later the U. S. Marines. McClure's comic artistry and sense of narrative make great fun out of all this stereotyped twaddle, and his drawings of such bizarre concepts as Lambert Leer and the Sinister Six all inside an absurdly elongated horse disguise (with a broomstick tail) are as visually memorable as anything on the comic pages of the time.

The art and story line became increasingly surreal as the strip rolled through its first year (McClure's vision of Russia in the 19th century is as fancifully funny as Walt Kelly's in a *Pogo* skit on czarist Moscow 20 years later), but McClure's pace was not as furious as in the first months. It is hard to say whether, when the strip was folded at the end of 1929 (with McClure going on to undertake *Little Annie Rooney* for Hearst's King Features), it could have continued its inspired foolery indefinitely. But while it lasted, *Vanilla and the Villains* was a tiny epic of concentrated spice and deft idiocy. It was a lively slice across the face of the average comic page of the time (overladen as it often was with domestic bickering and shopgirl romance), and it anticipated the avalanche of serious adventure and suspense strips shortly to come.

B.B.

VATER UND SOHN (Germany)

Vater und Sohn ("Father and Son") was created in 1934 by Erich Ohser under his pen name E.O. Plauen (combining the initials of his name with that of his hometown). Ohser had drawn cartoons for various newspapers and had illustrated the books of Erich Kästner. Having been introduced to the Berlin scene by Kästner ultimately led to Ohser's creating *Vater und Sohn* for publication in *Berliner Illustrirte*.

Vater und Sohn unquestionably belongs to the field of modern humorous drawing in Germany. Millions of readers followed the pranks and adventures of the bald-headed, mustachioed father and his round-headed, tousle-haired young son. Contemporary critics felt that Ohser's father-and-son stories were a humorous product of a specifically German nature, but they were proved wrong by the international appeal documented by reprints all over the world.

Ohser's work is a perfect example of the pantomime comic strip that does not make use of words except for subtitles. Thus, one strip from circa 1935, titled "Similarity (realization reached on visiting a zoo)," has father and son walking through the zoo. When a walrus lookalike breaks the surface of a pond, the flustered father ends the visit.

Father and son are full of love for each other and are devoid of any evil. Whenever dark clouds loom, they find the silver lining of easy reconciliation. Theirs is a quiet, sometimes wistful kind of humor that has lost none of its charm over the decades. *Vater und Sohn* was intended as a gift to youth, and children readily approved of it. They sent many enthusiastic letters, and when Erich Ohser occasionally visited a school, he was immediately surrounded by young admirers who asked him to give their regards to his real-life son Christian. As an introduction by Kurt Kusenberg in one of the *Vater und Sohn* books said: "Children realized that a kind man who loved nature, animals, pranks and the cunning little tricks just like they did was tending

"Vater and Sohn," E. O. Plauen (Erich Ohser). © Südverlag Constanz.

with loving care a corner of childhood paradise—their paradise that once also had been his."

Ironically, this gentle soul was driven to commit suicide in March 1944 after being arrested by the Gestapo following a denunciation for alleged defeatist remarks in an air-raid shelter. It makes the death of the quietly humorous creator of *Vater und Sohn* all the more deplorable.

W.F.

VELTER, ROBERT (1909-1991) One of the most prolific of French comics creators as well as one of the least celebrated, Robert Velter was born in Paris on February 9, 1909. He wanted to pursue art as a career, but family circumstances forced him to go to work at age 16, and he became a steward aboard an ocean liner of the French Line. He drew and painted during the long days and nights spent at sea; and his love of art and of the sea was to inform many of his later comics creations. It was during his many layovers in New York that he discovered the American newspaper strips—*Bringing Up Father, Barney Google, Moon Mullins*—that influenced his style. So enamored did he become with cartooning that he quit his seafaring job and in 1934-35 became an assistant to Martin Branner on *Winnie Winkle*.

His break came after his return to France in the mid-1930s. Under the pseudonym "Bozz," he created *Mr. Subito*, a daily newspaper strip distributed by the French syndicate Opera Mundi. The strip, about the

mishaps and contretemps suffered by a meek, middle-aged man always nattily attired in a black coat and wearing a bowler, was told in pantomime. It met with success from the start. The character's renown prompted the publisher of the newly established children's weekly *Le Journal de Toto* to call on Velter to create the paper's emblematic character: Toto, characteristically, was a spunky cabin boy who had many adventures at sea. Signed "Rob-Vel," the feature occupied the front page (in color) of the publication throughout its brief existence, from 1937 to 1940.

Again signing himself Rob-Vel, the artist created his most famous character, one that still lives today, Spirou, for the newfangled and eponymous Belgian weekly. The little hero was a bellboy this time, and the mix of humor and adventure proved irresistible to the paper's young readers. For the same publication Velter also originated *Bibor and Tribar*, about (what else?) the adventures of two rambunctious sailors.

Mobilized during World War II, Velter was wounded in 1940. Because of his wounds, which made it difficult for him to hold a brush, he sold the rights to *Spirou* in 1943. He resumed his cartooning career after the war, reviving *Mr. Subito* (which he had had to abandon in 1940) in January 1946. When his strip ceased publication in 1969, he went on to create a number of short-lived series. He then was asked to take over *Le Professeur Nimbus*, which he turned out under the house pseudonym "J. Darthel" from 1973 to 1977. He retired in the late 1970s, devoting his retire-

Robert Velter (Bozz), "M. Subito." © Opera Mundi.

ment to giving interviews and writing his lighthearted memoirs in order to counteract the oblivion into which his work had fallen. He died in 1991, feisty to the end.

M.H.

VERBECK (a.k.a. VERBEEK), GUSTAVE (1867-1937) American artist of either Dutch or Belgian origin, born in 1867 in Nagasaki, Japan. His father, Guido Verbeck, born in what is now Belgium at a time when it was a part of the kingdom of the Netherlands, was a missionary who headed the school in Tokyo that later became Japan's Imperial University. Gustave Verbeck grew up in Japan and later went to Paris to study art; while in Paris he worked as a cartoonist and illustrator for a number of European newspapers.

Around the turn of the century Verbeck immigrated to the United States, where an immigration officer miswrote his name as Verbeek on his official papers. Subsequently the artist signed his works with either name (his children were later officially named Verbeek), but Verbeck is the more commonly accepted spelling.

In the United States, Verbeck did illustration work for *McClure's, Harper's, American Magazine,* and *The Saturday Evening Post.* He later joined the staff of the *New York Herald,* for which he contributed three weirdly original series, *The Upside Downs of Little Lady Lovekins and Old Man Muffaroo* (1903), whose novel technique was never imitated; the nightmarish *Terrors of the Tiny Tads* (1905); and *The Loony Lyrics of Lulu* (1910), about a weird professor and his no-less-peculiar niece Lulu on a monster hunt.

In the 1920s Verbeck left the newspaper field and devoted himself to engraving and painting (several exhibitions of his works were held in New York and elsewhere). He died in New York in 1937.

Gustave Verbeck is one of the early comic strip artists whose work deserves to be saved from oblivion. His creations are full of a dark and sardonic humor that at times sounds curiously modern, and of a broad, fanciful penwork that seems deliciously passe.

M.H.

VERBEEK, GUSTAVE *see* Verbeck, Gustave.

VIC FLINT (U.S.) A routine detective strip, *Vic Flint* was introduced by NEA to its subscribing newspapers on Sunday, January 6, 1946 (the daily started the next day).

Flint was originally drawn by John Lane, with credit for the story line going to Michael O'Malley. O'Malley was in reality a cover name for the dozen or so writers who worked on the strip throughout its history. Lane was suceeded on July 31, 1950, by Dean Miller, who contributed some uninspired artwork. He, in turn, was followed by Art Sansom, who, fortunately for NEA, was as versatile with the pen as Russ Winterbotham was with his typewriter. The last artist to work on the feature was, ironically, the son of the first artist, John Lane.

The daily ended on January 7, 1956, exactly 10 years after its introduction, but the Sunday continued. On August 8, 1965, the title was changed to *The Good Guys,* with art by John Lane and a new, humorous angle and continuity by J. Harvey Bond (Russ Winterbotham). The feature expired on March 12, 1967.

Flint and *Good Guys,* especially the former, were designed as NEA's answers to other syndicates' successes in detective genre. But Flint was too routine, too stereotyped, too much the actor in a plot without interesting costars, to last. The feature went virtually unsold in papers that were not in the Scripps-Howard chain or heavy subscribers to other NEA features.

R.M.

"Vic Jordan," Paul Norris. © *Field Newspaper Syndicate.*

VIC JORDAN (U.S.) On December 1, 1941, a new kind of adventure strip appeared in the newly founded New York City newspaper *PM*. It was written by two staff men under the pseudonym Payne, and its first artist was Elmer Wexler.

Vic Jordan was the first newspaper strip depicting the struggle of the underground movement in Europe against Nazi occupation. Vic was originally a press agent for a French show that was closed down by the Germans. Among the cast was a girl who doubled as a spy for the British, and soon Vic found himself involved in the fight against the Germans. Bridges were blown up, trains derailed, and occupation troops ambushed in these grim tales of sabotage, violence, and torture.

Several times the Gestapo tried to infiltrate the underground group now led by Vic, but they were always outsmarted. As the months passed (and the war deepened), the strip became more and more realistic, showing the horrors of the occupation as well as the acts of heroism of the resistance fighters.

In 1942 Wexler enlisted in the U.S. Marines and was succeeded by Paul Norris, who was himself drafted in 1943. There followed David Moneypenny, a staff artist, and finally Bernard Bailey. The drawing, however, was always incidental to the spirit of the strip, with its stated sympathy for the occupied peoples of Europe.

On April 30, 1945, *Vic Jordan* last appeared, with the following epitaph: "The victory in Europe has been reflected on our comic page. *Vic Jordan,* our first comic strip, which was devoted to dramatizing the fight against fascism in the underground of Europe, has bowed to the fact that military victory is at hand. In the Sunday paper Vic made his exit. He was wounded, you remember, and has come back home for a rest."

M.H.

BEN JE ALLEEN?
VLUG DAN, NAAR
BINNEN!

"Vidocq," Hans G. Kresse. © Hans G. Kresse.

VIDOCQ (Netherlands) *Vidocq*, created by Hans G. Kresse, one of the big three among Dutch comic artists, was started in issue number 32 of the Dutch comics weekly *Pep* in 1965. Vidocq, the first detective in the world and founder of the French Sûreté, fits in nicely with Kresse's other historic heroes or, one should say, heroes whose adventures take place in a certain period of history, therefore making necessary extensive research if the artist wants to accurately re-create the mood of the times.

A lesser artist might get bogged down with all the research necessary for a historical strip like *Vidocq*. He might even feel tempted to draw the strip in a kind of academic realism that is sure to discourage a large part of the public. Not so Kresse. Although he can offer proof of the accuracy of details incorporated into *Vidocq*, he does not let himself get carried away with it. Instead, he concentrates on the storytelling and the dramatic effects. As might be expected, Kresse uses the interplay of light and shadow to perfection, just as in *Eric de Noorman*. Compared with *Eric de Noorman*, one cannot help but feel a kind of rejuvenation in Kresse's line work, and his use of speech balloons, unlike his earlier work, gives his art a somewhat changed look.

Nor does the writing fall behind the extraordinary artwork. One must even point out that Kresse has spiced the stories with humorous situations in order to fit in with the character of the French sleuth. The fact that the historic Vidocq is well known may have quickened the acceptance of the strip, and the Vidocq television series did not hurt it either.

The strip, which originally appeared in *Pep* magazine, was later reprinted in a comic book format, was published in other countries, and has since been reprinted in book form.

W.F.

VIRUS, IL MAGO DELLA FORESTA MORTA (Italy) Ten years after the appearance of *Buck Rogers*, the Italian comics produced their second science-fiction strip, *Virus, il Mago della Foresta Morta* ("Virus, the Magician of the Dead Forest"), written by the prolific scriptwriter Federico Pedrocchi, who, in 1937, had produced *Saturno Contro la Terra*. The artwork of Virus was done by Walter Molino, and the feature appeared in 1939 in the pages of the comic weekly *L'Audace*.

The chief character was a mad scientist, a not-uncommon figure in the fiction of the 1930s. Together with his mysterious Indu servant Tirmud, he schemed to conquer the world. This evil genius had his laboratory in the heart of a petrified forest. There, protected by an insurmountable electromagnetic barrier, Virus built a machine capable of calling the dead back to life. His plans were foiled by the handsome Italian hero Roberto and his youthful nephew Piero, who defeated Virus's army of ancient Egyptians.

Virus is one of the best-plotted and best-written science-fiction strips of the 1930s. Molino was especially brilliant in this tale of the strange and supernatural, his penwork rivaling the best efforts of the American cartoonists of the period in impact and intricacy. A second episode, "The Pole V," was published in 1940, after which the feature was suspended. In 1946, a third (and last) episode, "The Master of Darkness," appeared in the weekly *Topolino*, drawn this time by Antonio Canale. The effort was laudable but did not approach the high standard of the first two stories.

Considered today as one of the high points of Italian comic art, Virus's first two episodes have been amply reprinted: in the series *Albi d'Oro* in the 1940s, and more recently in the monthlies *Sgt. Kirk* and *L'Avventuroso*, as well as in the collection *Grandi Albi dell'Avventuroso*. In 1971 the definitive version of all three episodes of *Virus* appeared in the prestigious anthology *Le Grande Firme del Fumetto Italiano* ("The Great Names of the Italian Comics").

G.B.

VOIGHT, CHARLES A. (1887-1947) An American artist born in Brooklyn, New York, in 1887, Charles Voight was an accomplished illustrator and premier delineator of pretty women. Voight was primarily a cartoonist and is best remembered in comics for his long-running strip *Betty*.

The young Voight left school at 14 and joined the art staff of the *New York World*, where he eventually became sports cartoonist. His first strip was *Petey Dink*, which survived in different forms through the years but began in the *Boston Traveler* in 1908. He was later on the art staffs of the *Chicago Evening Post* and the *New York Evening Mail* before joining the New York Tribune Syndicate at its formation in 1919.

During his early period he was heavily involved with advertising art, refining his style and gaining a reputation; he appears to have been influenced by Wallace Morgan. He also drew a comic strip series for the old *Life* magazine in the late 1910s called *The Optimist*.

He contracted with the Tribune Syndicate to draw *Betty*, a pretty girl strip, evidently intended to compete with such entries as *Polly* and *Boots*. His work on the strip, like his work in advertising and his illustration in the major magazines, was impressive.

Voight's mastery of the pen inspires awe. His girls are the prettiest in the comics. If he had a flaw as a comic artist, it was his inclusion of panoramic scenes (usually a landscape of bathing beauties or café cuties) and the sublimation of the story progression. But this became a predictable device—also a trademark—and was forgivable because, though it might have interrupted the narrative, it was never visually offensive. Moreover, he had a real sense of humor (unlike such

"Voltar," Alfredo Alcala. © Alfredo Alcala.

other penmen as Gibson), and his pages were always lively and funny.

Voight left the Herald-Tribune Syndicate in 1942 to work independently. He died in Brooklyn on February 10, 1947.

R.M.

VOLTAR (Philippines) In the history of the comic book medium, most of the features that have become classics have been team efforts, with several people doing different facets of the production: scripting, breakdowns, pencilling, inking, lettering, publishing. The exceptions to this method, of course, are the underground comix, which are generally one-shot affairs slanted toward a specific audience. *Voltar* is unique in that it was a continuing series geared toward mass readership, yet it was written, laid out, pencilled, inked, lettered, and published by one man, Alfredo P. Alcala. The brush used to ink many *Voltar* pages was a special fountain-brush invented by Alcala, thus making the series even more noteworthy. Aside from the circumstances of its production, what makes the series stand out is the work itself. It is an astonishing display of sustained, artistic endeavor. Every chapter contains a spectacular center spread. Each panel is embellished in an etching style that rivals the works of the old masters. Inch for inch, it is probably the most detailed art ever to appear in comic books.

Voltar is the main character of Alcala's heroic epic. This graphic-novel encompasses elements of myths, legends, and actual history. It is high adventure dealing with extraordinary beasts and creatures such as winged unicorns, satyrs, and a white eagle. Ancient cities are sacked and plundered by wild tribesmen and barbarians, while young warriors perform deeds of bravery and valor. Love, hate, joy, sorrow, fear, and anger are expressed by the various characters in this tremendous saga. Plots and subplots are intertwined as the protagonist sets forth to seek his destiny.

The illustrations convey the feeling and mood of antiquity and bring to the viewer a glimpse of the beauty and splendor of the mythological past. The superb rendering of the young damsels and the youthful warriors provides a strong contrast to the withered and wrinkled rendition of the older characters. The brooding landscapes are filled with gnarled and twisted trees, ominous cliffs, mysterious caves, dark clouds, and the constant presence of vultures.

Voltar began in the first issue of *Alcala Fight Komix*, which appeared on July 9, 1963. With it were *Gagamba* ("The Spider"), by Virgilio and Nestor Redondo; *Virgo*, by Jim Fernandez; *Siopawman*, by Larry Alcala; *Alamid* ("Wild Cat"), by Tony Caravana; *Kagubatang Bato* ("The Rock of the Wilderness"), by Ruben Yandoc; *Kasalanan Daw* ("The Fault"), by Menny Martin; *Kapitan Limbas* ("Bird of Prey"), by Ding S. Castrillo; and *Ang Pagbabago Ng Mga San data* ("The Evolution of Weapons"), a three-page feature also by Alfredo Alcala.

For several years *Voltar* dominated the annual art awards presentation sponsored by the Society of Philippine Illustrators and Cartoonists. In 1971 a *Voltar* illustration was exhibited in a fantasy and science-fiction event that was held in the United States. The artwork took first place in the heroic fantasy division. And in 1974 *Voltar* was featured in *The Hannes Bok Memorial Showcase of Fantasy Art*, a book that compiled many of the finest works in the field of fantasy. It was edited by Emil Petaja. In the United States the feature appeared in the comic book *Rook* between 1979 and 1981, with texts by Bill Dubay.

O.J.

WAGS, THE DOG THAT ADOPTED A MAN (U.S.)

Billy Marriner, an emerging comic genius who cut his teeth on the pages of *Puck*, created *Wags, the Dog that Adopted a Man* for T. C. McClure in 1905.

McClure was one of a handful of protean syndicates that pre-printed sections of color comics for small hinterland papers, which bought them and surprinted their logotypes. Consequently, *Wags* and other Marriner strips achieved wide circulation in many markets.

Although another Marriner creation, *Sambo and His Funny Noises*, enjoyed greater longevity, *Wags* seems to have caught the public's imagination and deserves to be remembered for at least one contribution: It was among the first strips (*Buster Brown and Tige* was another) to have an animal, as an animal, talk.

Wags was a cute pup (all of Marriner's creations were cute without being syrupy) who attached himself to an animal-hater. Every week Wags succeeded in foiling My Nice Man's desperate efforts to lose him, or even to kill him. *Wags* was the only Marriner strip in which an adult figures prominently or permanently, and its style was in Marriner's striking mixture of thin, wispy lines; juxtaposition of blacks and masterfully used white space; and an enchanting atmosphere, of a slight distortion, that pervaded the whole work. *Wags* almost always ran full page.

Evidently Marriner tired of the one-gag strip and gave up *Wags* in 1908. But the public wouldn't have it, and Wags continued his efforts to adopt a master for several years thereafter, courtesy of boilerplate syndicates that reprinted old comic pages and distributed them to rural papers.

R.M.

WAKEFIELD, GEORGE WILLIAM (1887-1942)

British cartoonist and illustrator George William "Billy" Wakefield was born in Hoxton, London, in 1887. He was educated locally, winning a scholarship to Camberwell School of Arts and Crafts. He submitted cartoon jokes to Edwardian comic papers and was published in *Ally Sloper's Half Holiday* in 1906, then regularly in *Scraps* from 1907. He began to specialize in idealized girls, sweet yet saucy, and illustrated the spicy serial *Peggy the Peeress* in *Photo Bits* (1910). An interest in fairy-tale fantasy showed in his superbly detailed illustrations to *Prince Pippin*, a serial for *Young Folks' Tales* (1911). He also drew King Edward VII lying in state at Westminster Abbey for one of the illustrated papers (1910). His first strip, *Baron De Cuff and the Hon. Samuel Shiney* (1908), appeared in *The Comic Companion*, a pullout supplement to the weekly magazine *You and I*. This was followed by *Tap Room Tales* (1908) in *Scraps*. An introduction to Frederick Cordwell, an important editor at Amalgamated Press, led to an association with children's comics that lasted until his death.

Gertie Goodsort (1911), his first strip for Cordwell's new weekly, *Fun & Fiction*, featured the kind of flapper he drew so well, and this led to *Gertie and Gladys*, a flapper double-act, in *Merry and Bright* (1911). When

George Wakefield, "Laurel and Hardy." © *Amalgamated Press.*

Cordwell started *The Favorite Comic*, Wakefield contributed *Wott and Nott* (1913), then returned to girls with *Gertie Gladeyes* in *Firefly* (1914) and *Flossie and Phyllis the Fascinating Flappers* in *Favorite* (1914). In 1915 came a change of sex, and Wakefield illustrated the long-running *Boys Friend* serial *Rookwood*, by Frank Richards. He served in the 6th Lancers during World War I and was invalided out, returning to comics in 1917 with *Carrie the Girl Chaplin* for *Merry and Bright*. A number of new characters for this weekly and for *Butterfly* followed, until a new trend in his career was sparked in 1920.

Silent movies had so established themselves that Fred Cordwell combined them with comics and came up with a new weekly, *Film Fun*. Wakefield set the style of the paper, tapping an amazing ability to capture film stars' likenesses without resorting to caricature. He drew the strip adventures of *Baby Marie Osborne*, *Mack Swain*, and *Ben Turpin* for *Film Fun* (1920), then *Ford Sterling* and *Fatty Arbuckle* for *Kinema Comic* (1920), a companion paper, followed by *Jackie Coogan* (1921), some footballers for the short-running *Sports Fun* (1922), *Larry Semon* (1923), *Wesley Barry* (1924), *Grock* (1929), *Walter Forde* (1930), *Laurel and Hardy* (his best-remembered series, from 1930 to his death), *Joe E. Brown* (1933), *Wheeler and Woolsey* (1934), *Max Miller* (1938), *George Formby* (1938), and *Lupino Lane* (1939).

Other artists on the comics were required to model their style after Wakefield's, including his son, Terence "Terry" Wakefield, who took over many of his father's characters. Extremely prolific, yet extremely detailed and meticulous in finish, Wakefield also contributed melodramatic illustrations to stories in *Bullseye* (1931) and *Surprise* (1932), as well as adapting complete movies into strips for *Film Picture Stories* (1934), which were his only attempts at dramatic strips. He also drew the full-color series *The Jolly Rover* on the front page of *My Favourite* (1928), and *Freddie Flap and Uncle Bunkle* (1934) and *Teacher Trotter* (1935), both full pages, for *Sparkler* and *Comic Cuts*. In his spare time he executed excellent oil paintings. He died in Norwich Hospital in 1942 at the age of 54. For more than a decade his strips were reprinted in *Film Fun Annual*.

D.G.

WALKER, ADDISON MORTON (1923-) Mort Walker, one of America's most successful cartoonists by any yardstick, was born in El Dorado, Kansas, on September 3, 1923, and moved shortly thereafter with his family to Kansas City, Missouri.

A few lessons of the inevitable Landon Course was all the art training Walker received. Other schooling included elementary education in Kansas City public schools and enough various courses at Washington University and the University of Missouri to graduate with a B.A. in Humanities from the latter institution after World War II. Walker had been drafted out of college in 1943 and rose to the rank of first lieutenant, seeing action with the infantry in Italy.

After the war and college, he married and moved to New York as an editor with Dell. His experience as editor of the University of Missouri's *Show Me* humor magazine helped as Walker took charge of *1000 Jokes*, *TV Stars*, and a revived *Ballyhoo*, with another struggling cartoonist-editor, Charles Saxon.

Eventually his freelance cartooning superseded editorial activities and by the late 1940s he was recog-

nized as the most-published gag cartoonist. John Bailey, the *Saturday Evening Post*'s cartoon editor, suggested college kids as a theme and soon Spider, named after a fraternity brother of Walker's, was a regular character in his cartoons.

The syndication bug came to Walker in 1950, and he peddled *Spider* to King Features, which bought it—the last strip, in fact, personally approved by William Randolph Hearst. Two of the minor suggestions that Walker accepted, however, were taking Spider off the campus and putting him on an army base, and changing his name.

The name change was deemed necessary because King had just bought *Big Ben Bolt*, a major character of which was Spider Haines. Walker made an entomological switch and came up with Beetle. Soon the surname of the *Post* editor was added as a bow of gratitude and alliteration, and *Beetle Bailey* saw the light of day on September 3, 1950, Walker's 27th birthday. The Sunday page followed a year later.

The strip was an immediate success; Walker won the NCS Reuben award in 1954, the first of many other awards from NCS, the Banshees, and other organizations. He has served as NCS president and in other capacities, notably as editor of the newsletter, the magazine, and the periodic album.

Other efforts included his Museum of Cartoon Art in Greenwich, Connecticut, which opened in the summer of 1974. Another manifestation of Walker's life-long love of the art has been his association with other strips. He is the creator and author of *Hi and Lois*, *Mrs. Fitz's Flats*, *Sam's Strip*, and *Boner's Ark*.

Mort Walker's major contribution to the art is graphic, although his simple gags soon became the formula for many humor strips since the 1950s. He has always kept his artwork clean, stark, and simple. Many have criticized the lack of detail and seeming standardization of poses, but the success of *Beetle Bailey* speaks for itself.

The flavor of his strips can best be described as "stylized bigfoot"—modern and slick, but preserving the comic conventions of Frank Willard and other boyhood favorites of Walker's. The combined lists of Walker's various strips make him the most published comic strip artist in the world.

R.M.

Walker's latter creations have been *Sam and Silo* with Jerry Dumas (begun 1977); *The Evermores*, a historical feature done in collaboration with Johnny Sajem (1982-86); and *Gamin and Patches*, a kid strip he signed Addison and which Bill Janocha illustrated (1987-88). The International Museum of Cartoon Art, which Walker considers to be his greatest accomplishment, opened in Boca Raton, Florida, in March 1996. His sons Greg and Neal are also cartoonists.

M.H.

WALKER, BRIAN (1926-) One of the most successful comic strip artists to turn to the form late in life is Brian Walker, whose style—lively yet heavy in thick brushwork—has graced many comics since 1967, when Walker was 40. Previously he had been busy in many artistic fields, including calligraphy, painting, engraving, illustration, writing, and furniture design.

Brian Walker was born in Brislington, Somerset, on March 22, 1926. Her son's obvious affection for art prompted Walker's mother to enroll him in the Pitman's Press Art Course, a correspondence school, when he was 14. Finishing the course two years later, he left home for Bristol, where he applied for an art job on the *Evening World*. He drew war maps and joke cartoons while attending the West of England College of Art. After service in the Royal Air Force from 1944 to 1947, he was granted three pounds a week to return to the College of Art, from whence he won a *Punch* Scholarship. Soon he began writing articles for *Picture Post*, *Lilliput*, and *Cycling* (his favorite hobby), and in 1967 he illustrated a humorous book written by his friend George Haines, entitled *How to Be a Motorist*.

It was this book that changed the direction of Walker's artistic life. Upon seeing the book, the Scottish publishing house D.C. Thomson, one of two major children's comic publishers of the day, offered Walker trial work on several strips. Soon he was given the chance to take over the popular *I Spy* series. This he drew for some 130 weeks, but he later confessed that he had been unable to create story lines himself and that all his many pages for Thomson were scripted by a staff writer, Peter Clark. When Clark was promoted, his work for Walker fell off. A cartoonist friend of Walker's, Cliff Brown, was working for Amalgamated Press, a Thomson rival, and introduced him to Bob Paynter, editor of *Whizzer and Chips*. His first artwork for this weekly comic was *Three Story Sam* (1972), and the gruesome strain haunted many of his A.P. series from then on. There were *Fun Fear*, *Evil Eye*, and *Ghost Train* for *Whoopee*; *Misery Buckets* and *Plain Jane* for *Buster*; and *Wizards Anonymous* and *Old Boy* for *Whizzer and Chips*. His most popular was *Scream Inn*, an extremely Victorian strip laden with detail, which he drew for some 300 weeks (during its last period the title was changed to *Spooktacular Seven*). It also appeared in *Whizzer and Chips*.

His more recent work includes *Box-a-Tricks* in *Buster*, scripted by Roy Davis; and a newspaper strip, *Ar Little Uns*, in the *Bristol Evening Post*.

D.G.

WALLY AND THE MAJOR (Australia) Created by Stan Cross for the *Herald and Weekly Times Ltd.* in 1940, the strip was an offshoot of an earlier, unsuccessful strip, *The Winks*. Two of the characters from the strip, Wally (whose surname has never been given) and Mr. Winks (who became a major), were transferred to a new strip about army life that appeared daily in the *Melbourne Herald*. While not as blatantly Australian as *Bluey and Curley*, it was Australian in attitude and flavor and presented a far more subtle approach to digger-humor. It is, perhaps, this subtlety—often based on wordplay—that distinguished it from other areas of digger-humor.

In creating a strip about army life, Cross was determined to avoid the popular conception of the Australian soldier, much of which had been created by *Smith's Weekly*, where Cross had spent the previous 20 years. He went to great pains to see that his soldiers did not swill beer or have a cigarette dangling from their lips; where possible, they even avoided slang in preference to an educated vocabulary. By removing his characters from the firing line and making them part of a home-front army, Cross was able to leisurely unfold his humor, without the sense of active participation of other war strips.

The laconic, saturnine Wally made a limited contribution to the strip, particularly after the introduction of Pudden Benson as Major Winks' batman. The bald, tubby Pudden, when not playing the role of an obtuse buffoon, was often capable of flashes of cunning insight. More often than not, Pudden was the catalyst for the strip's punch line. He became a star in his own right, and when the Sunday page was published, it appeared in some states under the title of *Pudden*. The Major was a short, rotund, fatherly figure whose previous army experience qualified him for a commission. One suspects that his battle experiences were limited to wielding his pen in the war of red tape. He was a gentleman of the old school with a middle-class background, who had never come to grips with modern attitudes. He was constantly staggered by the assessments delivered by those around him. A highlight of the strip, under Cross, was the variety of expressions on the Major's face in the last panel. They ran the full gamut from anger, frustration, shock, disbelief, painful resignation, and, occasionally, beaming understanding. Cross was a master when it came to depicting an appropriate expression with an economy of line.

After the war, rather than take the characters back to city life, Cross located his team on the Queensland cane fields. With the Major still in charge, this locale was not very different from the army camp. However, it did allow greater scope for backblock/rural humor as well as the introduction of new characters such as Olsen, the thick-headed Swede. This shrewd relocation assisted the strip's continued popularity. When Cross retired in 1970, the strip passed to Carl Lyon, who had drawn the Sunday page for many years in addition to assisting Cross with the daily strip. Lyon never reached the level of skill and subtlety imparted by Cross, and *Wally and the Major* was retired in 1979.

J.R.

WANG SHUHUI (1912-1985) Wang had a profound knowledge of and skill in Chinese classical painting, being especially good at brushwork and at line drawings of Chinese women in ancient times. Her stylistic achievements came from blending images in paintings with the likenesses of real individuals from around her, as in her art for her tale based upon the well-known ancient novel *Xi Xiang Ji* ("The West Chamber"). It was made in 1958 and won the First Painting Award in the First National Comics Competition. "The West Chamber" is about the love between a poor young scholar, Zhang Sheng, and a girl from a rich family, Cui Yingying. Their love is thwarted by a powerful old woman, Cui's mother. But with the help of Cui's maid Hong Niang, the old mother is forced to accept their love.

At age 15, Wang began to learn drawing by copying the images from borrowed drawing books. Later in her artwork she mixed the skills she had studied with Western-style portraiture. Except during the Cultural Revolution (1966-76), when she was prohibited from doing artwork, she created comic books all her life. Most were based on stories written in ancient times: *Xi Xiang Ji*, *Yang Men Nu Jiang* ("Woman General in Yang's Family"), *Kong Que Dong Nan Fei* ("The Peacock Flies to the Northeast"), *Liang Shanbo yu Zhu Yingtai* (a tragic love story), *Meng Jiang Nu* (the story of a newly-wed whose husband is killed in battle), and many others. All of these stories are well known in literary form as well as in operas adapted from the books.

H.Y.L.L.

WANG XIANSHENG HE XIAO CHEN (China) Mr. Wang and Little Chen were two well-known figures in two respective comic strips, *Wang Xiansheng* ("Mr. Wang") and *Xiao Chen Liu Jing Wai Shi* ("Stories of Little Chen Staying in the Capital City"), which appeared at the same time and were created by Ye Qianyu (1907-1995). Both comic strips were initially published in *Shanghai Cartoons*, a large-size semi-monthly cartoon magazine started in May 1928. In June 1930 the magazine was merged with *Time Pictorial*, and Ye's strips continued to be published there, as well as in such publications as *Time Cartoons, Liangyou Morning,* and *Nanjing Morning News*. Ye's *Mr. Wang* and *Little Chen* lasted for 10 years, from the first issue of *Shanghai Cartoons* until the Sino-Japanese War broke out in 1937 and the publication of all journals was suspended.

Five interrelated figures in *Mr. Wang* and *Little Chen* were preeminent: Mr. Wang, his wife Mrs. Wang, and their daughter Miss Wang; and Little Chen and his wife Mrs. Chen. Though the relationships among these five characters never changed, the status of Mr. Wang and Little Chen did change according to the stories. Sometimes they were bullied by others, sometimes they were the ones doing the browbeating. Mr. Wang was a city dweller, and the stories in his strip focused on urban behaviors and problems, in addition to husband-and-wife feuds and other family affairs. Little Chen was a low-ranking official, and the episodes in his strip concentrated on government corruption and the effects of inflation and economic depression on the lives of the poor, for whom Ye had deep sympathy. Ye stopped cartooning entirely with the establishment of the People's Republic of China.

H.Y.L.L.

WARD, NORMAN (1906-1959) The comic art of Norman Ward, although never signed, was easily recognized by the young readers of *Film Fun*, the strips of several famous movie stars, which Ward took over after the death of the comic's virtual designer, George William Wakefield. Ward modeled his style very closely on Wakefield's, and only his distinctive lettering truly differentiated his work from his predecessor's. His strips included the front-and-back-page adventures of *Stan Laurel and Oliver Hardy* from 1944, his best-remembered work; *Joe E. Brown* and *Old Mother Riley and Her Daughter Kitty* (Lucan and MacShane), both from 1940; and *George Formby*, about the top comedy star in British films of the forties (from 1942). Ward's great success is unusual in that he took up the comic-strip form so late. He was 31 years old before he tried his hand at it, but after that he never looked back.

Norman Yendell Ward was born on November 30, 1906, in Page Bank, a colliery village in County Durham. His father was a coal mine policeman who had served with the Coldstream Guards and fought in the Boer War. Norman was nine years old when his father was killed in action at Ypres during World War I. Although he won a scholarship to a grammar school, his mother's destitution led him to leave school at 14 to become a telegraph boy at the local post office. Unable to progress higher than a telegraph-pole lineman, Ward emigrated to Australia in 1925 under the so-called Big Brother scheme. Returning to England in 1932, he tried several get-rich-quick schemes without success before taking a correspondence course in cartooning.

In a short while he had some of his cartoons accepted by the weekly magazine *Tit-Bits* (1933) and

then won a regular spot cartoon in *Detective Weekly* on the theme of criminals and convicts. (It has been said that he acquired the knowledge for this piece from unusually close contact with prisons and prisoners during the Australian era of his life.) His first comic strips were based on popular personalities of the period, a theme that would eventually lead him to a career at *Film Fun*. First came a strip based on a ventriloquist, *Arthur Prince and Jim*, in the boys' weekly *The Pilot* (1937), followed by *Wee Georgie Wood*, about a midget from the Music Halls, which was published in the new boys' paper *The Buzzer* (1937). Several of his strips turned up in the George Newnes/Arthur Pearson seasonal comics: *Unlucky Georgie* and *Dr. Hee-Haw* in *The Christmas Holiday Comic* (1937-38); *Dick's Quick Tricks* in *The Seaside Comic* (1938); *Milly and Billy* in *The Summer Comic* (1938); and *Ice Cream for All* in *Sunny Sands* (1939). He drew the front-page heroine *Jill Joy the Tomboy* in the short-lived comic supplement in *Favourite Weekly* (1938), then joined the new and instantly successful weekly *Knockout Comic*. For this quality comic book Norman supplied the silly serials *Stonehenge Kit the Ancient Brit* and *Sandy and Muddy* and filled in on Jos Walker's serial *Sandy's Steam Man* (all 1939). Later, he drew for the same comic book *Tough But Tender Tex* (1944) and took over the front-page Boy Scout strip *Deed-a-Day Danny* (1945). From 1940, however, he was best known as the leading *Film Fun* cartoonist, concluding his run of movie stars by drawing *Bud Abbott and Lou Costello* (1947).

Norman Ward continued to draw right up to his sudden and premature death at age 54 in 1959.

D.G.

WÄSCHER, HANSRUDI (1928-   ) German writer, artist, and graphic designer, born on April 5, 1928, in St. Gallen, Switzerland. While Hansrudi Wäscher's German parents lived in the Italian part of Switzerland, Wäscher learned Italian fluently. In 1936 he became acquainted with Italian comic books and was most impressed by *Tarzan, Mandrake,* and Alex Raymond's *Flash Gordon*. He also loved reading the novels of Italian writer Emilio Salgari. With his parents, he returned to Germany in 1940. After high school he became an apprentice decorator and completed his studies as a graphic designer at the Werkkunstschule in Hannover. He landed a job with the Hannover Municipal Transit Authority.

As early as 1950, Wäscher had drafted plans for German comic books. However, no publisher seemed interested. In 1953 Walter Lehning Verlag started publishing comic books in the pocket-sized Italian format of $6^5/8 \times 2^7/8$ inches. Somewhat flustered that his idea of entering the German comics scene on his own had been taken up by a publisher, Wäscher went to the Lehning offices and immediately sold his *Sigurd* feature. Since then, he has been in the comic business, writing and drawing more than 1,100 comic books in the Italian, or piccolo, format and some 450 normal-sized comic books; translating Italian comics into German; and drawing innumerable covers for Walter Lehning. Except for the first 40 issues of *Sigurd*, he has written all of the stories of his comic series, which include *Falk, Tibor, Nick, Gert Jörg,* and others. He started his own two series, *Nizar* and *Ulf*, when Lehning ceased publication in 1968. Since 1969 he has been working on the *Buffalo Bill* comic book of Bastei Verlag.

As most of Wäscher's comics show, he has a marked predilection for jungle tales (*Tibor, Nizar*) and for adventures involving knights (*Sigurd, Falk, Ulf*). He also feels at home with pirates (*Gert*) and science fiction (*Nick*). Wäscher's style at first glance seems to be simple and wooden. In part this is due to the fact that he had to do all of the artwork on the Lehning books in the same size that they were to be printed. Nevertheless, Wäscher manages to tell his stories well. The almost unending adventures of his heroes in the piccolo format still hold up today and are very much sought after by German collectors trying to recapture their childhood dreams and fantasies, gleaned from pocket-sized comic books eagerly devoured week after week to the chagrin of many a teacher. Wäscher's comic books, despite some of their artistic shortcomings, have helped to firmly establish comics in postwar Germany.

With fan interest in Wäscher continuing unabated, most of his work has been reprinted by Hethke Verlag with new artwork and new comic books and albums done for some of the old series. Wäscher's comic heroes have also been put on a series of telephone cards.

W.F.

WASH TUBBS (U.S.) The classic adventure and humor strip *Wash Tubbs* (originally titled *Washington Tubbs II*), by Roy Crane, began publication as an NEA Syndicate daily feature on April 21, 1924. The strip's pint-size hero-to-be, George Washington Tubbs II, curly-haired and with saucer-rimmed spectacles and an enormous penchant for women larger than himself (most were), sallied forth on the comic stage working in a small-town grocery called the Crabtree Emporium, run by a cracker-barrel philosopher type whom Wash simply called Boss. For the first few months, Wash and Mr. Crabtree were the principal characters, while Wash

had trouble with a rival named Bertram Speed for the attentions of a peroxide blonde called Dottie. Then, unexpectedly, on August 8, 1924, a wildly fresh element of mystery leading to buried treasure in the South Seas shattered the strip's story pattern. Before long Wash was aboard a ship called the *Sieve*, faced with a scurvy rogue named Tamalio, his life in danger, his future dubious; readers were shaken at their coffee.

NEA was by no means convinced that Roy Crane's novel experiment was worth repeating, and after Wash had returned home rich, he was again confined to relatively mundane exploits (crashing the movies; wooing a girl; riding the rails) for two years before Crane was able to fling him into a rough-and-tumble Wild West story (in a hell-town called Cozy Gulch) on July 15, 1926. Shortly after (on November 15, 1926), Wash met his buddy-in-arms, Gozy Gallup, and (as the strip title changed to *Wash Tubbs* in most papers in mid-1926) became involved in a medicine-show swindle, a circus, and then a brutal imbroglio with bandits in Mexico. Next came an excursion to Santo Domingo and Wash and Gozy's first encounter with Bull Dawson, who was to become Wash's worst enemy and a recurrent figure in the strip throughout the years. (Dawson's unshaven villainy first shadowed the strip on March 10, 1928.) By now, of course, the story line was pure adventure, and it was apparent Crane knew he was writing a kind of comic epic. In another year, the two-fisted adventurer, Captain Easy, had slugged his way into the strip, at the peak of a story of revolution and murder in central Europe. Easy (who entered the strip on February 6, 1929) was a man of mystery, obviously adventuring under a pseudonym, whose real and tragic story was not revealed for a number of years. (His true identity was William "Billy" Lee, framed by a rival for robbery in a staid southern town.) He became Wash's new fellow swashbuckler, while Crane retired Gozy to

"Wash Tubbs," Roy Crane. © NEA Service.

marriage and a family (a fate Wash was to share a few years later).

Easy was the hit of the strip. Although Wash continued as the central character (even adventuring a bit on his own, circa 1931-32), it was obvious that Easy had become the feature's true hero. And when NEA decided to give Crane a Sunday page on July 30, 1933, it was Easy who was the new strip's solo hero and source of the title: *Captain Easy*. (Ostensibly, the Sunday strip detailed Easy's escapades before he met Wash. A colorful, graphically freewheeling feature, *Captain Easy* quickly became the most eye-appealing page in the color comics, surpassing even the Foster *Tarzan* and Raymond *Flash Gordon* in the variety of layout and inventiveness of art. The story, simpler than the daily *Tubbs*, was still gripping and suspenseful.)

Then World War II split Wash and Easy for good. Tied down at home with a draft-exempting job and dependents, Wash had to watch Easy go into the service as a special agent behind enemy lines—which is where, after a number of graphically superb adventures, Crane left Easy when he turned the daily *Tubbs* and Sunday *Easy* over to his assistant, Leslie Turner, on June 1, 1943, to begin his *Buz Sawyer* strip for King Features.

Turner's work on the two strips differed materially from Crane's narrative approach, although his style was strikingly similar in its effective utilization of the basic Crane graphic techniques. Following the close of World War II, Turner developed an interesting narrative structure for the daily strip in alternating highly comic stories (involving such inventions of his own as the ghastly Kallikak Family and the master swindler J. Buckingham Ish, who never fails to hook J. P. McKee) and basically serious adventure stories, usually set in foreign locales and occasionally involving the old battler, Bull Dawson. The Sunday strip (which he turned over to Mel Graff for a long period of time) was generally humorous in tone when he drew it.

Essentially, however, Turner did a remarkable job of continuing a major strip without a really noticeable shift in style or story (aided in the transition, of course, by the watershed of World War II). After Turner retired, the daily and Sunday strips, now both called *Captain Easy*, were carried on by the team of Jim Lawrence and Bill Crooks. Theirs was a valiant effort, particularly in graphic style, but the result was a good deal further away from the Crane work than was Turner's rendition, without being interestingly innovative in its own right. *Wash Tubbs* finally ended its long run in 1988.

B.B.

WATCHMEN (U.S.) One of the most original and gripping stories to come out of the superhero genre in the last decade, *Watchmen* typically was the work of two British imports, the writer Alan Moore and the artist Dave Gibbons. It was published by DC Comics as a limited series over the span of 12 issues extending from September 1986 to October 1987.

Set in a parallel universe that took the reader back to the late 1950s, *Watchmen* opened on a murder mystery and closed on a nuclear holocaust. In this reinvented world superheroes did coexist with mere mortals and were the pawns (or perhaps the masters) of that society's power structure. The Watchmen were just such a group of superheroes, made up of the megalomaniacal Ozymandias, the paranoid Rorschach (whose face was

"Watchmen," Alan Moore and Dave Gibbons. © DC Comics.

a blot), the all-powerful Dr. Manhattan (who liked to move about stark naked), and a handful of others. After they came upon the body of their former associate, the Comedian, they realized that a sinister plot to start a world conflict was afoot, and they set out to save the planet from extinction in the 12 minutes remaining before the trigger point.

In every episode (each of which was posited to be only one minute in duration) there were radical shiftings of time frames, flashbacks within flashbacks, and enough plot twists to fill at least a score of ordinary comic books. The suspense was kept constant through different levels of storytelling (there was even a comic book within the comic book, a pirate series titled *Tales of the Black Freighter*, whose plot echoed some of the strands in the main story line). The oddly angled perspectives and asymmetrical compositions, as well as the surreal coloring, added to the mood of eeriness and dread.

Symbolism and irony abounded throughout the disturbing tales. In the course of an interview Moore averred, "What we were trying to do was to create something which has a structure that is multi-faceted enough and has enough layers to it so that each subsequent issue redefines bits of the ones that have come before." Rock-group covers were represented alongside snatches of classical paintings, and excerpts of Bob Dylan lyrics were juxtaposed with quotes from the

Bible. The work's title was itself based on a line by the Roman poet Juvenal, the author of the *Satires*, "Qui custodiet custodies?" ("Who watches the watchmen?").

Watchmen was a great (and unexpected) success as a comic book series, and it enjoyed even greater popularity when it was reprinted in paperback form. A unique tour de force, its excellence has never been replicated, and it lies like an erratic rock in the middle of the great comic book desert.

M.H.

WATSO *see* Mager, Gus.

WAUGH, COULTON (1896-1973) American artist, born in 1896 in Cornwall, England. Coulton Waugh's father, Fredrick J. Waugh, was a famous marine painter, and his grandfather, Samuel Bell Waugh, was the portrait painter of Presidents Lincoln and Grant. Coulton Waugh came back to the United States as a young man and worked variously as a textile designer, a newspaper and magazine illustrator, and a cartoonist in New York, while continuing to follow in his ancestors' footsteps as a painter. Waugh's hobby was sailing (he was once shipwrecked off Cape Hatteras), and he contributed articles and illustrations to various yachting magazines and to *Boy's Life*.

When the editors at Associated Press had to find a replacement for Milton Caniff on *Dickie Dare*, they selected Waugh, who started his long association with the strip in October 1934. In 1943 he married his assistant, Mabel Odin Burvik, to whom he had earlier relinquished the strip (her signature, Odin, started appearing in the spring of 1944). In 1945 Waugh started a new strip, *Hank*, about a war veteran, for the New York daily *P.M.*, but the experiment proved short-lived.

In 1947 Coulton Waugh published *The Comics*, a pioneering study of American comic art. From then on he divided his career almost equally among drawing, painting, writing, and teaching. From 1960 to 1970 he wrote and drew the daily *Junior Editors* panel for A.P.; taught art at Orange County Community College; had many one-man shows and participated in three Waugh family shows, along with eight other Waugh painters; served as first curator of the Storm King Art Center in Cornwall, New York; and wrote two art instruction books, *How to Paint with a Knife* and *Landscape Painting with a Knife*, both published by Watson-Guptill. Coulton Waugh died suddenly on May 23, 1973.

Waugh's fame now rests mainly upon his trailblazing study *The Comics*, still the most widely quoted work on the subject. His drawings for *Dickie Dare* exhibit an old-fashioned, easy charm reminiscent of more innocent days and youthful dreams.

M.H.

WEARY WILLIE AND TIRED TIM (G.B.) Weary Willy and Tired Tim, among the longest-lived of British comic strip heroes, were created by Tom Browne. They may be traced back to two prototype tramps identified by an anonymous caption writer as Weary Waddles and Tired Timmy in a strip entitled *Innocents on the River*, which filled the top half of the front page of *Illustrated Chips* number 298, dated May 16, 1896.

Intended for no more than a single appearance—standard strip practice of the period—the two complementary characters (one tall and thin, one short and

"Weary Willie and Tired Tim," Percy Cocking.

fat) caught the editor's attention, and he asked for more adventures. They reappeared five weeks later (number 303), then two weeks after that (number 305), and in another two weeks they filled the entire front page. Number 310 saw them rechristened *Willy and Tim* (the "Willie" came some time later), and from number 317 they became a front-page fixture until the final issue of *Chips*, number 2997, dated September 12, 1953.

Although there were regular comic characters before *Willie and Tim*, their success undoubtedly led to the establishment of the Victorian comic paper, and to the popularity of Tom Browne's style as a comic artist. His characters and style were widely copied by other cartoonists and editors hoping to cash in on the hobo bandwagon, and Browne was even paid well to imitate himself with *Little Willy and Tiny Tim* (the originals' nephews) and *Airy Alf and Bouncing Billy*, bicyclists in *Big Budget* (1898). Browne abandoned his "World Famous Tramps" in 1900, and other artists were tried, including Arthur Jenner. The strip finally was entrusted to the excellent pen of Percy Cocking around 1912, and he continued to draw it to the end, some 40 years later, happily retiring the characters at age 58 to the mansion of Murgatroyd Mump, Millionaire!

D.G.

WEB, THE (U.S.) *The Web*, created in July 1942, made its first appearance in MLJ's *Zip* number 27. Although its creators are not known, artists John Cassone and Irv Novick handled the bulk of the stories in the feature's short career. Making only a dozen short appearances, it was last seen in *Zip* 38 for July 1943. The character's appeal was his costume: a brilliant, half-green and half-yellow jumpsuit, a green domino mask, and a fascinating, weblike cape.

In his alter ego, the Web was really noted criminologist John Raymond, whose brother, Tim, was a criminal. After John helped police capture his escaping brother, he set out to avenge evil as the Web. Only Rosie Wayne, the strip's love interest, knew his secret. Despite his rather short tenure, the character managed to battle several inventive villains, including the Black Dragon, Captain Murder, and Count Berlin. Neither stories nor artwork on *The Web* was particularly outstanding, however, and MLJ quickly dropped the feature to concentrate on *Archie* and a horde of other humor concepts.

When MLJ (now Archie-Radio) made a short reentry into the superhero field in 1965, *The Web* made the most appearances, popping up in nine stories. And despite a rather inventive gimmick—Rosie Wayne had become John Raymond's wife, and she and her mother constantly nagged Raymond for coming out of retirement and resuming his career as the Web—the strip and the whole MLJ line collapsed the next year. Before it did, however, *The Web* appeared in a paperback, *High Camp Superheroes* (Belmont, 1966).

J.B.

WEBSTER, HAROLD TUCKER (1885-1953) The beloved creator of *The Timid Soul* and *The Man in the Brown Derby* was Harold Tucker Webster, born to middle-class parents in Parkersburg, West Virginia, on September 21, 1885. Tall at an early age (he stood six feet four as an adult), he moved with his parents to Tomahawk, Wisconsin, where he grew up, working at odd jobs while he went to school. To keep his mind off mathematics, which he hated, he began to draw at seven, persevered, and sold his first drawing, much to his amazement, to an outdoor magazine called *Recreation* in his teens. Deciding then to become a professional cartoonist, he saved his money and went off in 1901 to study at the Frank Holmes School of Illustration in Chicago, where Harry Hershfield and Roy Baldridge, the illustrator, were fellow students. The school went out of business 20 days after Webster enrolled, and the teenage artist, finding no interest in his work at the Chicago newspapers, followed a lead that took him first to the *Denver Republican*, then to the *Denver Post*, where he earned $15 a week drawing sports cartoons (which he later admitted were terrible).

Barely 20, he returned to Chicago and did freelance cartoon work for the *Chicago News* (illustrating the famed *Mr. Dooley* series for a time), then got a salaried job doing political cartoons for the front page of the *Chicago Inter-Ocean* at $30 a week. There he was spotted by an official of the *Cincinnati Post*, who hired him away from the Chicago paper at a princely $70 a week. Saving enough to take a European trip in 1911, Web-

ster did an illustrated account for the *Post*, which he thought impressive enough to get him a New York job. Arriving in New York in 1912, he met his future wife through cartoonist R. M. Brinkerhoff and promptly landed a fine job at the *New York Tribune*. At the *Tribune* he started the variously named series of daily cartoon gags (without continuing characters) on which his national reputation was quickly based.

Readers guffawed at such irregular series as *Poker Portraits* and *Life's Darkest Moment*, and Webster's syndicated fame mounted until he was hired away from the *Tribune* by the *World* in the early 1920s. There he continued the same daily cartoons and launched a Sunday page about a recurrent character and his wife, *The Man in the Brown Derby*. When the *World* collapsed in early 1931, the *Tribune* (now the *Herald-Tribune*) was glad to welcome Webster back, but suggested after a time that he base his Sunday page on the daily panel character who had become his most popular figure: the Timid Soul. So, in May 1931, the weekly *Timid Soul* page was launched.

Continuing to grow in wealth and reputation, Webster authored and/or illustrated a number of top-selling books through the 1920s and 1930s, among them *Our Boyhood Thrills* (1915), *Webster's Bridge* (1924), *Webster's Poker Book* (1926), *The Shepper Newfounder* (1931), *The Timid Soul* (1931), *To Hell with Fishing* (1945), and *Life with Rover* (1949). With his strips appearing in 125 papers, he was residing in a comfortable New England estate and still drawing his full output, with only minimal assistance from a coworker on the Sunday page, at the time of his death in 1953. Rather than having any of his intensely admired work continued by a ghost, the *Herald-Tribune* elected to circulate reprints of his earlier work to interested papers, where it continued to appear for several years. A really adequate memorial volume of Webster's still richly humorous work is long overdue.

B.B.

WEBSTER, TOM (1890-1962) British cartoonist and animator Gilbert Thomas Webster was born at Bilston, Staffordshire, on July 17, 1890. Educated at Wolverhampton, he started work as a booking clerk on the Great Western Railway at the age of 14. Although he received no formal art training (he drew in his pram as later publicity had it), he won a prize of five shillings offered by the *Birmingham Weekly Post* for comic drawings for six weeks in succession. His first sports drawing, a field he made his own, was a sketch of Bernard Wilkinson made while he and Aston Villa were playing on the Sheffield United football team. It was accepted by *Athletic News* for a guinea. He left the railway and joined the art staff of the *Birmingham Sports Argus*, where for four years he drew sports cartoons, evolving the running commentary style that became his worldwide trademark. Webster drew a form of strip, continuity with commentary, within a single, large-framed panel. Once established in the national press, his technique became widely copied and is still in use today.

Webster went to London in response to an advertisement for a political cartoonist and joined the *Daily Citizen*, a new paper, at six pounds a week, a considerable raise from his 50 shillings in Birmingham. He had eked out his living with experiments in cartoon film animation for a local company. Now he did freelance sports cartoons for *Golf Illustrated* and the

H. T. Webster.

Tom Webster, humor cartoon.

evening paper *The Star*. By the outbreak of World War I, he was earning 20 pounds a week.

In 1916, stricken with rheumatic fever, he was so desperate for work that he slept on the Thames embankment. Finally, the *Evening News* took a cartoon of the Tommy Noble-Joe Symonds fight, and Tom Webster was back in print. Soon he had sketches in seven Sunday papers. Tom Marlowe of the *Daily Mail* signed him exclusively in 1919, starting at 2,000 pounds a year, and he never looked back. He became part of the London sporting aristocracy and incorporated real-life persons into characters in his cartoons; these included Inman the billiards champ and, most famous of all, Tishy the Racehorse who crossed her legs. He created fictional heroes, too: the Horizontal Heavyweight and George, the common man and all-purpose spectator.

In 1936 he painted a Cavalcade of Sport, 12 panels, for the Cunard-White Star liner *Queen Mary*, a job that demonstrated his inborn artistry and certainly took longer to execute than his classic Beckett-Goddard fight cartoon, drawn for a *Mail* deadline in 18 minutes flat! He also made a brief return to animation in the 1920s, working with Brian White on a series featuring *Tishy and Steve*. The first collation of his drawings, *Tom Webster Among the Sportsmen* (1919), sold out its 70,000 copies in 20 minutes! Thereafter the *Tom Webster Annual* was published every autumn until 1939.

He retired in 1940, but chafed at enforced idleness. He joined the *Daily Sketch* in October 1944, then moved to the *News Chronicle* in 1953, retiring for the second, and final, time in 1956. He died in 1962 at the age of 71.

D.G.

WEE PALS (U.S.) For some time Morrie Turner, a black cartoonist, had an idea for an integrated strip, which he broached to Charles Schulz at a cartoonists' meeting in 1964. Schulz warmly endorsed the idea, as did black comedian Dick Gregory at a later meeting. Thus encouraged, Morrie Turner produced *Wee Pals* in 1965 for the Lew Little Syndicate (later merged into the Register and Tribune Syndicate).

As the title implies, the strip is concerned with a merry group of schoolchildren of all races and colors. Nipper is a bright black boy whose eyes disappear under the Confederate cap he is always wearing; Sybil, an enterprising, no-nonsense black girl. Their white companions are the long-haired, mischievous Wellington; the fat, bespectacled Oliver; Connie, the blonde tomboy; and Jerry, the Jewish intellectual. Special mention should be made of Polly, the culturally integrated parrot.

The setting is suburban, and the kids, when they do not feel self-conscious about their backgrounds, behave like any other bunch of high-spirited comic strip youngsters. Highly enterprising (Sybil tells fortunes, another black youngster spouts quotes for every occasion, and Jerry sells soul food from every nationality), they are also gregarious and hold regular meetings of the Rainbow Power Club. To sum it up, the Wee Pals are a cross between Schulz's *Peanuts* and Branner's *Rinkey-dinks*.

Wee Pals had the merit of presenting to the American public the thorny problems of black and white integration in an entertaining package. As Charles Schulz once stated: "When Morrie draws about children trying to find their way in an integrated community, the results show that Morrie has been more than a mere observer. Of course, the best part of it all is that *Wee Pals* is a lot of fun."

A number of *Wee Pals* strips have been reprinted in paperback form by Signet, starting in 1969. There have also been a number of *Wee Pals* animated cartoons; and in the 1980s a children's show called *Wee Pals on the Go* was broadcast on a local television station. Now distributed by Creators Syndicate, the strip enjoys a stable, if relatively small, circulation.

M.H.

"Wee Pals," Morrie Turner. © Register and Tribune Syndicate.

WEE WILLIE WINKIE'S WORLD (U.S.) The same year that saw the appearance of *The Kin-der-Kids*, Lyonel Feininger contributed a second feature to the *Chicago Tribune*. Taking its title from the well-known nursery rhyme (already used by Rudyard Kipling), *Wee Willie Winkie's World* first saw print on August 19, 1906.

Wee Willie Winkie is less turbulent and more lyrical than *The Kin-der-Kids*. In this strip Feininger does not make use of balloons but inserts a printed narrative, illuminated by allegorical, floral, or abstract motifs, between the panels.

The strip's diminutive hero is a winning and naive little boy named Wee Willie, who finds himself in the midst of an enchanted universe (the theme is not unlike *Little Nemo*'s) where inanimate objects spring to life, familiar landscapes take on fantastic shapes, in a whimsical symphony of lines, colors, and forms. A metamorphosis, at times gradual, at times sudden and startling, transforms trees and clouds, rocks and buildings into tentacular monsters and threatening demons, or conversely into benevolent genies and hospitable havens.

Wee Willie Winkie's is a world of fantasy and whimsy, of sweetness and shadows, of marvel and terror. The last page of this remarkable series was published on January 20, 1907, and with *Wee Willie's* disappearance Lyonel Feininger's promising career as a comic strip artist came to a premature end.

M.H.

WEISINGER, MORT (1915-1978) American comic book writer and editor, born April 25, 1915, in New York City. After several years as a pulp writer, magazine editor, and literary agent, Weisinger joined National Comics in 1940. Although he originated a slew of superhero strips like *Green Arrow* and *Airwave*, he is best known for his long tenure as editor of the *Superman* family of magazines (1940-70). More than creators Siegel and Shuster, it was Weisinger who fashioned what is now known as the Superman legend.

As originally conceived and executed, *Superman* was artistically crude and totally humorless. But Weisinger stepped in with a new direction; he made the Superman of the late 1940s and 1950s a super-powered slapstick artist. It was not odd for the Weisinger Superman to be perplexed by the most bizarre of villains. No longer would he allow Superman to battle and defeat the second strongest man in the world. Weisinger made him battle imps and frivolous ne'er-do-wells. Villains like the Toyman, the Prankster, and the fifth-dimensional Mr. Mxyztplk began to appear, launching attacks of toys, gags, novelties, magic, and anything but muscle in attempts to best the Man of Steel.

Weisinger also must be credited with securing numerous talented artisans to chronicle the character's adventures. Artistically, Weisinger leaned most heavily on Wayne Boring, Al Plastino, and Curt Swan for *Superman*, Jim Mooney for *Supergirl*, and Kurt Schaffenberger for *Lois Lane*, but Jack Burnley, Irwin Hasen, and others of merit were also used. For the text, writers like Otto Binder, Edmond Hamilton, Al Bester, Bill Finger, and Manly Wade Wellman were used.

It was under Weisinger's aegis that concepts like kryptonite were developed; he also expanded the list of survivors of Krypton considerably. Argo City, The Phantom Zone, and the bottled city of Kandor all survived the planet's destruction, along with Weisinger-conceived characters like Supergirl, MonEl, Krypto, and

Super-Robot. During the 1950s Weisinger was also responsible for overseeing the creation of the Fortress of Solitude, the Bizarro world, Lex Luthor, Brainiac, the Legion of Super-Heroes, and many other bits of Supermania. He personally scripted the Superman motion picture serials starring Kirk Alyn and acted as story editor for the Superman television program.

Weisinger left *Superman* and comics in 1970 to devote his full time to a burgeoning book and magazine writing career. His novel *The Contest* was purchased by Columbia Pictures, and Weisinger's byline appeared in *Esquire, Argosy, Reader's Digest*, and many other magazines. He died in June 1978.

J.B.

WELLINGTON, CHARLES H. (1884-1942) American artist, born in 1884 in St. Louis, Missouri. Duke Wellington's first published work appeared in the *St. Louis Post Dispatch* and *St. Louis Republic*. He accepted, in 1908, an offer to draw for the *Memphis News-Scimitar* and later moved to Nashville for a six-month stint on the *Tennessean*. Wellington's work, though crude, was just good enough to impress Colonel Henry Stoddard of the *New York Evening Mail*, who offered him a contract (a year earlier Stoddard had lured another young cartoonist, Rube Goldberg, to New York City). Wellington drew spots and editorial cartoons for the *Mail* and dabbled in short-lived strips.

Also at this time, for syndication, Wellington drew *Pa's Imported Son-in-Law* for the McClure service; he quit in 1914, and under Ed Carey it became *Pa's Family and Their Friends*, which briefly capitalized on the Charlie Chaplin rage, featuring that comedian. Meanwhile Wellington revived his characters in the *Tribune* (for Hearst's Newspaper Feature Service) under the title *That Son-in-Law of Pa's!* and, finally, *Pa's Son-in-Law*. Except for the oafish English son-in-law, the strip was patterned after Sterrett's earlier *Polly*. In 1920 Wellington switched to the Tribune Syndicate.

Pa's Son-in-Law became a staple of the *Tribune* (and later *Herald-Tribune*) comic section, along with *Mr. and Mrs. Peter Rabbit* and others. It was syndicated with steady but modest success through the years and continued to Wellington's death in 1942.

C. H. Wellington, "Pa's Son-in-Law."

Wellington's drawing style never progressed past the advanced amateur stage. His knowledge of anatomy was limited; figures were stiffly proper. Gags were always wordy and the humor subdued, if not obscure. The strip never progressed, in art or character development, beyond the level of its early days.

Wellington died of pneumonia in Hollywood, California, at the age of 58.

R.M.

WERNER (Germany) *Werner*, a creation of Brösel ("Breadcrumb"), whose real name is Rötger Feldmann, was a surprise success on the German comics market. Among the elements that might have been expected to hinder the strip's popularity, but didn't, are the fact that the strip originally appealed to an underground audience, that its main character is a beer-guzzling biker (somewhat of an alter ego of the artist), that it is done in a very loose graphic style, and that it is written in North German dialect. *Werner* was first adopted by a sturdy group of devoted biking fans, then spread out to a large mainstream following among comic readers from all walks of life. Strangely enough, part of the success of the series stems from its use of dialect instead of "high German." *Werner* (whose first print runs these days are in the neighborhood of 150,000 copies) may even have inspired the highly salable dialect editions of *Astérix*.

Werner was first published in 1981 by Semmel Verlach, a publishing house originally founded for publication of *Werner* comics. The success of the strip has been nothing short of phenomenal. In 1992 the album *Ouhauerha* ("Oopsy Daisy") was the best-selling book of the year. It was almost inevitable that *Werner* should hit the silver screen. A first animated motion picture,

"Werner," Rotger Feldmann ("Brösel"). © Rotger Feldmann.

Werner beinhart ("Werner Bone Hard"), was produced in 1990. It mixed animation with a real-life story contrasting Brösel's reality and Werner's fictional adventures. A second, broadly humorous feature film, *Werner, das muss kesseln* ("Werner, It's Gotta Hum"), this time all animation, was released in 1996. Like its predecessor it was successful at the box office and then did a brisk business on videocassette.

Brösel draws and coauthors the *Werner* comics, which, after first being published in book form, have subsequently been published in magazines. The work of plotting and writing the stories is shared by Brösel's brother, Andi Feldmann. Girlfriend Kirsten Staack serves as business manager. When Semmel Publishing got into financial trouble, the *Werner* line of comics went independent in 1991. It is now being published by Achterbahn Verlag, a venture Brösel is involved in personally.

Werner also is used in merchandising T-shirts, calendars, phone cards, and other items. There is even a beer that takes its name from the beer drunk by the protagonists: Bölkstoff ("burp stuff"). In 1988 Brösel raced a revved-up four-motor Horex motorcycle of the kind Werner drives in the strip. The event was witnessed by 200,000 fans, and a film of the media event was made. Although Brösel failed to win the race, *Werner* shot to new heights of popularity.

W.F.

WESTOVER, RUSSELL (1886-1966) The creator of one of the most successful working-girl comic strips of all time, *Tillie the Toiler*, Russell (Russ) Westover was born into a large, middle-class family in Los Angeles on August 3, 1886. Following his merchant business in Oakland, the elder Westover sent his son to school there at the turn of the century. Russ went on to art school in San Francisco in the early 1900s, and at the time of the 1906 quake and fire, he had already been sports cartoonist on the *San Francisco Bulletin* for two years. Subsequently, he worked on the *Oakland Herald*, the *San Francisco Chronicle*, and the *Post*. During this time, he developed a style very similar to that which Rube Goldberg had made famous in sports cartooning on the East Coast, often turning out work that was very funny and memorable in its context.

Moving to New York on the strength of his Bay Area success at the time of World War I, Westover joined the cartooning staff of the *New York Herald*, where he created his first nationally syndicated strip, the Sunday page *Snapshot Bill*, based on the early shutterbug craze. Freelancing in the early 1920s, he sold King Features Syndicate on the idea of *Tillie the Toiler*, which was released in 1921 in both daily and Sunday editions of a number of Hearst newspapers. Based in part on the experiences and appearance of Westover's wife, Jenesta, the strip quickly became a hit with readers (one midwestern madman literally fell in love with Tillie, and he wrote long letters begging her not to get involved with Mac, her office boyfriend, and to consider his own proposals of marriage). By the mid-1920s, numerous newspapers were printing the strip. Hearst himself thought highly of it, and his Cosmopolitan Pictures made a film of *Tillie the Toiler* in 1927 with Marion Davies, which was widely promoted in the Hearst papers. Cupples and Leon published a series of *Tillie* books at this time, too. In 1926 Westover added a family-squabble strip to his Sunday page; it was to become *The Van Swaggers* and would run weekly with *Tillie* until the 1950s.

Moving in the 1930s to California, Westover retired from King Features in 1954. His still-popular strip was continued by Bob Gustafson until 1959. Westover died in San Rafael, California, of heart failure, on March 6, 1966.

B.B.

WHEELAN, EDGAR (1888-1966) A major contributor to the concept of comic strip continuity and a great satirist of the movie serial, American artist Ed Wheelan was a product of San Francisco, California, as were so many other great cartoonists of the early years. Wheelan, a Cornell University graduate, was inspired to become a cartoonist by his mother, Albertine Randall, who drew a strip in the 1910s called *The Dumb Bunnies*. He first drew spot and editorial cartoons for the *San Francisco Examiner*, then transferred to another Hearst property, the *New York American*. In April 1918 he created *Midget Movies*. It lasted nearly two years and mimicked the dramatic format of movies of the time, just as Chester Gould, with *Fillum Fables*, and Elzie Segar, with *Thimble Theater*, were both to do for Hearst soon afterward.

Wheelan broke with Hearst around 1920 and would harbor a lifelong conviction that Hearst was bent on his destruction. Ron Goulart records that on his deathbed Wheelan saw the black hand of Hearst in every misfortune that overtook him. Leaving Hearst proved a profitable move, however: Wheelan's *Minute Movies*, created for the George Matthew Adams Service in 1921, was an instant hit. Readers cherished the chattiness of the feature, wrote fan letters to the characters, and followed the day-to-day continuity with unflagging devotion, to the delight of editors.

Wheelan's story line, until he adapted the classics, was puckishly self-effacing. His art was somewhat crude but drippingly melodramatic, in keeping with the tone of the feature. In later years, Nicholas Afonsky's art prettied the strip up and give it a bit more of a comic flavor; Jess Fremon was another ghost for the strip. In the late 1930s Wheelan drew a circus feature, *Big Top*, and carried *Minute Movies* to *Flash Comics*. He then faded into obscurity in his later years. Wheelan died at Ft. Myers Beach, Florida, in 1966.

R.M.

WHEN A FELLER NEEDS A FRIEND (U.S.) Clare Briggs's best-known daily cartoon feature was almost certainly the occasional gag panel series called *When a Feller Needs a Friend*, which ran between 1912 and 1929 in the *Chicago Tribune* and the *New York Tribune* (later the *Herald-Tribune*). This widely popular feature about individuals (usually boys, dogs, and businessmen) caught helplessly alone in embarrassing and threatening domestic situations appeared at weekly intervals, between such other Briggs standby features as *Kelly Pool*, *The Days of Real Sport*, *Oh Man, Ain't It a Grand and Glorious Feelin'*, and *Somebody's Always Taking the Joy Out of Life*. Without recurring characters or continuity, *Feller* was not a comic strip: in fact, only one of Briggs's daily panel features (which carried no day-to-day linking title of any kind) had a vestige of a reappearing character, and that was the always-unseen Skin-nay of *The Days of Real Sport*. *Feller* itself seems to

"When a Feller Needs a Friend," Clare Briggs. © New York Tribune.

have first appeared in the *Chicago Tribune* on November 28, 1912, but this cannot necessarily be called the first example drawn by Briggs, since subscribing papers of the time, including Briggs's syndicating paper, the *Chicago Tribune*, simply did not run all of the panels he drew for distribution at the rate of seven a week.

After publishing a hardbound collection of *Feller* in 1914 through the Volland Company, Briggs took his panels to the *New York Tribune* in 1917 and remained there until his death in 1929. (The *Chicago Tribune*, however, continued to run his work by buying the *New York Tribune* cartoons.) A posthumous volume of *Feller* was published in 1930 by William H. Wise and Company as part of a seven-volume memorial set bound in leather. Many of Briggs's panel series were reprinted in newspapers after his death without being labeled as such, so that it is difficult to assign his last *Feller* panel. Greatly popular during his lifetime, Briggs's work was a development of early George McCutcheon material and was reflected in the similar work of H. T. Webster, Gaar Williams, Frank Beck, and others.

B.B.

WHERE I'M COMING FROM (U.S.) In September 1991, Barbara Brandon became the first African-American female cartoonist ever to have her comic strip syndicated by a major American newspaper syndicate. That's when Universal Press Syndicate debuted her Sunday feature *Where I'm Coming From*.

The weekly feature had first appeared in the *Detroit Free Press* in 1989. It stars a cast of seven black women who drift in and out of the artwork, usually talking to each other on the phone about life, men, single parenthood, sexism, and racism. The format owes much to

"Where I'm Coming From," Barbara Brandon. © Universal Press Syndicate.

the style of characters speaking out of the strip directly to the reader, a style developed by Jules Feiffer.

Usually just the characters' heads and hands are shown. Brandon, a daughter of Brumsic Brandon Jr., the creator of *Luther*, has as one of her goals debunking stereotypes about African-American culture and black women in particular.

Where I'm Coming From is designed to deliver only the occasional belly laugh. Brandon works as a kind of visual columnist, presenting her take on social issues and life. While she usually puts this in a humorous context, Brandon does not suffer fools or injustice lightly. Several reprint collections of *Where I'm Coming From* have been published, and there has also been a line of greeting cards.

B.C.

WHITE, BRIAN (1902-1984) British cartoonist and animator Hugh Brian White was born in Dunstable, Bedfordshire, on April 4, 1902. Educated at local schools, he was self-taught as an artist. He joined the local newspapers *Luton Reporter* and *Luton News* as a sports cartoonist and caricaturist in 1916. In 1924 he joined G. E. Studdy and William Ward as an animator on the *Bonzo* cartoon films, moving to *Pathé Pictorial* to animate Sid Griffiths' *Song Cartoons* (1926) and Joe Noble's *Sammy and Sausage* series (1928). With Griffiths he produced animated advertisements for Superads (1929), then made a sound cartoon, *Topical Breezes* (1930), featuring *Hite and Mite*. His last cartoon, *On the Farm* (1932), from H. M. Bateman drawings, was made in the Raycol color system.

White's first strip was *Mr. Enry Noodle* (1924) in *Pearson's Weekly*; it was followed by *Jolly Jinky* (1931) in the same journal. His first daily was *Adam and Eva* in the 1930s in the *London Evening Standard*, followed by the *Weather Pup* panel (October 1932) in the *Daily Mail*. This led to the acceptance of his most successful strip, *The Nipper*, which began a long run in the *Mail* from August 30, 1933, and brought such ancillaries as postcards and annuals. With the wartime paper shortage the strip was discontinued, and White tried strips for children's comics, taking over *Deed-a-Day Danny* from Hugh McNeill and creating *Little Tough Guy*, both in *Knockout* (1942).

He did war service with the police in Liverpool and Luton (1942-44), and in 1945 formed a publishing company, B. & H. White Publications, with his cousin. He reprinted the *Nipper* strips in painting-book form and produced a new *Nipper* comic, *Careful Nippers*, about

Brian White, "Double Trouble." © Associated Newspapers Ltd.

road safety, and *Nipper's A-Z Animal Book*. In 1948 he published *Bernard Shaw Through the Camera*. He produced *Nipper* filmstrips for Pathé (1951) and illustrated the Focal Press series of books on how to animate (1955).

In 1955, in an unprecedented move, London agent Frank Betts bought the rights to Bill McLean's American strip, *Double Trouble*, then syndicated in *The Star*, and White was contracted to continue it in a completely British version. When *The Star* was purchased by the *Evening News*, the strip was continued from October 16, 1960, until 1967. White returned to drawing strips for D. C. Thomson's children's comics in 1956 with *Shorty* in *Beezer*, followed by a revival of Allan Morley's character *Keyhole Kate* in *Sparky* (1968-74), *Tich and Snitch* in *Buzz* (1973), and *Plum Duffy* in *Topper* (1974). Although less ingenious and inspired, White's later kid strips carried the stamp of his good-humored *Nipper*. He died on November 4, 1984.

D.G.

WHITE, HUGH STANLEY (1904-1984) British cartoonist Hugh Stanley White was born on October 6, 1904, at Kilburn, London. He was educated at Arlington Park College, Chiswick, and then studied art at evening classes at Chiswick Art School. After six months in advertising with the Gordon and Gotch Agency, a chance meeting with Walter Booth while sketching at the Natural History Museum led to his becoming Booth's assistant, first on weekends, then full-time. For two years he assisted Booth on inking, backgrounds, lettering, etc., on *Rob the Rover* and other adventure strips. When his mother died, he visited Norway on her legacy, sketching whaling, Viking history, and other themes. Upon his return he interested Frank Anderson, an editor at Amalgamated Press, in his work. In 1929 he did his first solo strip, a weekly complete picture-story for the nursery comic *Bo-Peep* (1929), expanding into serials with *Ranji's Ruby* (1932) and *In the Days of Drake* (1933).

He became a pioneer of the British newspaper comic section with his complete adventure strips for *Boys & Girls Daily Mail* (1933) and serials for *South Wales Echo & Express Supplement* (1933-34): *Jimmy in Java*, *Peter in Pygmy Land*, etc. When the Walt Disney organization instituted *Mickey Mouse Weekly* in Britain, White was in at the start, contributing two dramatic serials to the first issue (February 8, 1936): *Ginger Nick the Whaler* and *Ian on Mu*. Subtitled "Pioneer of the Mystery Planet," the latter was a landmark, the first British science-fiction serial (apart from individual episodes of *Rob the Rover*). Planet Mu, inhabited by Chinese pygmies, Viking giants, hollow robots, and a cute little six-legged Hexpod, was frankly inspired by the film *Metropolis* and by *Flash Gordon*, but White's curious blend of Victorian Jules Verneisms and years of drawing for very young readers made the strip unique. It ran 15 weeks.

In 1938 came *Phantom City*, *Flashing Through*, and *Oil and Claw*, for the same Disney weekly; all were similarly fantastic. In 1939 he returned to Amalgamated Press to draw the science-fiction serial *Into Unknown Worlds* for *Butterfly*, and *John Irons, Lone Fighter* for *Triumph*.

After war service in civil defense and the Royal Air Force, White joined forces in the printing trade with a wartime acquaintance to edit and publish *Merry Maker* (1946), a monthly comic using his own art and that of his old friends Walter Booth and Basil Reynolds. Then came two comic books in the American style, *Xmas Comic* and *Atomic Age Comic* (1948), for which he tried some superheroes: *The Bat-Man*, etc. He took on Bob Monkhouse's *Tornado* for *Oh Boy* (1951), then did episodes of *Young Marvelman* (1952) and a science-fiction series in *Space Comics* (1953), all for Mick Anglo. But his style had become too dated to appeal to modern tastes, and after a spell in Kenya during which he did advertising art, he returned home to retire. He died on September 21, 1984, aged 88.

D.G.

WHITE BOY (U.S.) A Sunday half-page strip first appearing in the *Chicago Tribune* for October 8, 1933, and shortly thereafter in the *New York Daily News*, Garrett Price's *White Boy* was a curious, stunningly drawn, often wildly imaginative narrative about a white boy captured by an Indian tribe in the late 19th century. Much of its potential was blunted by Price's obvious conformity to the syndicate stricture that the Sunday strip should appeal to young readers. The attendant naiveté of dialogue and situation seems to have been a burden for the sophisticated *New Yorker* cartoonist and magazine fiction illustrator.

Loved and succored by an Indian girl named Chickadee, the strip's hero is known only as White boy for much of the early continuity, even after a scout named Dan Brown enters the story and would logically have been privy to his true name. In between purely educational episodes about Indian ways and arts, and gag pages about White boy's pet bear cub, Whimper, Price managed to introduce a weirdly gripping story about a young white "Moon Queen" who ruled over the local Indians with a tyrannical hand and who lived in a cavern palace guarded by gigantic bobcats and a grizzly bear.

Following this genuinely enthralling story, however, Price turned to more juvenile gag material and adapted a less realistic style to introduce caricatured comic horses and Indians and then abruptly, on April 28, 1935, switched the theme and period of his strip to a dude ranch in the West of the 1930s. He gave White boy the name of Bob White, dropped Chickadee and all of the earlier strip's characters, and introduced a new heroine in the first episode, Doris Hale. The renovated strip, which was called *Whiteboy in Skull Valley* (reduced later to *Skull Valley*), dealt with tenderfoot joke material, rustlers, and similar continuity at first, then developed a visually exciting narrative about cavemen for a time. It finally subsided into tired gag routines until the strip folded on August 16, 1936. Price drew a small-paneled gag strip called *Funny Fauna* to accompany his half-page for a time. It was an animal pratfall vignette without recurrent characters.

B.B.

WIEDERSHEIM, G. *see* Drayton, Grace.

WILDEY, DOUG (1922-1994) American comic book and strip artist, born on May 2, 1922, in Yonkers, New York. Lacking formal art training, Wildey began cartooning for his base newspaper in the service during World War II. In 1949 he got his first professional art job, drawing *Buffalo Bill* for the Street and Smith comic book publishing house.

For the next 10 years, Wildey did freelance work for a wide variety of comic book publishers, including National, Lev Gleason, and Dell/Western. He was most often assigned Western stories and strips, such as *Hopalong Cassidy* and *Lash LaRue* for Fawcett and *The Outlaw Kid* for Atlas (later Marvel). Wildey's photographic art style, based heavily on his morgue of picture clippings, made *The Outlaw Kid* a popular feature. It originally ran for three years, from 1954 to 1957, and was revived in reprints by Marvel in 1970. The resurrected book proved so popular that Marvel attempted to introduce new stories by a new artist after exhausting the supply of reprints. The readers preferred the Wildey stories, however, and Marvel was forced to drop the new series and reissue the old ones for the third time.

In 1959 Wildey followed Bob Lubbers as artist of *The Saint* newspaper strip (New York Herald-Tribune Syndicate) and drew it until the strip folded in 1962. He then joined Hanna-Barbera studios and created the prime-time animated adventure series *Johnny Quest*. The series enjoyed a healthy afterlife in off-network reruns, and Wildey remained in the animation industry, doing layouts and art direction. He designed the *Sub-Mariner* cartoons for the Grantray-Lawrence *Marvel Super-Heroes* TV show and returned to Hanna-Barbera for layout work on such shows as *The Fantastic Four, The Mighty Mightor,* and *The Herculoids.* He was also involved in the creation of presentation pieces for projected shows and feature films, for Hanna-Barbera and for other studios.

Along with his television work, Wildey drew *Korak, Son of Tarzan* in 1966 and *Tarzan* in 1968-69 for Gold Key/Western. He did freelance work for National and Skywald before beginning a new syndicated strip of his own creation in 1972. The strip, *Ambler,* for the Chicago Tribune-New York News Syndicate, gained a loyal but insufficient following and ended at the beginning of 1974. Wildey then returned to comic books, drawing *Kid Cody* for Atlas/Seaboard and *Jonah Hex* and *Sgt. Rock* for National. The stark realism of his characters made him very much in demand for strips of a mysterious or historical nature.

M.E.

In 1977 Wildey was a contributor to Joe Kubert's short-lived comics magazine *Sojourn.* Between 1983 and 1992 he published several comic books starring a Western hero called Rio. During his last years he worked mostly for television, notably on the *Johnny Quest* animated series. He died in Van Nuys, California, in October 1994.

M.H.

WILDMAN, GEORGE (1927-   ) George Wildman was born in Waterbury, Connecticut, in 1927, two years before Popeye would make his first appearance in Elzie Segar's *Thimble Theatre.* However, it is Wildman's inspired work drawing the *Popeye* comic book that King Features licensed to Charlton Comics of Derby, Connecticut, that remains one of the enduring accomplishments in cartooning.

A graduate of Whitney School of Art (now Pairer Art School) in New Haven, Wildman served in the navy toward the end of World War II. He was recalled to active service for the Korean War and served on the battleship *New Jersey.* After leaving the navy he worked as an art director for several Connecticut advertising agencies for 16 years.

Wildman entered the comics field in 1969, when he joined Charlton Comics. Within a relatively short period of time, he had become Charlton's comics editor. Wildman recalls that the best part of the job was dealing with cartoonists on their way to making it big. Charlton was unique in that it both edited and printed its own comics, all under one roof. Its parent company also published a series of pulp and music magazines. It was a starting place for many cartoonists, including John Byrne, Pat Boyette, Mike Zeck, Phil Mendez, Warren Statler, and Joe Staton (whose creation of *E-Man* was one of the superhero high points of Wildman's tenure as editor). Wildman was also blessed with a series of talented assistant editors, including Nick Cuti, Bill Pearson, and John Wren.

For King Features, Charlton published *The Phantom, Beetle Bailey, Blondie, Sarge Snorkle,* and *Flash Gordon* comic books. Of these the comics written by Bill Pearson and drawn by Wildman for Popeye's 50th anniversary in 1979 stand out. Wildman's Popeye birthday-special drawing was picked up by King and used worldwide in publicity.

Charlton also published *The Flintstones, Yogi Bear, The Jetsons, Hong Kong Phooey, Top Cat,* and *Scooby Doo* for Screen Gems. Connecticut cartoonists Ray Dirgo and Frank Roberge were stalwarts in this endeavor. Wildman signed Neal Adams to draw *The Six Million Dollar Man,* which was issued as a black-and-white magazine, as were *The Bionic Woman* and *Space 1999.* He published John Byrne's *Rog: 2000.*

By the early 1980s, however, Charlton Comics was in decline. Wildman left in 1984 when the company was only publishing reprints of old stories, some over and over. What brought Charlton Comics down was a direct result of its magazine distribution operation. When girlie magazine publisher Larry Flynt needed national distribution for his fledgling *Hustler* magazine, he struck a deal with Charlton. A few years later he dropped Charlton, and the company never recovered. Charlton Comics closed shop about 1986.

Wildman went on to draw many freelance cartoon projects for Random House, including *The Popeye Pop-Up Book* and books featuring *Annie, The Smurfs, Nancy and Sluggo,* and *The Snorks.* He currently has a commercial art and animation studio in Connecticut with his son Karl.

B.C.

WILLARD, FRANK HENRY (1893-1958) The man who took a notion by Joe Patterson and slammed it over the left-field wall for a home run, Frank Willard—whose *Moon Mullins* was one of the great comic strip hits of all time—was born near Chicago on September 21, 1893, the son of a physician. His early life is obscure (Willard keeping it that way in interviews), but apparently there was no support from home when the young Willard worked nights in a Chicago department store to keep himself in art school during his early twenties. His talent, however, was marked, and he was placing humorous and political newspaper panels in Chicago papers by 1914, following this freelancing with a permanent job on the *Chicago Herald* in 1916 (where he worked side-by-side with the then-unknown E. C. Segar and Billy De Beck). While with the *Herald,* Willard drew a Sunday page about a bunch of school kids called *Tom, Dick, and Harry.* When the *Herald* was purchased by Hearst for consolidation with the Chicago *American,* Willard went along with Segar and De Beck to the new paper. After a stint in the Allied Expeditionary Force during World War I, Willard began a daily strip for King Features called *The Outta-Luck Club,* about a family man and office worker named Luther Blink who relaxes from personal pressures at his club. Not particularly inspired, this was nevertheless the strip that Captain Joseph Patterson, publisher of the *New York Daily News,* saw and liked before he called Willard in to do a strip for the *News* and *Chicago Tribune* about an opportunistic, jovial young roughneck who would wear a derby (as Blink did) and knock about a big city's suburbs after a quick buck. Willard liked the idea, the initial money, and the name Patterson suggested: *Moon Mullins.*

The sample episodes the News-Tribune Syndicate circulated in 1923 intrigued a number of newspapers from coast to coast, and *Moon Mullins* began with a sizable circulation outside of its parent papers. Once again, Patterson had brought the right man and strip idea together, and the ebullient Willard put much of his own raffish character into Moon and his poolroom associates in the strip. Working with a gifted assistant,

Frank Willard, "Moon Mullins." © Chicago Tribune-New York News Syndicate.

J. R. Williams, "Out Our Way." © NEA Service.

Ferd Johnson, from the mid-1920s, Willard quickly built *Moon Mullins* into the kind of strip people read first in a newspaper each morning. (Many small-town dailies in the 1920s ran no other strip.) Together, Willard and Johnson were able to turn out an almost invariably funny, witty, and captivating continuity for the strip, and all this time Willard put in endless, exhausting hours at his obsession, golf, while Johnson turned out a Sunday page of his own called *Texas Slim* (later *Lovey Dovey*).

By 1934, Willard was able to hold his enormous audience enthralled in comic suspense while he maneuvered two of his principal characters, Emmy Schmaltz and Lord Plushbottom, into a marriage held at the Chicago World's Fair. By this time his annual income was over $100,000, *Moon Mullins* was in more than 400 newspapers, and many *Moon Mullins* books were in print. Later in the 1930s, Willard moved west, but his true home remained the golf course, his unending game taking him to all parts of the country, where he drew, near deadline, strip episodes in hotel rooms (which were sometimes lost, forcing Johnson to draw others or the syndicate to substitute old episodes). During World War II, *Moon Mullins* was one of the few strips to steer clear of war involvement for its principals: Moon stayed a bum throughout, as did the other characters in the strip. Never filmed, *Mullins* did make the radio in 1940.

Willard's death in Los Angeles at the age of 64 was sudden: he died a week after a stroke in the Cedars of Lebanon Hospital on January 12, 1958. Ferd Johnson, of course, continued *Moon Mullins*, and is still drawing it.

B.B.

WILLIAMS, JAMES ROBERT (1888-1957) American cartoonist, born August 18, 1888, in Nova Scotia, Canada, to American parents. His father, an executive with a public utility company, moved his family to Detroit after finishing his temporary assignment in Canada. J. R. Williams was raised with an early understanding of the importance of holding a job. A husky kid, he was playing football at 14, had worked as a fireman on the Pennsylvania Railroad at 15, and felt more than able to make his own way when, stirred by a spirit of adventure, he ran away from home (with no ill feelings) in his mid-teens.

Working his way to Little Rock, Arkansas, he got his first independent job as a mule skinner on a railroad grading gang. A little later, in southern Kansas, Williams did menial work on a ranch, getting his first real taste of cowboy life. Moving on to Fort Sill, Oklahoma, he signed up with the U.S. Cavalry for a three-year hitch, again playing football on the cavalry team, with the young Lieutenant George Patton as a fellow player.

Discharged at Fort Sheridan, Illinois, Williams returned to his parents in Ohio, married, and went to work for a nearby crane manufacturing company, where he drew his first published work: a cover design for the company catalog. He stayed with the crane company for seven years, all the while seriously polishing his style and submitting strip ideas to syndicates everywhere. Finally, in 1921, NEA put Williams to work doing his basic panel idea—the *Out Our Way* that is still running today.

Asked by NEA to do a Sunday page in the mid-1920s, Williams felt that his small-town family group, named the Willits, would be the most widely appealing of his character groups, and *Out Our Way, With the Willits*, was then launched. Williams never cared for the extra chore of the multipaneled Sunday page, and several cartoonists worked on it for him, first George Scarbo, and later his ultimate replacement on the strip, Ned Cochran. Widely syndicated by the late 1920s, Williams followed up a boyhood ambition and bought his own ranch near Walnut Creek, Arizona, moving there from Cleveland (the location of NEA) in 1930.

After a long period of ill health, Williams died of a chronic heart ailment in Pasadena, California (where he had moved in 1941), on June 18, 1957. It can certainly be said of Williams, though of few other cartoonists, that there is not a single one of his professionally published drawings, whether done for *Out Our Way* or for advertising use (Sunday page aside), that does not merit permanent reprinting in a complete set of his work.

B.B.

WILLIAMSON, AL (1931-   ) American comic book and comic strip artist, born on March 21, 1931, in New York City. After growing up in Bogota, Colombia, Williamson returned to New York and trained with Burne Hogarth. His first comic book work appeared in Eastern's *Heroic* number 51 in 1948, and even then the heavy influences of Alex Raymond were

Al Williamson, EC Science Fiction Panel. © William M. Gaines, Agent, Inc.

evident. During his early years, Williamson worked for many comic book houses, among them ACG (1951-52), Eastern (1948-52), for which he drew *Buster Crabbe* with Frank Frazetta; and Toby (1950-53), for which he drew *Billy the Kid* and *John Wayne*. Although his illustrative approach was rapidly maturing, his work did not really begin to solidify until he joined the E.C. group in 1952.

The youngest artist in an incredibly talented stable that already included Davis, Wood, Kurtzman, Severin, Frazetta, and Ingels and that would later include Crandall and Krigstein, Williamson began improving immediately. His slick, photographic style developed rapidly, and he was assigned to E.C.'s much-heralded science-fiction stories. Often working with Frazetta and Krenkel, an older artist who drew the most intricate backgrounds in the field, Williamson became popular with the rabid E.C. fans.

When E.C. folded in 1955, Williamson moved on to Atlas and spent six years drawing war, romance, adventure, and horror tales. Also during this time, he freelanced for ACG (1958-59), Charlton, Dell, and Harvey (all 1958), and Prize (1955-58). Much of his work was erratic, however, and few of the stories showed the flair and verve his E.C. work had exhibited.

Williamson then became John Prentice's assistant on the *Rip Kirby* newspaper feature in 1961. His work here was mainly backgrounding, but Williamson picked up valuable composition and layout pointers from the slick, clean Prentice. He continued with Prentice until 1964, and then returned to comic books, contributing material to Warren's black-and-white horror books (1964-66), Dell (1965), and Harvey (1962-67), some of it with Jack Kirby. In 1966, he drew three issues of King's *Flash Gordon* comic book, and like his idol Raymond before him, Williamson produced Flash's stories with dynamic conception, brilliant draftsmanship, and an eye-pleasing layout. He won the NCS's 1967 Story Comic Book plaque for his efforts.

Perhaps because of his stellar *Flash Gordon* work, King offered him a chance to replace artist Bob Lubbers on the *Secret Agent X-9* syndicated strip, another old Raymond feature. The title was soon changed to *Secret Agent Corrigan*, and Williamson drew it for 13 years, beginning on January 20, 1967. His superb use of blacks and zip-a-tone, combined with his solid layouts and Archie Goodwin's scripts, made *Corrigan* one of the few high-quality adventure strips of the time.

J.B.

Williamson quit *Corrigan* in 1980. Aside from drawing the *Star Wars* newspaper strip from 1981 to 1984, he has devoted his career to comic books for the last decade and a half, starting with the adaptation of *The Empire Strikes Back* in 1980. Since that time his work has appeared in many more movie adaptations (*Return of the Jedi*, *Blade Runner*, etc.) and in graphic novels such as *Predator and Prey*. From the late 1980s on he has concentrated on the *Daredevil* and *Punisher* comic book titles.

M.H.

WILSHIRE, MARY (1953-   ) American illustrator and comic book artist, born in New Jersey in 1953. Her work in comic books is only one aspect of Mary Wilshire's career. She currently is doing more illustration than cartoon work and is regularly published in the National Geographic Society's children's magazine *GEO World*. The mother of two daughters, Wilshire is especially interested in artwork for children. She was one of the artists drawing *Barbie* for Marvel Comics; that comic book ended in 1995, by some accounts a good product that fell victim to poor marketing.

Wilshire planned on a career in commercial art and studied at the Pratt Institute of Art in Brooklyn, New York. Her comic book career developed first as a lark in underground comix. In 1978 she had a four-page story published in *Wet Satin #2*, the comix of women's erotica edited by Trina Robbins. She also contributed to the underground comix *Young Lust* and *After Shock*.

She had grown up a fan of *Mad* magazine and of animated and newspaper comics and was influenced by the work of Jack Davis, Stan Drake of *The Heart of Juliet Jones*, Alex Kotzky of *Apartment 3G*, and animator Chuck Jones. Her first work for Marvel Comics came around 1980, when she contributed to *Crazy*, the *Mad* clone that never really caught on. Larry Hama, with whom Wilshire had worked on *Crazy*, asked her to take over the drawing of one of Marvel's stars, the barbarian swordswoman created by pulp fiction writer Robert E. Howard, *Red Sonja: She-Devil with a Sword*. Wilshire, who loves drawing people best of all, knew little of Red Sonja but liked the concept of a beautiful battling barbarian in a chain-mail bikini.

The character of Red Sonja had been redefined in the mid-1970s by Frank Thorne's tour de force drawing and Roy Thomas's scripts. Cartoonist, writer, and *Elfquest* creator Wendy Pini had become the first woman creatively involved with *Red Sonja*, writing some scripts, but it was Mary Wilshire who captivated fans, often teenage boys, as the beautiful woman cartoonist who drew the beautiful woman warrior.

Wilshire brought her own interpretation to *Red Sonja* in a style that was less ornate than Thorne's. Her skill at drawing the human form was displayed in full flower. No matter what else she does in her career, her work on *Red Sonja* has won her a place in comic book history as the character's definitive artist.

Wilshire's other work for Marvel included drawing such titles as *Power Pack*, *Spider-Man*, *Ka-Zar*, *New Mutants*, and a four-book miniseries of *Firestar*, a superheroine from the children's *Spidey* animated television show. Her magazine illustration work includes pieces for *National Lampoon*, *Heavy Metal*, and general-interest publications such as *Good Housekeeping* and *Reader's Digest*. She has also done extensive licensed-product artwork for the World Wrestling Federation.

B.C.

WILSON, ROY (1900-1965) British cartoonist Royston Warner Wilson was born in Kettering, Northamptonshire, on July 9, 1900. Educated at Norwich and trained at Norwich School of Art, he was apprenticed to Trevor Page as a furniture designer for three years, then appointed as a junior draftsman on the air board staff in London. Conscripted into the army on November 10, 1918, the day before the armistice, he served in the King's Royal Rifle Corps in Cologne until March 13, 1920.

A chance meeting in a pub led to his becoming assistant to Norwich cartoonist Donald Newhouse, who paid Wilson three pounds a week to help him pencil and ink the characters he drew for the comic papers published by Amalgamated Press. On the side, Wilson contributed single-joke cartoons and also painted some color postcards for Jarrold's (1923). Working in Newhouse's style, which followed that of the earlier Tom Browne and G. M. Payne, Wilson soon passed his tutor and became the finest exponent of the traditional British comic style. His earliest work is difficult to identify, as Newhouse did all the lettering, but it is certain he worked on all Newhouse strips from 1920, including *Monk and Jaff*, an animal strip in *Comic Life; Cuthbert the Carpenter* in *Funny Wonder; G. Whizz* in *Jester;* and *Tickle and Tootle* in *Sparks*.

In 1921, for the new nursery comic *Bubbles*, he worked on *Pickles the Puppy*, *Bunny the Rabbit*, and *Micky the Mouse*, also doing *Jacko and Jerry* in *Comic Life*. Animals would, in the years ahead, play an important part in Wilson's work, and some of his finest series featured comic animals: *George the Jolly Gee Gee* (October 15, 1938) and *Chimpo's Circus* (October 8, 1938). The latter strip was his first designed for full color and ran on the front of *Happy Days*, the new gravure comic, making it the finest weekly of the golden age of British comics.

Wilson's other color work was confined to annuals, for which he often painted covers and frontispiece plates: *Chips Annual, Butterfly Annual*, etc. These minor masterpieces and *Chimpo* were the only works he was allowed to sign by his publisher, Amalgamated Press. (He worked for no other.) In his later years he drew many star personality strips for *Radio Fun, Film Fun*, and *T.V. Fun*, but although his likenesses were excellent, their style restricted his natural humor. He was better with the sheer slapstick of *Pitch and Toss* or the wild fantasy of *Stymie and his Magic Wishbone* (1938). Outside comics his only artwork was a weekly painting-competition panel for *Woman's Own*, which he drew from 1947 until his death at age 65 from lung cancer in June 1965. His last strip, *Morecambe and Wise*, was published on January 30, 1965.

His strips include: 1920—*Beside the Seaside*; Funny Films; 1921—*Jolly Jacko; Pretty Peggy; Reel Comedies; Phil and Bert; Roland Butter and Hammond Deggs; Willie Evergrow*; 1922—*Joyland Express; Peter the Pussy Policeman; Mossoo Marmalade; Pitch and Toss*; 1923—*Basil and Bert* (first full-page solo); *P. C. Blossom; Rosie and Rex*; 1924—*Good Knight Gilbert* and *Folio the Page*; 1925—*Oozee the Wonder Bird*; 1926—*Chip and Jerry; 3 Jolly Sailorboys*; 1927—*Happy Family; Fred and Freda*; 1928—*Tango the Terrier*; 1929—*Sir Toby Tinribs*; 1930—*Steve and Stumpy* (the first official Wilson strip without Newhouse); *Fun and Frolic at Fitzpip Hall* (the first Wilson front-page series, in *Comic Cuts*); 1931—*Molly and Mick*; 1932—*Augustus Topping; Chief Chucklehead*; 1933—*Happy Harry* and *Sister Sue* (the first full-color front page); 1934—*Tiddlewink Family; Jerry Jenny and Joe* (the first adventure strip); 1935—*Jack Sprat and Tubby Tadpole; Twiddle and Nobb; Peanut and Doughboy*; 1936—*Lieut. Daring and Jolly Roger; The Captain, the Kid and the Cook; Robin Hood*; 1937—*Daydreaming Don; Honey Potts*; 1938—*Dimple and Dumpling*; 1939—*Vernon the Villain; Happy Andy and His Playful Pets*; 1941—*Tommy Handley*; 1944—*Billy Muggins*; 1946—*Sweet Rosie O'Grady*; 1947—*Dragamuffin*; 1948—*Wildflower and Little Elf*; 1949—*Jimmy Jolly's Magic Brolly; Hook Line and Singer*; 1953—*Keeper Nyon*; 1954—*Smarty*; 1955—*Reg Varney*; 1956—*Derek Roy*; 1957—*Jerry Lewis*; 1958—*Terry Thomas*; 1960—*Harry Secombe*; 1961—*Cloris and Clare*; 1962—*Bruce Forsyth*; 1964—*Morecambe and Wise*.

D.G.

WINNER, CHARLES H. (1885-1956) American artist, born in 1885 in Perrysville, Pennsylvania. Doc Winner began drawing on clay slates on the family farm and soon decided on a career in cartooning. In his early twenties, after an unhappy stint in art school, Winner secured a position with the *Pittsburgh Post*, succeeding Will De Beck, who was to lose several jobs and establish a cartooning school in order to survive before creating *Barney Google*.

Winner drew for the *Post* for a few years, but attracted national attention through the re-publication of notable editorial cartoons (he also drew sports cartoons). In 1914 he left to dabble with animation (as many of his contemporaries did) and draw a series of women's suffrage cartoons on contract. In 1918 Winner accepted an offer from the Hearst organization to join its comic art staff, beginning a 38-year association with Hearst, which is his main contribution to comic history.

Winner was perhaps the most talented and certainly the most utilized of the King Features bullpen crew, which included such workhorses through the years as Paul Fung Sr., Joe Musial, Bob Naylor, Bud Sagendorf, Bela Zaboly, Vern Greene, Paul and Walter Frehm, Austin Briggs, Charles Flanders, Nicholas Afonsky, Lou Sayre Schwarz, and Paul Norris. Most of these men did creditable jobs filling in on established comics anywhere from one day to several years. There were exceptions (Musial, for example, was adequate on *Barney Google* but a butcher with *The Katzies*).

Winner filled in on *Thimble Theatre* during Segar's last days and approximated the artwork; other assignments included work on *Barney Google* and (after Knerr's death) *The Katzenjammer Kids*.

Besides *The Katzies*, Winner was permitted to sign one effort: *Elmer*. Having inherited the strip in 1926 from A. C. Fera, whose strip had been titled *Just Boy* (perhaps after James West's very funny book), Winner proceeded to do consistent, homey, and gently humorous work. Elmer, whose constant exclamation was "Crim-a-nentlies!", was a quiet but solid favorite of two generations of readers.

Winner's style was versatile, but his early newspaper work was more reserved and solid than the work of his conscious influence, De Beck. His syndicate work, too (as in *Popeye* and *The Katzies*), is a little stiff and uncomfortable; action was not his forte. Neither was expression; the faces in *Elmer* are all slightly empty. The top strips to this feature, *Daffy Doodles* and *Alexander Smart, Esq.*, showed a little more looseness. Winner died on August 12, 1956, of cancer.

R.M.

WINNETOU (Germany) Winnetou, the noble Apache chief, was originally the creation of the prolific German novelist Karl May (1842-1912), whose books over the decades have sold 50 million copies in Germany alone and have been translated into 25 languages. May first introduced the character of Winnetou in an 1879 novel, but he did not start the *Winnetou* trilogy until 1893. Although he did a lot of research on America, it was not until 1908 that he actually visited the United States. Nevertheless, several generations took May's Western novels for gospel truth, and these novels laid the groundwork for a German fascination with the Western genre, a fact attested to by, among other things, the large number of German cowboy clubs.

The success of the books beckoned comic artists to try their hands with the material. They were especially alerted to Winnetou when a series of Karl May movies hit the screens in the early 1960s. The *Winnetou* saga was done in one way or another by Juan Arranz, by Studio Vandersteen, and by Walter Neugebauer for a special Kauka album. The best of these, staying closest to the original novels, started in February 1963 and was produced by Lehning Verlag, with the able hand of Helmut Nickel providing the artwork. It is largely due to Nickel that the flavor of the novels was still felt in the comic strip version. As with other strips he had done (e.g., *Robinson*, *Hot Jerry*, *Peters seltsame Reisen* ["Peters Strange Journeys," a comics parody]), Nickel used realism with just an inkling of comic relief, a characteristic of his style.

After the publication of the first eight issues, the series was split up into two alternating ones. Besides Western adventures with Winnetou, there were also comic books with adventures in the Orient. Of these only the *Winnetou* artwork was worthwhile. It is too bad that Nickel withdrew from comics at the time because the story was spread thin over a large number of *Winnetou* issues until 1965. The strip has also been reprinted in foreign countries.

W.F.

WINNIE WINKLE (U.S.) Created by Martin Branner and distributed by the News-Tribune Syndicate, *Winnie Winkle, the Dread Winner* made its first appearance as a daily strip on September 20, 1920. Winnie was a vivacious young woman (modeled after Branner's own wife, Edith) who worked as a stenographer for one Barnaby Bibbs in order to support herself, her father Rip, and Ma. Winnie's daily vicissitudes on her job constituted the thick of the plot until April 2, 1922, when Winnie blissfully announced in the first panel of her newly created Sunday page: "Folks, I want you to meet my adopted brother Perry."

For the next 25 years, *Winnie Winkle* was to display a split personality (as was the case with many other newspaper strips of the 1920s and 1930s). During the week (as becomes a working girl), Winnie remained the heroine of the strip. She had a string of suitors with whom she flirted outrageously before finally marrying Will (Mr.) Wright in 1937 and settling into the dull felicity of many other domestic strips. Branner saw the trap, however, and Will mysteriously disappeared in the 1940s, leaving Winnie free again to play the field (after a suitable time during which she searched in vain for her vanished husband).

On the other hand, the Sunday page was almost entirely given over to the antics of Perry and his merry gang of pals known as the Rinkey-dinks. In the 1940's, unfortunately, Perry came to be gradually replaced by the newcomer Denny Dimwit (the name tells it all), and the charm of the Sunday feature faded along with him.

In the 1950s the strip (now shortened to simply *Winnie Winkle*) was devoted entirely to Winnie's romantic adventures, and Perry, all grown up now, made only intermittent appearances. In 1962, Branner retired and left the strip to his former assistant, Max van Bibber, who did it in the same soap-opera vein, giving Winnie a new rival in the person of her own daughter Wendy.

In 1980 Frank Bolle took over *Winnie Winkle* from the retiring van Bibber. In an attempt to make the feature more relevant to the times, he introduced continuities dealing with crime, corruption, and illicit drugs. Despite his efforts the strip only barely kept afloat during his 16-year tenure. Ironically, when it was finally

"Winnie Winkle," Martin Branner. © *Chicago Tribune-New York News Syndicate.*

discontinued on July 28, 1996, the syndicate gave as the reason for its demise the fact that Winnie was "not recognized as a contemporary role model for the '90s."

Winnie Winkle had her own comic book in the 1940s, but the strip was never popular enough to be made into a motion picture.

M.H.

WINTERBOTHAM, RUSSELL (1904-1971) An American writer and editor born on August 1, 1904, in Pittsburg, Kansas, Winterbotham was a speedy novelist and facile editor. During his career he turned out dozens of paperback novels under the name J. Harvey Bond.

He joined the Newspaper Enterprise Association of Cleveland as a book editor and soon found himself writing strips. His work on Walt Scott's Sunday *Captain Easy* was adequate, but not up to the level of Crane, Turner, or even the recent Crooks and Lawrence humorous stories.

But he did turn in solid comic strip storywriting on *Chris Welkin*, several years of *Red Ryder*, and *Vic Flint* (and *Flint*'s latter-day metamorphosis, *The Good Guys*) under the Bond name.

Winterbotham wrote the brief but classic pamphlet on comic production, *How Comic Strips Are Made*. He retired from NEA in February 1969 and died in 1971 after a long illness.

R.M.

WIZARD OF ID, THE (U.S.) Johnny Hart created *The Wizard of Id*, in collaboration with Brant Parker for the drawing, on November 9, 1964. Like Hart's earlier *B.C.*, *The Wizard* is distributed by Publishers-Hall Syndicate.

In the forsaken kingdom of Id there once lived a midget of a monarch, grouchy, greedy, cruel, nasty,

and craven. His greatest satisfaction in life lay in the debasement and exploitation of his equally unlovable, loutish subjects. He was flanked by his cowardly knight Brandolph and by the Wizard, a magician of dubious achievement, whose spells, as often as not, backfired lamentably when they worked at all. Yet, in the dark recesses of the royal palace, the Wizard experimented untiringly with formulas and potions, under the watchful eye of the spirit that he sometimes succeeded in conjuring. (The Wizard was, along with Bang, the inebriated jester, the only man who could play tricks on the diminutive king with impunity.)

The mood of the strip swings from black humor ("What is bread?" asks an unwashed prisoner when told he has been put on bread and water as punishment for some offense) to oft-repeated inside jokes ("The king is a fink!"—the populace's protest cry—appears in the most unlikely places and in the most outlandish forms) to verbal and visual puns (in answer to the king's peremptory order to bring rain, the Wizard calls forth a cloudburst just over the king's head).

Johnny Hart's unique brand of humor is precisely captured by Brant Parker's simple yet sophisticated style. Using the same graphic conventions as Johnny Hart on *B.C.*, Parker brings to his drawings a more rounded, more humanized look, and his visual depiction of the characters is well-nigh flawless.

The Wizard of Id has been reprinted in paperback form by Fawcett. There are now more than 30 collections in print. The Wizard and his acolytes have also been featured in a number of animation specials. The strip, now distributed by Creators Syndicate, received the Reuben Award in 1984.

M.H.

WOLINSKI, GEORGES (1934-   ) French cartoonist and writer, born in 1934 in Tunisia, of a Polish

"The Wizard of Id," Johnny Hart and Brant Parker. © Field Newspaper Syndicate.

father and an Italian mother. In 1946, Georges Wolinski's family moved to Briancon, in southeastern France, where the young boy attended grammar and high school. In 1952 he went to Paris and studied at the School of Architecture for a while (by his own admission, Wolinski stayed in school only to avoid being drafted and sent to Algeria). In 1960 he started his long collaboration with the satirical monthly *Hara-Kiri*, to which he contributed cartoons, illustrations, and a series of comic strips on political or erotic themes: *Ils Ne Pensent Qu'à Ca* ("They Only Think of One Thing"), an extremely funny and ribald variation on the eternal war between the sexes; *Histoires Inventées* ("Invented Stories"); *Hit-Parades* (in which Wolinski indulged his own sardonic views of men, women, politics, literature, history, and the arts).

Wolinski played an active role in the May 1968 student revolt, making speeches, issuing manifestos, and founding with his colleague *Siné L'Enragé* ("The Rabid One"), one of the most mordant satirical magazines born during this turbulent period, and the only one to survive. He also expressed his philosophy in a new comic strip series, *Je Ne Veux Pas Mourir Idiot* ("I Don't Want to Die an Idiot," 1968), in which the slogans of the Establishment were pitilessly dissected and lampooned, with the inevitable punch line: "I don't want to die an idiot." Later, disillusioned by the failure of the student movement, he created a new series, *Il N'y A Pas Que la Politique Dans la Vie* ("There Is More to Life Than Politics"), whose title says it all.

In 1969 Wolinski became the editor of the newly created comic monthly *Charlie*, and he made quite a reputation for himself as a playwright with several plays adapted from his comic creations (*Je Ne Veux Pas*

Georges Wolinski, magazine cartoon.

Mourir Idiot was one of the hits of the 1970-71 theater season in Paris).

Georges Wolinski has often been called the French Jules Feiffer, and there are a number of similarities. Both men use their comic strips as vehicles for social and political criticism, their drawings are reduced to their simplest expression, their characters are often abject, and their dialogues are bitter. They both enjoyed somewhat similar careers (cartoonist, editor, playwright). But, while Feiffer has always played it safe, Wolinski never hesitated to do as he preached, making his art and his life one. That this made Wolinski the superior artist (as some in France contend) is a dubious proposition.

Since 1977, when he became political cartoonist of the Communist daily *L'Humanité*, Wolinski has devoted most of his efforts to editorial cartooning. His drawings have appeared in a variety of publications, from the liberal daily *Libération* to the conservative weekly *Paris-Match*. He has also written skits for television and has continued to produce stage plays. His comic-strip output has become sporadic, principally appearing in the pages of the humor magazines *L'Echo des Savanes* and *Charlie Hebdo*.

M.H.

WOLVERTON, BASIL (1909-1978) American comic book artist and writer, born July 9, 1909, in Central Point, Oregon. Although Wolverton had no formal art training, he soon became one of the most respected and innovative creators in the comic book field. His work was so offbeat, intricate, and personalized that *Life* magazine's editors once called his material work from "the spaghetti and meatball school of design"; many underground cartoonists cite Wolverton as a profound influence on their style.

A former newspaper artist who sold his first cartoon to *America's Humor* in 1926, Wolverton saw his first comic book work appear in Globe's *Circus* number one (June 1938). His first major strip was a fantasy/science-fiction/superhero feature entitled *Spacehawk*, which premiered in Novelty Press's *Target* number five in June 1940. His early scripts were violent and brutal, with retribution being substituted for justice. Spacehawk, an interplanetary crime-fighter, was more likely to kill a captured criminal than to bind him over for proper punishment. Artistically, the feature showcased Wolverton's creative genius. Although some of the work was crude and cramped, it showed brilliant flashes of Wolverton's unsurpassed storytelling. The feature lost its fantasy base by editorial fiat in 1942, and the strip disappeared after December 1942's *Target* number 34.

By that time, however, Wolverton had already entered his humor period and created *Powerhouse Pepper* for Timely in April 1942. The strip was an instant success and appeared sporadically until 1948. Powerhouse Pepper himself was a near-perfect physical specimen with an eye for beautiful women; he was, however, somewhat lacking in mental prowess. Wolverton used a cast of grotesque-looking characters in the strip. This was to become his trademark, but he also utilized a textual device that has yet to be successfully duplicated: all the *Powerhouse Pepper* characters spoke in outrageously zany rhymes and alliterations. Combined with his exaggerated anatomy, Wolverton's rhymes made the strip one of the most cherished features of the 1940s. Wolverton created several other outstanding humor strips during this period, including *Scoop Scuttle* (Lev Gleason), *Mystic Moot and His Magic Snoot* (Fawcett), and *Inspector Hector the Crime Detector* (Timely). Then, after creating 17 outstanding science-fiction and mystery stories for Atlas between 1951 and 1953, Wolverton left comic books until 1973, when he began drawing covers of appropriately grotesque characters for National's weird humor book entitled *Plop*.

In 1946, United Feature sponsored a contest that invited *Li'l Abner* readers to submit drawings of Lower Slobbovia's ugly woman, Lena the Hyena. Wolverton won the contest handily with a patently repulsive drawing, and he began drawing a long series of highly detailed caricatures of important people of the day. Also during his career, Wolverton drew a handful of well-received features for *Mad*, was active in the commercial art field, and created a beautifully rendered adaptation of the Bible for Ambassador Press.

Graphic Story Magazine, a limited-edition magazine produced by comic art fan William Spicer, devoted two complete issues to Wolverton and his career in 1970 and 1971. In it, *Mad* associate editor Jerry DeFuccio commented that, in recognition of Wolverton's contributions, the ACBA awards should rightfully have been named the Basil. He died in Vancouver, Washington, in 1978.

J.B.

Basil Wolverton, "Lena the Hyena." © Basil Wolverton.

WONDER WOMAN (U.S.) Wonder Woman was created by writer William Moulton Marston (under the pen name Charles Moulton) and first illustrated by H. G. Peter for National Comics' *All-Star* number eight (December 1941). The next month she began appearing in *Sensation* (where she adopted her civilian identity of Diana Prince); and she began in *Wonder Woman* comics in the summer of 1942.

Marston was not a comic book writer but rather a well-known psychologist and inventor of the polygraph. He created *Wonder Woman* to express his theories about male-female relationships. The strip has received heavy scrutiny over the years, being adopted by the woman's liberation movement as an early manifestation of their philosophy. On the other hand, Dr. Fredric Wertham's controversial *Seduction of the Innocent* (Holt, Rinehart and Winston, 1953) saw *Wonder*

"Wonder Woman," William Moulton Marston. © National Periodical Publications.

Woman as a "crime comic . . . found to be one of the most harmful."

Wonder Woman's origin had several versions, but the most widely accepted claimed she was an Amazon princess and daughter of Queen Hippolyte. She lived on Paradise Island, where no men were allowed and ostensibly came to America to help fight the World War II. Wearing a star-spangled costume of red, white, blue, and yellow, she was almost omnipotent, unless her bracelets of submission were chained together by a male.

It would be impossible to cite all the various psychological interpretations scholars have drawn from *Wonder Woman,* but they include sadomasochism, lesbianism, and literally dozens of other allegedly aberrant "isms."

After Marston died in 1947, the strip began ignoring pseudo-psychology and became a straight adventure strip. More emphasis was placed on Wonder Woman's gadgets: her invisible robot plane, her golden lasso, and her bracelets. By the late 1960s, she was just another superheroine. One of the few interesting interpretations came when Denny O'Neil became the writer and editor. He stripped Wonder Woman of her powers and traditional costume and made her a disciple of I Ching. The change did not last, however; she was soon back at her former status.

She still appears in *Wonder Woman* comics, now having published over 200 issues. And besides her numerous comic book appearances, she has also had a short-lived newspaper strip, made cartoon appearances, and is a sought-after property.

The strip's greatest recent achievement, however, was the publication of the *Wonder Woman* hardback anthology (Holt, Rinehart, 1972). Besides reprinting several of the classic Marston-Peter strips, the book carried an outstanding introduction by Gloria Steinem, renowned journalist, feminist, and editor of *Ms.* magazine. Dr. Phyllis Chesler, a psychologist and feminist, contributed an interpretative essay that captures the character's original concept more faithfully than anything published after Marston's death.

J.B.

Wonder Woman in the late 1970s and the 1980s experienced a series of ups and downs (with a majority of downs), culminating in the cancellation of the title in February 1986. She came back to her roots in the miniseries *The Legend of Wonder Woman* (May to August 1986), leading to a reprise of the *Wonder Woman* monthly comic book in February 1987. George Perez ably guided the Amazon Princess through her paces for the first couple of years, but aside from a brief interim by John Byrne, the title has again become mired in mediocrity.

Wonder Woman has been the subject of a number of media adaptations through the years. Aside from the aforementioned newspaper strip (1944-45), there was a live-action series on ABC-TV (1976-77), later transferring to CBS (1977-79), with Lynda Carter in the title role.

M.H.

WONG, TONY (1950-   ) Born in Canton, Tony Wong moved to Hong Kong at the age of six. There he became familiar with the only comics available, those from Japan. At 14 he quit school to support his family, working as an office boy and, later, as an artist for several firms. At 20 he started the comics company Yuk Long ("Jademan"), which by 1972 had become Hong Kong's leading comic-book publisher, a position it retains to this day. Wong's books used kung fu, science-fiction, ghost, and humor stories. His first big hit was the kung fu book *Siulauman* ("Street Fighter"), whose title was changed in 1980 to *Dragon and Tiger Heroes*; it is still a best-seller.

By the mid-1980s Jademan controlled 70 to 90 percent of Hong Kong's comics trade, amassing a total circulation of 2.1 million for its 15 titles. A feature Wong adopted from the Japanese publishers was their factory style of operation; he refined the system, using five times more artists per book, tiering his art staff, and building in bonuses as incentives for high production.

Wong was at the height of his career in 1987-88, when he listed Jademan on the Hong Kong Stock Exchange, diversified into other ventures, and eyed a large overseas market. He bought parts of daily newspapers, magazines, and other properties and expanded his distribution networks deeper into Asia, the United States, and other English-speaking countries, before running into a series of troubles that saw him lose control of Jademan in 1989. Shortly after, he was convicted and sent to jail for fraudulent business practices.

Upon his release from prison in 1993, Wong launched a new comics company that attracted back some of his old audience, as well as some former Jademan employees. Jademan itself had continued to thrive, evolving into a holdings firm of 14 companies, 2 of which published up to 20 comics titles by 1992.

Among Wong's major contributions, aside from igniting the comics industry of Hong Kong, were highlighting the international marketing possibilities for Asian comics, creating the martial arts genre for which the colony became known, and training a number of excellent artists, including Ma Wing-shing and Chris Lau, who went on to start their own comics companies.

J.A.L.

WOOD, ROBIN (1944-   ) Although he is generally considered to be an Argentinian author, Robin Wood was actually born in 1944 in Nueva Australia, a colony founded in the jungles of Paraguay by Australian immigrants, and he lived and worked in Brazil, Argentina, and Italy before settling in Copenhagen, Denmark, in 1993. After a childhood not too dissimilar from that of the young narrator of Paul Theroux's *The Mosquito Coast*, he moved with his parents to Buenos Aires. His love of adventure led him to work successively as a prizefighter in Argentinian boxing rings and as a truck driver through Brazilian jungles.

His first foray into comics occurred in 1965 when he started work, first as a cartoonist, then as a scriptwriter, for Editorial Columba in Buenos Aires. His first success in the field came with *Nippur de Lagash*, an adventure strip he created in 1974 and continues to produce today. An incredible succession of titles followed, from *Gilgamesh* (an epic saga set in ancient Mesopotamia) to *Merlino* (recounting the exploits of the fabled wizard from the Arthurian legends).

The author's fame spread internationally, especially to Italy, where most of his series were published in the monthly *LancioStory*. There he confirmed his success in 1981 with *Dago*, drawn by Alberto Salinas. The protagonist is a Venetian aristocrat named Cesare Renzi, the only member of his family to survive a murderous conspiracy of Venetian noblemen and Saracen pirates. The hero crisscrosses medieval Europe, under the contemptuous nickname "Dago," in search of his family's killers. Along the way, he meets such worthy opponents as Vlad Tepes the Impaler, better known as Count Dracula. In addition to the titles he has done using his own name, Wood has, under a variety of pseudonyms (including Robert O'Neil, Carlos Ruiz, and Roberto Monti), written innumerable series, ranging from Gothic tales (*Dracula*) to military yarns (*Il Cosacco, Qui la Legione*) to romance stories (*Amanda*).

Wood has been the recipient of many distinctions and honors for his work, including the Lifetime Achievement Award from the 1996 International Comics Salon in Rome.

M.H.

WOOD, WALLACE (1927-1981) American comic book and comic strip artist and writer, born June 17, 1927, in Menahga, Minnesota. A self-taught artist, Wally Wood received his only professional training during short stints at the Minneapolis School of Art and Burne Hogarth's Cartoonists and Illustrators School. Breaking into comic art as a letterer, he did not see significant amounts of his artwork appear in print

until 1949. His best early work came in 1950, when he drew three weeks of Sundays for Will Eisner's *The Spirit*. Entitled "Denny Colt in Outer Space," the episode gave the earliest indication of Wood's amazing ability to interpret science-fiction material.

Wood also entered the comic book field in 1949, freelancing for many groups, including Ziff-Davis, Avon, Charlton, and EC. He finally settled down with EC about the time Bill Gaines and Al Feldstein introduced the New Trend line in 1951 and became their main science-fiction illustrator. Wood had perfected his talent with science-fiction material: he drew intricate spaceships, startling monsters, and beautiful space scenes; he was a master of lighting; he created intriguing and innovative alien planet scenes; and he topped it all off by drawing luscious and incredibly well-endowed women. His page composition and tight line work made him the acknowledged dean of comic book science fiction. He later went on to illustrate for science-fiction digests like Galaxy.

At the same time, however, Wood was also contributing heavily to EC's irrepressible *Mad*. Along with Will Elder and Harvey Kurtzman, Wood was a pioneer in *Mad*'s cluttered panel technique, and one had to really strain to catch all the sight gags and jokes Wood crammed into each panel. He appeared in every *Mad* magazine and comic produced during the book's first 12 years.

After EC folded its non-*Mad* line in 1956, Wood branched out and started a successful advertising art career, but he also found time to assist on syndicated strips such as *Terry and the Pirates*, *Flash Gordon*, and *Prince Valiant*. On September 8, 1958, he and Jack Kirby began a well-received syndicated science-fiction strip entitled *Skymasters*, which ran for 18 months.

Wood has since gone on to work for almost every comic book company while continuing to do advertising art. In 1964, he did some highly acclaimed work on Marvel's *Daredevil* book, and he later worked for National, Warren, Gold Key, King, and several others. In 1965, he created the *THUNDER Agents* for Tower with the aid of artists Steve Ditko, Dan Adkins, Reed Crandall, Gil Kane, and others; though short-lived, it was one of the best features of the 1960s.

In 1966, Wood founded *Witzend*, a fanzine in which professional artists wrote and drew strips they normally could not produce for the mass-market-oriented comic book companies. Stricken with an incurable illness, he took his own life on November 3, 1981, in Los Angeles.

J.B.

WOOLFOLK, WILLIAM (1917-   ) American comic book writer, editor, and publisher, born in June 1917 on Long Island, New York. After attending New York University, Bill Woolfolk began his writing career in 1936 by contributing to some of the many small literary magazines of the time. He then moved on to bylined pieces at slicks such as *Liberty* and *Collier's*, became an advertising copywriter, and finally entered the comic book field in 1941 as a writer for the MLJ line.

Unlike most writers of the time, who simply wrote the story and dialogue and gave it to the artist, Woolfolk used a style that would eventually become prevalent at Marvel in the 1960s. He would first produce a plot synopsis, allow the artist to draw the plot (Marvel art director John Romita once called it a visual plot), and then add dialogue to the finished artwork.

More than anything else about Woolfolk's comic career, however, was the amazing number of top-notch strips he wrote for various publishers simultaneously. At MLJ, he was writing for the entire line, including major features like *Black Hood* and *Shield* when, in 1942, Warren King introduced him to Fawcett and *Captain Marvel* and *Captain Marvel Jr.*; the same year, Fawcett editor John Beardsley moved to Quality and introduced Woolfolk to *Blackhawk*; after a short stint in the army in 1943, he returned to comics and added Timely strips *Captain America*, *Human Torch*, and *Sub-Mariner*; and, finally, in 1944, Woolfolk added National to his accounts and started on *Superman* and others. During most of this time, his works were appearing on the five all-time best-selling strips.

His best work undoubtedly came on *Blackhawk* and *Captain Marvel*. For the latter, he created the villain

Captain Nazi, a durable Axis menace who ranked just below Dr. Sivana and Mr. Mind as the Captain's greatest foe. On Quality's *Blackhawk*, Woolfolk teamed with artist Reed Crandall and guided the strip through its glorious years (1941-45). Unlike some of the feature's other writers, he concentrated on giving distinct characters to the seven Blackhawks, who frequently were allowed to fade in deference to their military hardware.

In 1946, Woolfolk started his own publishing company, O. W. Comics, with J. G. Oxton, but the effort was short-lived. After another fling at comics writing with Orbit, Woolfolk began another, non-comics publishing business. Several years later, he went to Hollywood and became a successful television writer, then a story editor on the then-popular *Defenders* show. He finally retired from television and has since been writing mainstream novels.

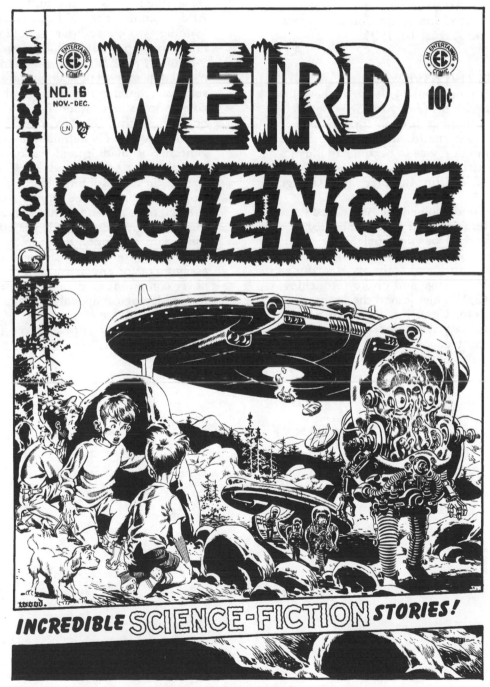

Wally Wood, "Weird Science." © *William M. Gaines, Agent, Inc.*

His wife, Dorothy Rubichek, is also a former comic book writer and editor.

J.B.

WROBLEWSKI, JERZY (1940-1991) Jerzy Wroblewski was born in 1940 in Bydgoszcz, Poland, where he was educated at the Fine Arts Gymnasium. His career in comics began in 1959, when he drew and wrote a strip for his hometown newspaper, *Dziennik Wieczorny*. In 1967 Wroblewski drew the police story *Risk*, which became Poland's longest serial, composed of 53 segments. A propaganda strip, *Risk* starred a superbrave, educated, and intelligent policeman.

In the early 1970s, Wroblewski worked on another propaganda piece, *Underground Front*, about the Polish resistance movement, and from 1973 he worked on *Captain Zbik*, another police adventure strip. Prolific as an artist, Wroblewski also contributed many stories to *Relax* magazine, which debuted in 1976, and later to *Awantura* magazine. In the 1980s, he published his own albums of adventure, historical, sensational, and Western-style comics. He was considered Poland's most popular comics artist during the Communist era.

Wroblewski died on August 10, 1991.

J.A.L.

WUNDER, GEORGE (1912-1987) American artist, born in New York City on April 24, 1912. While still a boy Wunder moved with his family to Kingston, New York. He received art training through correspondence lessons from the International Correspondence Schools. His early ambition was to become an illustrator or commercial artist, although he closely followed the comic strips of Martin Branner and George McManus.

On July 1, 1936, Wunder joined the Associated Press as a staff artist (he remembers a vow of poverty as a prerequisite) and worked beside Noel Sickles, Bert Christman, sports cartoonist Tom Paprocki, editorial cartoonist Hank Barrow, and others. His duties included sports spot drawings and photo retouching.

At the end of 1942, Wunder joined the army, serving until February 1946. Upon his discharge he was informed by AP friend Jay Alan (*Modest Maidens*) that the syndicate he was trying to crack, the Chicago Tribune-New York News Syndicate, was looking for a

George Wunder, "Terry and the Pirates." © Chicago Tribune-New York News Syndicate.

replacement for Milton Caniff on *Terry and the Pirates*. After a conference with comic editor Mollie Slott, Wunder was chosen over a field of competitors. His first *Terry* appeared on December 29, 1946.

Wunder maintained a consistently varied parade of characterizations. His dialogue (always written by himself) was among the most sophisticated, taut, and cinematic—albeit Grade B—of the story strips. The body of criticism about Wunder, however, has focused on his artwork. He definitely maintained the AP conventions of shading and backgrounds and even the wrinkles that are the trademark of AP graduates like Caniff, Sickles, Robbins, Toth, and so many others. Upper lips disappeared from virtually all of the *Terry* characters in a manner that annoyed many fans, and the seemingly mesmerized eyes on all of the faces also cast a sameness upon the strip.

Filling Milton Caniff's shoes would be an unenviable assignment for any artist, and to Wunder's credit, he never compromised details in art and the strip's traditional ideological appeal at a time when pressures to modify both were extreme.

The last *Terry* appeared on February 15, 1973. Wunder died in 1987.

R.M.

X-MEN (U.S.) *X-Men* first appeared in *X-Men* number one (September 1963), the creation of writer-editor Stan Lee and illustrator Jack Kirby. The story introduced a band of teenaged mutants, each gifted with a particular superpower. The wheelchair-confined Professor X, gifted with amazing mental powers, brought them together at his private school to guard against the schemes of evil mutants, notably of their arch-foe, Magneto. The X-Men consisted of Cyclops, whose eyes emitted a powerful blasting beam; The Angel, born with operative wings; Iceman, a reverse Human Torch, able to hurl snow and ice bombs; The Beast, an apelike being whose erudite speech was in marked contrast to his bestial appearance; and Marvel Girl, able to levitate objects and command a force field.

Kirby was the artist for the first 11 issues and remained on layouts for several more. After one issue by Alex Toth, Werner Roth became the principal artist and remained in that post until 1969, despite fill-in art jobs by Jack Sparling, Barry Smith, Jim Steranko, Don Heck, Ross Andru, Dan Adkins, and George Tuska. In 1966, writer Roy Thomas joined Roth on the book to continue the tales of the mutant band and their encounters with others born with bizarre powers. Despite the best efforts of all involved, the book remained one of Marvel's least-noticed titles. In 1967 and 1968, various gimmicks were used to try and boost sales, such as new uniforms for the team and the death of Professor X. Scripting chores passed on to Gary Friedrich and Arnold Drake.

In May of 1969, Thomas returned to the writing and joined with artist Neal Adams in an attempt to bring about a new look for the X-Men. New supporting characters were brought in, but this did little good. In March 1970, with issue number 66, Marvel announced the book's discontinuation.

In December of that same year, the title was revived in reprint form, and the success of the old stories prompted talk of attempting new stories. The X-Men appeared in other Marvel comics, and a series starring the Beast (albeit in highly altered form) enjoyed a brief run in *Amazing Adventures*. But it wasn't until 1975 that the new stories were finally undertaken. A revamped team, featuring several new members, was introduced by artist Dave Cockrum, first in a one-shot *Giant-Size X-Men* and then, replacing the reprints, in the regular *X-Men* comic book beginning with number 94 (August 1975).

M.E.

The second version of *X-Men* really took off in 1977 when John Byrne was entrusted with the artwork and contributed some needed pyrotechnics to the title.

"X-Men," Jim Lee/Bob Wiacek. © Marvel Comics.

Since that time the comic book (retitled *The Uncanny X-Men* in 1981) has been the favorite playground of some of the best artists in the field, including Neal Adams, John Buscema, Walt Simonson, Barry Smith, and Jim Lee. There have also been a number of entertaining plot developments (often involving the destruction of entire worlds) and the addition of several interesting newcomers to the group, such as Phoenix, Nightcrawler, Storm, and Colossus. The series has become Marvel's most successful line of comics, with innumerable spin-offs, all starting with the letter *X* (*X-Factor*, *X-Terminator*, *X-Men Classic*, *X-Force*, ad nauseam).

M.H.

YEATS, JACK B. (1870-1957)

YEATS, JACK B. (1870-1957) An Anglo-Irish cartoonist, author, and painter, John Butler Yeats was born in London on August 19, 1871, the son of the Irish painter John Butler Yeats, and the brother of the poet William Butler Yeats. He was educated in County Sligo, Ireland. His first published drawing appeared on April 7, 1888, and he became a regular contributor of horse sketches to the magazine *Paddock Life* (1891-93). He illustrated his brother William's book *Irish Fairy Tales* (1892), and the same year began drawing joke cartoons for *Cassells' Saturday Journal* and the boys' weekly *Chums*.

Several tries at gags in strip form led to his creation of the first regular character in the Alfred Harmsworth comic weeklies, a burlesque on Conan Doyle's *Sherlock Holmes*, which he titled *Chubb-Lock Homes*. His great detective was assisted by another burlesque character, Shirk the Dog Detective, a takeoff on *Dirk the Dog Detective*, a serial story in *Illustrated Chips*. Chubb-Lock Homes made his debut in *Comic Cuts* on June 16, 1894, and the character transferred to *Funny Wonder* in August of that year. Homes's adventures turned into a weekly serial from December 22, 1894, and after an interval reappeared in the same paper as a full front-page feature in 1897.

By that time Yeats's work had developed considerably and had a lively, sketchy quality, with an artistic use of solid black and white spaces that set him immediately apart from the followers of Tom Browne. His love for horses came out in *Signor McCoy the Circus Hoss*, a remarkable creation for *Big Budget* (June 19, 1897). For the same weekly he created *John Duff Pie* (1897) and *Little Boy Pink* (1898) and revamped his detective character as *Kiroskewero the Detective* (1899). Meanwhile, for *Funny Wonder* he created *Mrs. Spiker's Boarding House* (August 22, 1896); a comic Yankee, *Hiram B. Boss* (December 18, 1897); a smuggler, *Ephraim Broadbeamer* (June 10, 1898); and *Convict 9999* (1899).

Jack Yeats, "Chubb-Lock Homes."

Yeats wrote and drew two children's books, *James Flaunty or the Terror of the Western Seas* (1901) and *The Bosun and the Bobtailed Comet* (1904), then returned to comics with a new, neater style, signing his strips "Jack," followed by either a small bee or a small black bird. For Harmsworth's first weekly comic in color, *Puck*, he created *Dr. Up-To-Dayte's Academy* and *Sandab the Sailor* (both 1904) and some new series for the revamped *Jester and Wonder*: *Skilly the Convict* and *Licketty Switch* (both 1904), *Fandango the Hoss* (1905), and *The Jester Theatre Royal* (1907). Also in 1907 he did *Dr. Patent* and *The Little Stowaways* for *Puck*; then in 1909 *Roly Poly's Tours* and a crazy creature, *The Whodidit*, for *Comic Cuts*. His interest in the stage emerged more fully through *Carlo the Jester* in *Comic Cuts* (1912), *Jimmy Jog the Juggler* (1914), *Eggbert and Philbert* (1915), and his last strip, *Bill Bailey* (1917). The last three were for *Butterfly*.

Yeats left comics to continue his career as a writer and painter. His books include *Sailing Sailing* (1933), *The Amavanthers* (1936), and *The Careless Flower* (1947). Among his plays are *Apparitions*, *The Old Sea Road*, and *Rattle*. His watercolors and paintings, famous for their color qualities, are collectors' items, and a London exhibition was staged in March 1975. He died on March 28, 1957, aged 86.

D.G.

YEH HUNG CHIA (1913-1990)

YEH HUNG CHIA (1913-1990) Although considered the giant of Taiwan's golden era of cartooning in the 1950s, Yeh Hung Chia did not gain widespread popularity until 1958, when the good times were already drawing to a close. During the 1940s, Yeh sneered at Taiwan's social conditions in political cartoons but quit doing them after the conflict between China and Taiwan in February 1947. For nine years he worked as a designer, until in 1956 he began cartooning Chinese folktales.

Yeh's big break in comics came in 1958, when he created *Chuko Szu-lang*, about a character with a mighty double-edged sword. It was based on two Chinese historical figures: Chuko Kung Ming, a sage in the Three Kingdoms Period (220-265), and Yang Szulang, national hero and dutiful son of the Northern Sung dynasty (960-1127). Both embodied loyalty and filial piety. The first installment of what would become 55 books appeared as *Chuko Szu-lang Struggles with Evil Party* in *Cartoon Weekly*. Yeh's character, which filled 32 of the periodical's 72 pages, quickly became popular. Eventually Yeh's comic books sold 100,000 copies weekly, while at the same time inspiring songs and films.

Yeh had the zeal of a teacher, using his books to educate about good and evil. Other Yeh stories were included in *Silang and Zhenping* and focused in part on a comic strip hero named after the Chinese-language characters for sincerity and honesty. Yeh handled his

"The Yellow Kid," R. F. Outcault.

stable of comics through Hung-Chia Publishers, which he established.

His career nosedived after 1960, when the government began looking at his work less favorably; a car accident in 1974 left him handicapped. During the latter part of his life, he reorganized his old scripts and sought loans to reprint them.

J.A.L.

YELLOW KID, THE (U.S.) The hero of the first true comic strip, R. F. Outcault's Yellow Kid first appeared in two gag panels, one in color and one in black and white, in the same issue of the Sunday *New York World* on May 5, 1895. The color panel was called *At the Circus in Hogan's Alley* and was one of several similar slum kid panels Outcault drew through the middle of 1895 for the *World*, with varying locales given in the titles: Reilly's Pond, Casey's Alley, Shantytown, etc. On the sidelines in both of the May 5 panels is a large-headed, jug-eared boy of about six or seven, clad in a plain dress or nightshirt smudged with dirty handprints; in the color panel the nightshirt is blue. In a number of subsequent back-street kid panels, the nightshirted kid, who acquired the bald head he would later be famed for, plays either a subordinate role or is altogether missing. By January 5, 1896, however, the kid is more noticeable, and he wears a yellow nightshirt for the first time. Since his prominence in the panel series and the first use of yellow more or less coincided, from the public's point of view, they began to talk about the otherwise nameless child who had caught their amused fancy as the yellow kid. Outcault, however, used *Ho-*

gan's Alley as a general running title for the weekly panels, and neither he nor the *World* ever referred to the feature figure as the Yellow Kid while Outcault was employed there.

The Kid himself began to talk to his public with his nightshirt, emblazoning saucy and irreverent messages more or less related to the theme of the week's other panel action, but he never spoke otherwise (although some minimal dialogue balloons appeared in the *World* panels from time to time). The last *World* panel in this form by Outcault appeared on May 17, 1896, just after Outcault's departure for William Randolph Hearst's *New York Journal*. (George B. Luks continued the panels for the *World*, using the *Hogan's Alley* running title and dropping the yellow nightshirt for other hues on several occasions.) Hearst immediately applied the popular *Yellow Kid* label to the panel, trumpeting his acquisition everywhere in New York and encouraging Outcault to abandon the gag-panel format in favor of progressive panel narration, which other Hearst cartoonists were using in different features in the *Journal*'s *American Humorist* Sunday section. Outcault did so later in 1896, and with the addition of relevant balloon dialogue vital to the point of the weekly anecdote, he formed what amounted to the definitive comic strip for the first time.

But Outcault was not happy with the Kid, despite the financial harvest he was reaping. He and his wife were sensitive to the views of the "better people" in New York, and these people regarded *The Yellow Kid* as a public disgrace, even applying the color of his nightshirt to the sensational "yellow journalism" they despised (then largely centered in the New York *World* and *Journal*). The furor kicked up by the widely publicized legal battle between the *World* and the *Journal* over the rights to the *Hogan's Alley* characters (which resulted in Outcault retaining the right to continue the characters and the *World* holding control of the *Hogan's Alley* name and figures as well) irked him also. He dropped the Kid (and Hearst) to return to freelancing in 1898, later joining the staff of the *New York Herald* to introduce *Poor Li'l Mose* and, in effect, begin a new career.

But the memory of *The Yellow Kid* lingered forcefully. Not only were there dozens of artifacts, buttons, statuettes, games, puzzles, a joke magazine with the strip name (but containing no strips), and books (one, *The Yellow Kid in MacFadden's Flats*, consisting of Hearst strip reprints with an accompanying text, constituted the first true comic book), but Outcault himself used the Kid figure in advertisements well into the new century (usually pairing the Kid with his pet goat), and drew him in various guises in his later *Buster Brown* strip. Curiously, however, there has never been a *Yellow Kid* collection in this century, despite the fact that the entire oeuvre would run to only about 125 pages. It is vital, and long overdue.

B.B.

YOKOYAMA, RYŪICHI (1909-   ) Japanese cartoonist, born May 17, 1909, in Kochi. After graduation from Kōchi Jōtō Chūgakkō of the former school system, Ryūichi Yokoyama went to Tokyo in order to take the entrance examination to the Art Academy, but he failed to gain entrance for two consecutive years (1927-28). In 1928 he became a pupil of the famous sculptor Hakuun Motoyama, while contributing cartoons to various magazines in order to support himself. On the advice of Motoyama, Yokoyama decided on a cartooning career, and before long he made a success of it.

In 1932 Yokoyama and some of his fellow cartoonists (Hidezō Kondō, Yukio Sugiura, Fukujirō Yokoi, Zenroku Mashiko, Ryū Osanai, and other Young Turks) founded the Shin Mangaha Shūdan ("New Cartoonists' Group") to fight against the older cartoon establishment (in 1945 the association dropped the "New" in its name to become simply the Manga Shudan). Yokoyama became the leader of the new group. In 1936 he created his first famous comic strip, *Edokko Ken-chan* ("Ken from Edo"); later the title was changed to *Fuku-chan*, and the title character became one of the most famous characters in Japanese newspaper strips. *Fuku-chan*'s success was followed by more famous creations: *The Beggar King* (1946); *Doshako* and *Peko-chan* (both 1947); and *Densuke* (195). Densuke had been a second banana in *Peko-chan*, but, like Fuku-chan earlier, he graduated to star status. Other Yokoyama creations of note are *Chakkari Densuke* (1953); *Yuki* (Courage , 1966); and *Hyaku Baka* (1968).

In 1955 Yokoyama established his own company, Otogi Pro, for the production of animated films. Among the many cartoons he produced, the more noted are *Onbu Obake* (1955); *Fukusuke* (1957); *Hyōtan Suzume* (1959); *Instant History* (1964); *Kokki* ("The National Flag," 1965); and *Dobutsu Gomanbiki* (1966). Yokoyama has also contributed many cartoons, illustrations, and covers to newspapers and magazines, and he has also created a number of picture books.

Ryūichi Yokoyama, "Fuku-chan." © Asahigraph.

Lyman Young, "Tim Tyler's Luck." © *King Features Syndicate.*

Ryūichi Yokoyama was greatly influenced by American films as well as by American and European comic strips, and he reflected these influences in his strips and cartoons, bringing a fresh outlook to the Japanese comic strip scene before the World War II. Yokoyama's influence played a great role in the shaping of younger cartoonists, beginning with Yokoyama's own brother Taizō.

H.K.

YOKOYAMA, TAIZŌ (1917-   ) Japanese cartoonist, born February 28, 1917, in Kochi. While on vacation from Kōchi Commercial School in 1931, Taizō Yokoyama went to Tokyo to pay a visit to his elder brother Ryūichi and decided to remain in the capital. While there, he attended Kyōko Commercial School during the day and Kawabata Art School at night. Called into the army, Yokoyama was sent to China in 1938 but returned to Japan in 1941. That year he entered Teikoku School of Fine Arts, graduating in 1944 and exhibiting at several national art shows during that time.

Yokoyama was again drafted in 1945, but the war ended before he saw any action. Soon after his discharge, he started to do illustrations for the daily *Shinyūkan* and became a professional cartoonist in 1946 for *Shinyūkan* (that same year he joined the Manga Shudan, the cartoonists' association founded by his brother in 1932). To *Shinyūkan* and other publications, such as the satirical magazine *Van* and the humor magazine *Hōpu*, Yokoyama contributed a great number of cartoons. In 1952 he created his famous newspaper strip *Pū-san* (later made into a motion picture). More successes followed: *Shakai Gihyō* (an editorial panel which he created in 1954 and which is still in existence); *Shinjinbutsu Gihyō* (in which he caricatures celebrities) in 1957; *Gihyō no Tabi* (an illustrated travelogue, 1963). In 1965 he expanded the adventures of Pu-san further into a weekly magazine format. In the meantime, he had been instrumental in the founding of *Ehe*, a satirical magazine run by professional cartoonists, and in 1965 he was named chairman of the cartoon department of the Tokyo College of Design. He is now retired.

Taizō Yokoyama revolutionized the art of the Japanese cartoon after World War II: he drew cartoons that were extremely stylized with a sharp and geometric line. His political cartoons were direct and to the point, in contrast to the shilly-shallying of editorial cartoons before the war. His graphic style was influenced more by Saul Steinberg than by any Japanese artist. In addition to his cartoons, Yokoyama has also done illustration, covers, and oil paintings.

H.K.

YOU AND ME *see* Potts, The.

YOUNG, LYMAN (1893-1984) American cartoonist, born in 1893 in Chicago. Along with his younger and more famous brother Murat ("Chic"), he showed an early talent for cartooning, and later went to the Chicago Art Institute. After service in World War I and a short stint as a salesman, Lyman Young, prodded by his brother, started his cartooning career in 1924 by taking over *The Kelly Kids*, a sister-and-brother strip that had been created by C. W. Kahles in 1919. In 1927 he created his first strip, *The Kid Sister* (an offshoot of *The Kelly Kids*) for King Features Syndicate. In 1928 his most famous feature, *Tim Tyler's Luck*, appeared as a daily strip, to be followed in 1931 by a Sunday version (with *The Kid Sister* as its top). In 1935 *Curley Harper*, a reporter-detective strip, replaced *The Kid Sister* on the Sunday page.

From then on Lyman Young's career was exclusively devoted to the production of his strips, with which he strongly identified. (Young himself stated in a 1942 interview that *Tim Tyler* was his attempt at recapturing his childhood dreams of thrilling adventures in faraway places.) Many ghosts labored under Young's direction, but however many the people involved in the strip's production, *Tim Tyler* (Young's most memorable creation) was unmistakenly one man's vision. In the late 1950s Young relinquished the daily strip to his son Bob and the Sunday page to Tom Massey and retired, first to Florida (where he lived next to his brother Chic), and then to California. He died in Port Angeles, Washington, on February 12, 1984.

M.H.

YOUNG, MURAT (1901-1973) American cartoonist, born in Chicago on January 9, 1901. Young's mother, a painter, encouraged her two sons (Murat and his brother Lyman, who was also to become a cartoonist) to pursue artistic careers. Murat Young studied art in Chicago, New York, and Cleveland. In 1920 he went to work for the Newspaper Enterprise Association, where he originated his first comic strip, *The Affairs of Jane*. Moving to the Bell Syndicate, he created, in 1922, *Beautiful Bab*, the comic adventures of a pretty blonde in a girls' school.

In 1924 Young joined King Features Syndicate as an assistant. At King he created another girl strip, *Dumb Dora*, in 1925 (it was then that he signed his now-famous nickname, "Chic"). In September 1930, having left *Dora*, he originated the widely acclaimed *Blondie*. Among Chic Young's other strips, mention should be made of *The Family Foursome*, which served as *Blondie's* top and related the doings of a middle-class couple and their two teenaged children. In 1934, with Blondie start-

Murat (Chic) Young, "Beautiful Bab." © Bell Syndicate.

ing a family of her own, *The Family Foursome* was replaced by *Colonel Potterby and the Duchess*, an underrated strip, full of whimsy and a wry, lunatic humor.

From 1930 on, Chic Young devoted himself entirely to his comic strip work, making *Blondie* into the most popular strip of all time. In 1948 he received the Reuben Award, and throughout his career, he has been the recipient of many more citations and awards. His style has been widely copied, and his theme (the matriarchal family viewed with knowing sympathy and tender irony) has inspired countless other strips, not to mention scores of TV situation comedies.

Chic Young died on March 14, 1973, in St. Petersburg, Florida.

M.H.

YOUNG ALLIES (U.S.) Leo Gorcey and Huntz Hall made the 1937 motion picture *Dead End* a phenomenal success, and their Bowery Boys (née Dead End Kids) spawned a horde of imitators in all media. The comic books were no exception, and the very first kid group was premiered in Timely's *Young Allies* number one during the summer of 1941. Created by editors Jack Kirby and Joe Simon, writer Otto Binder, and artist C. Wostkoski, the Young Allies were Bucky, Captain America's sidekick; Toro, The Human Torch's sidekick; and a group of youths unendowed with superpowers who had originally appeared as the Sentinels of Liberty. These boys were Percival O'Toole, alias Knuckles, a ruffian who hailed from New York's Lower East Side; Jeff Sandervilt, who seemed to be nondescript as a profession; Henry Tubby Tinkle, the group's fat kid; and a most unfortunate black caricature, Whitewash Jones. Whitewash had the archetypal rolling eyes, zoot suit, and dialogue complete with drawl.

The group made its first appearance as the Young Allies in a battle against the dreaded Red Skull, and their inexperience necessitated the aid of Human Torch and Captain America, both of whom were added to hype sales just in case the buying public wasn't sure it

could identify with its peer group. But the book was moderately successful, lasting 20 issues until 1946. The team also made about a dozen other appearances in other Timely titles and even spawned a Timely take-off, the ill-fated *Tough Kid Squad*.

Most of the scripts were written by Stan Lee and Otto Binder and concentrated on fast action; it was standard fare for the book-length story to be divided into several parts with the tide of battle switching from the good guys to the bad at the drop of a chapter change. But the most intriguing plot device surfaced when Toro and Bucky fought for control of the group. After six issues of haggling, Bucky finally prevailed.

Many fine artists contributed material to the strip, including Al Gabriele, Frank Giacoia, Mike Sekowsky, Syd Shores, Don Rico, and Alex Schomburg.

J.B.

YOUR UNCLE FEININGER *see* Feininger, Lyonel.

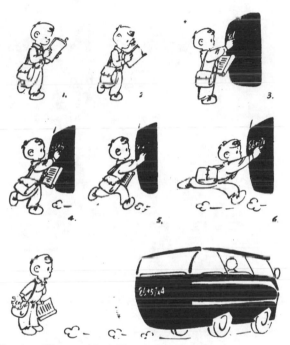

Yue Xiaoying, "Engrossed in Arithmetic." © Yue Xiaoying.

YUE XIAOYING (1921-1985) Born in Zhenhai, Zhejiang Province, in 1921, Yue studied commercial art in Zhenhai Business School in 1938, and, the next year, studied New Year's painting in Shanghai under Wu Guangzhi, a master of that specialized art form. Yue taught himself cartooning. After the founding of the People's Republic of China, he concentrated on comics for children. In the 1950s his comic strip *The Colorful Road* (coauthored with others) was awarded first prize at the First National Exhibition of Comic Art. As art editor for the *Little Friends* magazine and *Xinmin Evening News* in Shanghai, he was a member of the National Chinese Artists Association. His comics work was published in *Selected Comics for Children by Yue Xiaoying.*

Although some of Yue's political cartoons from the 1940s were quite critical of the government, in later years his comics mostly extolled the "new people and new scenes in new China." Children were always dear to Yue's heart, and children warmly welcomed his comics. He was called, with honor, "an old friend of the little friends."

H.Y.L.L.

ZIG ET PUCE (France) One of the most important and influential of European comic strips, Alain Saint-Ogan's *Zig et Puce* first appeared in the pages of the French weekly *Dimanche Illustré* on May 3, 1925. *Zig et Puce* started as a last-minute editorial replacement and was not supposed to run for more than a few weeks, but to everyone's (including the author's) surprise the strip met with an enthusiastic reception and was soon to become the star attraction of *Dimanche Illustré* until 1937, when the feature was transferred to *Cadet-Revue*.

Zig and Puce are two enterprising young boys, one short and chubby, the other tall and skinny, whose love for adventure takes them to the far corners of the earth and into outer space. In the course of their adventures they successively meet the penguin Alfred, who becomes their mascot (and will nearly steal the strip from them); Dolly, the young American heiress whom they repeatedly save from the clutches of her criminal uncle Musgrave; Marcel, the bad-tempered but resourceful dray-horse; Princess Yette of Marcalance, who will name them cabinet ministers after they have saved her throne; and a host of lesser characters.

"Zig et Puce," Alain Saint-Ogan. © Alain Saint-Ogan.

During the war and the years after, *Zig et Puce* was to know a somewhat checkered existence, passing from one ephemeral publication to another. These included *Benjamin, France Soir Junior, Ima, Zorro,* and its own short-lived *Zig et Puce.* Its success, challenged by newer, more suspenseful features, accordingly declined. In 1963 Saint-Ogan relinquished the characters to the Belgian cartoonist Greg, who tried to re-create the strip in the magazine *Tintin,* but he encountered only moderate success and finally abandoned it in the late 1960s.

Zig et Puce was the first European strip to make exclusive use of balloons to carry dialogue, and as such it heralded an important breakthrough in European comic art and storytelling. *Zig et Puce* upheld the tradition of quality in the French-language comic strip and provided the aesthetic link between Forton's *Les Pieds-Nickelés* and Hergé's *Tintin.*

"I have achieved many things in my life," Alain Saint-Ogan wrote in his memoirs. "I have created innumerable characters, like Prosper the bear. I have illustrated the book for the centennial of the Military Medal; but all that people want to talk about is Zig and Puce." The success of the strip in the 1920s and 1930s was phenomenal: all the stories were reprinted in book form by Hachette, the strip was made into a play and a series of animated cartoons, and it was adapted to the radio and later into a series of records. The characters themselves had their likenesses made into toys, key rings, and countless other gadgets.

M.H.

ZIGOMAR (Yugoslavia) Zigomar was a popular hero of Serbian comics between World War I and World War II; his tales were also translated into other languages and published abroad. He grew out of the rivalry between two publishers. Milutin S. Ignjačević was the editor of the most popular Belgrade comics magazine of the time, *Mika Miš* ("Mickey Mouse"), between 1936 and the beginning of 1939. Because of disagreements with the owner-publisher, Aleksandar J. Ivković, Ignjačević quit his job and started his own magazine, *Mikijevo carstvo* ("Mickey's Domain"), which debuted on February 23, 1939. As he had treated authors well, many continued to work for him.

Because Ivković held the rights to publish *The Phantom* in Yugoslavia, Ignjačević ordered his tried-and-true team of Branislav Vidić and Nikola Navojev to produce another masked hero. They did. The first page of the new serial, *Zigomar,* appeared in *Mikijevo carstvo* number 28, on May 28, 1939. Because they didn't want readers to know the strip was a domestic product, the name of the scriptwriter was omitted. The reader response was overwhelming.

There is no denying that the Phantom prompted the creation of Zigomar. The resemblances include the fact that both are masked, never reveal their true identity,

"Zigomar," Branko Vidić and Nikola Navojev. © Vidic and Navojev.

a sect of mystics lives in the Himalayas; secret rituals are performed in Egypt. . . .

After Navojev's death on November 9, 1940, Vidić continued to write scripts for *Zigomar*. Episode six is *Leteći Zigomar* ("The Flying Zigomar"). The artwork was done single-handedly—and successfully—by Dušan (Duško Bogdanović). But Zigomar never completed his flight. The Luftwaffe bombarded Serbia in the early-morning hours of April 6, 1941, and in two weeks Serbia was defeated and occupied by the forces of the Third Reich. Publishing virtually ceased. The last issue of *Mikijevo carstvo*, number 217, had appeared on April 8.

During his short career (he was 27 at the time of his death) Navojev produced some other outstanding features. Among them were *Dve sirotice* ("The Two Orphan Girls"); *Mladi Bartulo* ("Young Bartulo"), a pirate story; *Mali moreplovac* ("Sailor Kid"), a seafaring tale; and *Taras Bulba*. On most of these titles he worked closely with scriptwriter Branislav Vidić.

S.I.

ZORAD, ERNÖ (1911-   ) Hungarian graphic artist, painter, and comic strip artist. After secondary school he attended the Hungarian School of Applied Arts, where his classmates included the well-known Hungarian artists Amerigo Tot and Michel Gyarmathy. He dropped out after two years to become a gallery painter and a painter of horses. After military service in World War II, he became a book illustrator.

He contributed illustrations to a number of magazines and newspapers, including *Magyar Vasarnap*, *Pesti Izé*, and *Szabad Szaj*. Later on the editor in chief of the newspaper for the Hungarian Pioneer (Communist) Association asked him to draw a picture-story about a badly behaved Pioneer who enjoyed comics too much. (During the 1950s up until the revolution of 1956, drawing and reading comics was forbidden.) Since 1957, Zorad has drawn comics almost continuously for the magazine *Fules*, using a unique collage technique.

The comics he has drawn for *Fules* and other magazines and for daily and weekly newspapers now total more than 300. Since each of these comics consists of at least 16 pages and there are at least five panels to a page, it has been calculated that Zorad has done a minimum of 3,800 pages and 19,000 drawings, an incredible number. His work has also been anthologized in two albums, he has been amply written about, and in 1993 he completed a successful volume of memoirs as told to an interviewer.

K.R.

ZOZO (Belgium) *Zozo* was an animal strip created in 1935 by C. Franchi (of whom nothing else is known) for an obscure children's paper, *Le Journal de Francette et Riquet*, published in Liège, Belgium. In all probability, the strip would never have attracted anyone's attention had it not been regularly reprinted in book form by Editions Touret in Paris, thereby reaching a wide audience all over France and in other French-speaking countries.

Zozo, a tar-black, monkey-like creature, and his human companion Croquefer, a bearded sailor of herculean strength, were a pair of freewheeling adventurers always ready to embark on some farfetched enterprise. In the first episode Zozo and Croquefer single-handedly captured a crew of pirates who had hijacked a millionaire's yacht on the high seas. Further

have no superhuman powers, and love women from New York high society. Zigomar rescues his beloved Laura Morgan from distress on the first page of his first episode. And it turns out that she was a schoolmate of the Phantom! But there are key differences between the two masked characters. To begin with, Zigomar is a modern urban hero. He has a permanent underground shelter in New York City, from which he monitors events and activates himself as necessary, sallying forth to fight evildoers in the Big Apple or abroad. Secondly, in his operational center he has some advanced technology at his disposal. Thirdly, while the Phantom is a loner whose main partners in action are a horse and a wolf, Zigomar has an associate, the little Chinese boy Yang.

In sum, Zigomar more resembles another masked hero, one at a higher stage of evolution than the Phantom: Batman. Though the resemblance is astonishing, plagiarism is out of the question; *Superman* started in the United States in June 1938 and was unknown in Serbia in 1939, and *Batman* started in the United States in the same month as *Zigomar* debuted in Serbia, May 1939.

Five *Zigomar* episodes were published. The first was titled simply "Zigomar." Next came "Zigomar versus Phantom," "Zigomar and the Bride of Gods," "Zigomar, the Whip of Justice," and "Zigomar and the Mysteries of Egypt." (The last two episodes appeared in 1940.) The stories (and their weaknesses) were typical of action-adventure comics of the 1930s: a rich heiress is kidnapped; secret plans of a new submarine are stolen from some ministry and the search for them begins;

"Zozo," C. Franchi. © Editions Touret.

adventures took the duo to Mexico, Hollywood, Indochina, Ethiopia, and even the North Pole, where they rescued the members of a stranded scientific expedition. One of the most entertaining stories featured the invention of their friend Dr. Microbus: the autofish, an extraordinary all-purpose vehicle.

In all, seven albums of *Zozo* were published; the first six were reprints, but the seventh (released in 1942) was an original story. A paperback edition was also published after World War II, but around 1948 *Zozo* disappeared again, this time for good.

Zozo was aimed at a childish audience, and its plots were as unsophisticated as its drawing. The author was obviously inspired by the two strips of humorous adventure most popular in France at the time: *Mickey Mouse* and *Zig et Puce*; and while his efforts do not put Franchi on a par with either Gottfredson or Saint-Ogan, they certainly deserve to be noted here.

M.H.

More About the Comics

A History of Newspaper Syndication
by Richard Marschall

"The Comic Paper in America"
by William Henry Shelton

"The Humor of the Colored Supplement"
by Ralph Bergengren

Glossary of Comic Strip Terms

A History of Newspaper Syndication
By Richard Marschall

The newspaper syndicate has been of inestimable value to the acceptance, growth, and development of the comic strip. It has served simultaneously as showcase and sounding board for the creators, and the syndicate business itself—although frequently subordinating creativity to commercialism—has given birth to almost all of the formats, conventions, devices, and techniques used in the modern comic strip. And it is to a handful of syndicate giants from the days of journalistic moguls that the whole experience known as the newspaper comic strip is most indebted.

Briefly, the syndicate concept started with the thirst for fast news about important events. In 1841 Moses Y. Beach of the *New York Sun* had messengers deliver President John Tyler's inaugural address to his pressroom, where he ran off preprints for local papers throughout New York State. Six years later the *Staten Islander* bought whole sections ("insiders") from the *Sun* for inclusion in its own editions.

In 1861 Ansel Nash Kellogg of the *Baraboo* (Wisconsin) *Republican* bought preprinted war news from the *Wisconsin State Journal*, a practice capitalized on by the latter as it began the first large-scale regular distribution of newspaper material, including advertising. Kellogg himself picked up the idea and, in 1865, founded the first real syndicate, the A. N. Kellogg News Co., which originated features and jokes for subscribers.

Much of this activity was centered in Chicago, and hundreds of papers throughout the Midwest suffered when Chicago burned in 1871. But in the recovery the first continued stories appeared, the first illustrated syndicated articles came in 1872, and the first stereotyped plates ("boiler plates"), whereby papers could fit preset type into a page, debuted in 1875.

Most of the primitive syndicate activity to that time was confined to rural papers unable to offer their own feature material. But in the 1880s, distributed material went to town. Irving Bacheller sold big-name interviews to major papers and established the New York Press Syndicate, later contracting famous writers. Major Orlando Jay Smith in Chicago operated similarly in 1882. *The New York Sun* again shone by syndicating its fiction around the country, and the *New York World* sent Bill Nye, the most popular humorist of the day, and cartoonist Walt McDougall around the country to sell their reports to other papers.

Unable to persuade his employers to syndicate material from *Century* and *St. Nicholas* in 1884, S. S. McClure decided to establish his own syndicate. On a shoestring he did so, with one paper receiving material free in exchange for galley proofs, which were sent to other subscribers. Soon McClure had the biggest names in fiction and public life in his stable.

It was at that point that a now-obscure group of men introduced comic strips, just at their birth in the mid-1890s, to the syndicate process. As color was added to newspapers, major cities generally kept their comic sections to themselves,

George Herriman, "Major Ozone." (1906)

Clarence Rigby, "Little Ah Sid, the Chinese Kid." (1906)

but enterprising preprint and boiler-plate syndicates introduced the nation to the comic strip.

Following is a list of the major syndicates and their features. The comics often changed artists; some cartoonists were idea men, originating features and letting others continue them. Today, these old sections are delights—abounding in features, some in color, all with a freer and sometimes more amateurish look than their big-city counterparts, Hearst and Pulitzer. Familiar names of later greats often appear, too, mass-produced with large audiences in client papers such as the *Bellefontaine* (Ohio) *Index-Repository*, instead of in New York or Chicago papers.

Foremost among these concerns was the World Color Printing Co. of St. Louis, no relation to the *New York World*. It was the longest-lived of its contemporaries, supplying rural Sunday papers with preprinted color comics until 1937. Its president was Robert Sterling Gravel, and often artists—as they switched from feature to feature—would sign his middle name to a strip as an umbrella nom de plume.

The World Company's stable was the largest and most talented of any; its star idea man for years was George Herriman; its preeminent strip was *Slim Jim*. Herriman created and drew, among others, *Butch Smith, the Boy Who Does Stunts*; *Bud Smith* (continued by Bart and later Johnny Gruelle); *Major Ozone, the Fresh Air Fiend* (continued by Clarence Rigby, Bart and Ray Nottier); *Handy Andy* (continued by Gruelle); *Bruno and Pietro* (later drawn by Rigby); and *Alexander the Cat*, on which he was succeeded by Rigby and Alexander, among others.

Clarence Rigby was also prolific, contributing his own features, including *Little Ah Sid, the Chinese Kid* and *Pinky Prim the Cat*. George Frink drew Herriman's *Rosy Posy—Mama's Girl*, in addition to *Circus Solly* and *Slim Jim*. Dink (Dink Shannon) had a style similar to James Swinnerton's and produced *Sammy Small* and two comics taken over by Jack Rogers, *Uncle Ned* and *Mooney Miggles*. The classic *Hairbreadth Harry*, begun in the *Philadelphia Press*, was first syndicated by the World Company.

Raymond C. Ewer, "Things as They Ought To Be." (1909)

Other creations and their artists were *Mr. Smarty* by Collins, *Foolish Questions* by Rutledge, *The Almost Family*, *Jingling Johnson the Poet*, and *Fitzboomski the Anarchist* by Bradford (he later became a radical himself), *Brown the City Farmer* by Raymond Crawford Ewer, *Sleepy Sid* by Paul Plashke (who became an editorial cartoonist), *Cousin Bill from the City* and *Jocko and Jumbo* by Goewey (*Cousin Bill* was originated by Jack Farr, later a cartoonist for *Judge* and comic books), *Mama's Girl—Daddy's Boy* by Bart, *Willie Westinghouse Edison Smith* and *Muggsy* by Frank Crane, and *Teacher's Pet*, among a host of strips created by Carl Anderson of later *Henry* fame. Most of the foregoing were created before 1915.

The mainstay of T. C. McClure Syndicate's bullpen was Billy Marriner. He created *Wags, the Dog that Adopted a Man*, *Sambo and His Funny Noises*, and *Mary and Her Little Lamb*, among others. After Marriner's death, Pat Sullivan, who drew *Fadder und Mamma Lade* for McClure, continued some of his work before entering animation with *Felix the Cat*. Bray, another pioneer animator, drew an absentminded character, and Kate Carew, sister of Gluyas Williams, drew *Handy Andy*.

Simon Simple was one of the most popular early strips; its creator, Ed Carey, was paid more than $500 a page in 1905. The redoubtable C. W. Kahles drew *Clarence the Cop*, *Billy Bounce*, and many other strips for McClure (for various services he once had seven strips running simultaneously). Pioneer Walt McDougall drew *Hank the Hermit* and *Hank and His Animal Friends*, and A. D. Reed drew *Uncle Pike* and other farmer strips. J. A. Lemon drew perhaps the first henpecked-husband strip, *How Would You Like to Be John?*, for McClure.

From the *Philadelphia Inquirer*, Otis Wood ran the Keystone service and the syndicate that bore his name. Marriner contributed heavily to its offerings: *Irresistible Rags*, a black character; *Mr. George and Wifey*, continued by Jack Gallagher and Ernie McGee; and *The Feinheimer Twins*, a copy of Hans and Fritz that Marriner drew between 1902 and 1905 and which was then drawn, until 1914, by H. H. Knerr.

Other graduates of this class included Charles Payne, who drew *Bear Creek Folks*, *The Little Possum Gang* (later taken over by Joe Doyle and Jack Gallagher),

Billy Marriner, "Sambo and His Funny Noises." (1909)

BILLY BOUNCE PUTS HIS FIRE DEP'T THROUGH THE LIFE DRILL

C. W. Kahles, "Billy Bounce." (1904)

and *Kid Trubbel*, foreshadowing his later *S'Matter, Pop¿*; Sidney Smith; Clare Victor Dwiggins (Dwig); and two Hearst favorites, Rudolph Dirks and R. F. Outcault. Dirks drew *The Terrible Twins*, an obvious approximation of his *Katzies*, for a handsome sum until Hearst made him stop, and Outcault, while still with the *Herald* between stints with Hearst, moonlighted on *Barnyard Fables* in Philadelphia.

Some larger cities had their own comic sections and made modest efforts to distribute them in the hinterlands. *The Boston Globe*, for instance, introduced *Kitty and Percy* by George H. Blair and *That Li'l Rascal Rastus* by Maginnis. *The Boston Herald* came out with *Bolivar* and *The Kid Klub* by Hal Coffman and Wallace Goldsmith respectively; both artists later became successful editorial cartoonists. Also from Boston came very handsome newspaper versions of Peter Newell's charming children's stuff, *Polly Sleepyhead*, and Palmer Cox's *Brownies*.

The *Philadelphia North American* was active in the early comic field, and Walt McDougall, already a veteran in the first two decades, was a mainstay. He drew *Handsome Hautrey*, *Fatty Felix*, *Peck's Bad Boy*, *Absent-Minded Abner* (daily), and perhaps the first continuity strip, *The Wizard of Oz*, for four months in 1904. The fine magazine artist W. O. Wilson drew *Madge, the Magician's Daughter*, and the great Zim (Eugene Zimmerman) drew two strips, one about two Dutch boys and another about a luckless reporter.

The *Philadelphia Record* presented Ernie McGee's *Mechanical Toys*, and the *Philadelphia Press* introduced Hugh Doyle's *Lazy Lew Casey*.

Other comics from the early days abound: Everrett E. Lowry, later an editorial cartoonist, drew *Binnacle Jim* for T. C. McClure; Carl Anderson's first of many strips for McClure was *Spiegleburger*; Dink drew *Jones—His Wife Can't Boss Him* for the World Company and was followed by Armstrong before he worked on *Slim Jim*; Louis Dalrymple, a *Puck* magazine veteran, drew for the *Boston Post*; Karl's *Dem Boys* was a straight imitation of *The Katzenjammer Kids* between 1914 and 1917. At the same time, both Dirks and Knerr were drawing the kids in their own versions—and Hearst was also reprinting original Dirks pages from a decade before!

The *Chicago Tribune* thrived with its own comic section for years, kicking off with Lyonel Feininger's classic surrealist creations showcasing such names as Clare Briggs and F. M. Howarth (after the latter was fired by Hearst), and culminating in the pre-*Gasoline Alley* comic creations of Frank King just before syndicate organization.

Other titles, proving that the development of strips was not a slow process, include *Mrs. Rummage* and *Mr. Gouch and His Beautiful Wife* by Hy Gage; *Isador*

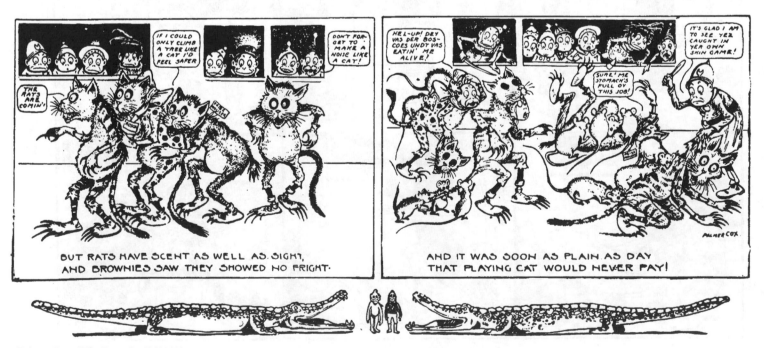

Palmer Cox, "The Brownies." (1907)

Walt McDougall, "Peck's Bad Boy." (1906)

Knobb Almost Keeps a Job by Honhorst; *Grandma's Girl* (yet another Herriman creation) by C. H. Wellington; Rigby's *Imaginative Clarence*; *Doubting Thomas* and *Pretending Percy*, two more from the active C. W. Kahles; and *Brainy Bowers*, another Ed Carey classic.

The early preprinters and boiler-plate syndicates served as valuable training grounds for both themes and artists. And, in the first two decades of this century, broad segments of the American public may have only vaguely known *Alphonse and Gaston* and *Foxy Grandpa*, but they warmly identified with *Hairbreadth Harry*, *Slim Jim*, and *Simon Simple*.

Back in the big cities, comparatively slow progress was being made with syndication. In 1895 the *New York Herald* was selling its features; later *Little Nemo* was an offering. The same year Hearst began distribution when the *Pittsburgh Press* requested reprint rights to certain features. But it was not until 1915 that Hearst consolidated all of his various syndicate operations into a large-scale syndicate. In that year the Newspaper Feature Service, International News Features, King Feature Syndicate, Premier Syndicate, and the Star Company, among others, were combined under the autocratic Moses Koenigsberg, with King Features the sales agent.

Of course, William Randolph Hearst's personal affection for and involvement with comics is well documented. He was a guiding genius who found, bought, and developed talent; he and his lieutenants displayed an uncanny knack for finding formulas and hitting popular tastes. Before syndicate operation, Hearst comics were seen around the nation in his many newspapers and in limited preprint offerings. Before 1920 Hearst's biggest stars were R. F. Outcault, Rudolph Dirks, F. B. Opper, James Swinnerton, Bunny (Carl Schultze), Winsor McCay, Cliff Sterrett, and George McManus.

The *New York World*, never far behind Hearst, began its syndicate operation in 1898. Of course many of its artists were bought away by Hearst (including Outcault and McManus), but by the 1910s the *World*'s publisher, Joseph Pulitzer, had lured Bud Fisher and Rudolph Dirks to his side. The early *World* offerings constituted a merry bunch of comic strips: R. W. Taylor's *Yens Yenson, Yanitor* and *Uncle Mose*; Gene Carr's long-running *Lady Bountiful* and *Stepbrothers*; Dwig's *Ophelia and Her Slate* and *Willie Fibb*; William J. Steinigans's *Splinters the Clown* and *The Bad Dream that Made Bill a Better Boy*; the talented F. M. Follett's *See-See Kid*; and the ubiquitous Kahles's *Billy Bragg*—all danced happily across the *World*'s pages with a wide array of McManus creations.

By the 1910s Pulitzer was heavily involved with preprints, starring *The Original Hans and Fritz—by the Creator of the Katzenjammer Kids*. When the *World* folded in 1931, its syndicate, the Press Publishing Co., merged with Max Elser's Metropolitan Features into United Feature Syndicate, an outgrowth of United Press's

W. O. Wilson, "Madge the Magician's Daughter." (1906)

literary agency, founded in 1891. When Hearst's International News merged with UP, Hearst received part ownership of United Feature.

In 1901 Robert F. Paine of the *Cleveland Press* founded the Newspaper Enterprise Association and then in 1909 the NEA Service—the service sells complete packages of comics rather than offering and contracting individual strips to client papers. It remained the last vestige of the boiler-plate system and provided many rural papers (and ultimately the affiliated Scripps-Howard chain) with quality comics. *Doings of the Duffs, Freckles and His Friends, Mr. Skygack from Mars, Everett True,* and *Adolph and Osgar* were early favorites.

In 1907 George Matthew Adams signed big names to report on big events and contracted famous writers to produce short works that he syndicated. The early syndicate ventures were very successful, with Edwina Dumm and Ding Darling as two of his stars. Later the George Matthew Adams Service was absorbed by the Washington Star Syndicate, which in turn affiliated with King Features. The Central Press of Cleveland, founded in 1910 by V. V. McNitt, was a local feature service also ultimately swallowed by Hearst. However, McNitt was later the main drive (with Charles McAdam) behind the McNaught Syndicate, founded in 1922. In 1912 Victor Lawson of the *Chicago Daily News* arranged for Adams to establish The Associated Newspapers, composed of several large-city dailies. As a syndicate it later merged with Consolidated News Features and Bell and North American Newspaper Alliance. All finally merged with the McClure Syndicate, only to sell out to United Feature.

Bell Syndicate was the creation of John Wheeler, the father of modern syndication, who perfected many of the technical and sales aspects of the business. By sheer audacity, talent, and force of personality this former sports reporter was able to lure Bud Fisher away from Hearst and got the *New York World* to guarantee $50,000 a year for *Mutt and Jeff*. Fisher, Fontaine Fox, Charles Payne, Gluyas Williams, and Wally Carlson worked for Bell.

The Ledger Syndicate of Philadelphia was organized in 1915 to distribute features from the *Saturday Evening Post* and *Ladies' Home Journal; Hairbreadth Harry* and Frank Godwin's strips were its mainstays.

In 1919 Joseph M. Patterson of the *Chicago Tribune* started selling his paper's features on an active basis and moved to New York to establish the *Daily News*. Comics were created for the paper's debut and for distribution by the new Tribune-News Syndicate; soon the distributors had the most well-rounded and consistent offerings of any syndicate until the 1940s. Captain Patterson was an unequalled genius. He often took average artists, suggested titles, changed characters, and outlined themes to create classic comics. In the stable were Harold

Gray, Chester Gould, Frank King, Frank Willard, Sidney Smith, and, later, Milton Caniff.

Also in 1919 in Chicago Eugene P. Conley founded Associated Editors, which provided teenage features. In 1925 he joined with H. H. Anderson and launched Publishers Syndicate; it soon became a leader in the story-strip field as *Apple Mary* and *Chief Wahoo* turned serious. In 1962 Publishers was bought by Field Enterprises, which had entered the syndicate field as the Chicago Sun-Times Syndicate and had only recently bought up the Herald-Tribune Syndicate. The latter had an anachronistic offering, with old wheezes like *Mr. and Mrs.*, but also had new comics like *B.C.* and *Miss Peach*. It was itself the combination of two great namesake syndicates and was beginning to show signs of creativity when its parent newspaper died.

Field Enterprises went on to acquire the Hall Syndicate in 1967. Bob Hall, a former United salesman, had founded his syndicate in 1949 with the help of the *New York Post*, and he quickly compiled a list of such hits as *Pogo*, *Dennis the Menace*, and *Andy Capp*. Publishers-Hall (now Field Newspaper Syndicate) has since become one of the largest modern-day syndicates, and it still employs H. H. Anderson's techniques of polling and scientifically planning features and continuities.

Today the major syndicates have whittled down to five in number: King, United Media Services (regrouping United Feature and NEA), Tribune Media Services, Universal Press Syndicate, and Creators Syndicate. But, as various independent attempts have shown, syndicates are necessary for the distribution of an artist's work. It remains to be seen in these days of newspaper mortality whether syndicates will accommodate just one more time—this time with realism—and explore new outlets for the comic strip.

Richard Marschall

REPRINTED FROM *CRITIC*, SEPTEMBER 1901, 227-34

The Comic Paper in America
By William Henry Shelton

My past recollection of an American comic paper is of a sheet somewhat larger than *Puck*, printed on very coarse paper with grotesque figures in outline on the cover, which used to appear in the fifties in the window of Aldrich & Fairchild's bookstore in Canandaigua, along with *Gleason's Pictorial* and *Ballou's Dollar Monthly*. I was not much interested in the comic paper and have quite forgotten its name, but *Gleason's Pictorial*, with the shipping in Boston harbor at the head of the first page, was in high favor with a little coterie of us who met one evening of each week to copy its fascinating pictures.

In the autumn of '71 I came to New York to set up as an artist with no training whatever.

My very first commission was for a page in *Wild Oats*, then published in Beekman Street by Winchell & Small. The firm soon became Collier & Small, the last-named being the editor under the pen name of "Bricktop," which, it is needless to say, referred to the color of his hair. The page consisted of imaginary heads of Brigham Young's wives and was drawn in pencil over India ink washes, on a block of boxwood, glued and bolted together, of many small pieces. The engraving was of the coarsest and the drawing of the weakest. Times were good, however, and the public not over-critical. *Wild Oats* paid as high as $25 for a full-page drawing and $20 for a front page, which was about half the minimum prices ruling at Harper's.

Among the draughtsmen whom I met at that time in the little office in Beekman Street a few are living, but more are dead. Frank Bellew, who signed his drawings with a triangle, was a middle aged Englishman of polished manners, and rather seedy dress, resulting from too convivial habits. "Mike" Woolf, genial and bubbling over with brilliant jokes, dropped in with as many comic sketches of children as he might have left after supplying the joke market at Harper's and Frank Leslie's. Tom Worth did the darkies sleigh-riding in dry-goods boxes behind grotesquely spavined horses. Sol. Ettynge also did darkies about Christmas time, but I never remember to have seen him, only hearing that he lived somewhere in Jersey and had a famous thirst with all his cleverness. Howard, who made comic valentines for a firm of lithographers in Nassau Street, and may do so still, was among the contributors, and there was also a small man, whose name I have forgotten, with premature gray hair, who got in a drawing occasionally and who was reputed to be particularly hard up. I had almost forgotten Wales, who was quite the most successful of us all in securing boxwood block from *Wild Oats*.

It was whispered at the time that he was on familiar drinking terms with Bricktop in a neighboring saloon. Wales was a cartoonist of much originality, whose professional career was cut short a few years later as a result of intemperance. Collier was the member of the firm with whom we bargained for our work. He was so easily imposed upon that it often became necessary for Bricktop to cut in with a veto from his office window behind which he ground out editorials and railway jokes. In '74 *Wild Oats* published a German edition, under the name of *Snedderadaugg*.

Phunny Phellow was a comic paper of the same period, published, if I remember, by Street & Smith, which afforded a convenient market for some of the cartoons that were not available elsewhere. "Not available," by the way, was a formula much in use by Mr. Parsons, then at the head of the art department at Harper's.

Another comic sheet which lived a short life and not a very merry one while *Wild Oats* was at the height of its prosperity, was the *Fifth Avenue Journal*. It was published during its troubled career from a bleak office in Newspaper Row by a

" YANKEE NOTIONS "

"VANITY FAIR"

young man who sported very large cuffs and paid his bills in very small installments. His was an early and fatuous attempt to intrude the comic paper, with suitably tempered jokes, upon the exclusive circles of the smart set.

The comic papers that have preceded the successes of to-day have strewn the literary prairie with their whitened bones since the early forties. A year and a fraction has compassed the ordinary span of a comic paper's life. In going over the lists of failures we find the names of men now famous in literature, art, and journalism associated with a curious crowd of notables-in-their-day.

Mr. Brander Matthews, in the *American Bibliopholist* for August, 1875, mentions thirty-four comic papers that had been started in this city previous to that date.

In the December number of the same publication Mr. L. W. Kingman adds eight more to the list. Mr. Matthews's list included the Galaxy, which had a humorous department, and the *Salmagundi*, edited by David Longworth, and written by William and Washington Irving and J. K. Paulding, which appeared as a periodical on Saturday, January 24, 1807, and ended with the twentieth number.

Excluding these two, and adding Mr. Matthews's list to Mr. Longworth's, we find that forty comic papers had been started in New York before 1875. The year 1872 seems to have been a banner year for such ventures, as no less than twelve were launched here, including *Wild Oats*, before mentioned, and its ephemeral predecessor, *The Brickbat*.

The Pictorial Wag, published about 1842, by Robert H. Elton, a wood engraver, and edited by Thomas L. Nichols, a water-cure doctor, has the honor of being the pioneer of comic periodicals in the city of New York.

Mr. Elton's unpopularity is said to have been too heavy a load for the *Wag* to carry, and the paper only published a few numbers. Mr. Elton afterwards went into real estate and built Morrisania and Eltonia.

Yankee Doodle appeared in 1845, as a sixteen-page quarto, published by Cornelius Matthews, whose funny name was "Puffer Hopkins." G. G. Foster, known as "Gaslight" Foster, Richard Grant White, and others were interested in the publication. Horace Greeley, then a young man of twenty-four, was at the same time a contributor and an object of caricature. N. P. Willis was another contributor, and the artist was one Martin. Puffer Hopkins was a man of wealth, but with all the talent enumerated his paper expired within the year.

Judy, an imitation of *Punch*, made its appearance a few weeks after *Yankee Doodle*. Its publisher was George F. Nesbitt, then known as the "Nassau Street Punster." Harry Grattan Plunkett, an actor, who was equally well known as Harry Plunkett Grattan, was editor, assisted by Dr. W. K. Northall, from the Olympic Theatre Company. One of the chief artists was a Mr. Wolfe, afterwards leader of the orchestra of Burton's Theatre. Over-burdened with comedians *Judy* came to a tragic end a few weeks before *Yankee Doodle*.

Following *Judy*, *The Bubble* appeared and burst after the second number.

The New York *Picayune*, started in 1847, lasted until 1858. Its phenomenal longevity is accounted for by the fact that it was published by a Dr. Hutchings to advertise his patent medicines. Its editor until 1854 was Joseph A. Scoville, an erratic character who quarrelled with the proprietor and started *The Pick*, which lived a little over a year.

Robert H. Levison, one of the subsequent editors of the *Picayune*, added to the reputation of the paper by publishing "The Comic Sermons of Julius Caesar Hannibal." In 1858 Frank Bellew, "The Triangle," who had been the artist of *The Reveille*, another short-lived periodical, became the editor of the *Picayune*, and associated with him appeared Mortimer Thompson,—G. K. Philander Doesticks.

In 1852 Dr. Hutchings started a second comic paper, *The Lantern*. At one period of its short career Jno. Broughton was its editor, assisted by one Thomas Powell, an Englishman, who was said to have been the original of both Mr. Pecksniff and Mr. Micawber. FitzJames O'Brien and Charles Seymour, theatrical critic of the *Times*, were contributors. With so many wags in control *The Lantern* did well to keep its light burning for eighteen months. This is evidently the same paper that appears in some lists as conducted by John Brougham, who was a persistent promoter of comic journalism, under the name of "Diogenes hys Lanterne."

Young Sam had had a career of twelve months following *The Lantern*, and *Young America*, started in 1853, existed a few months longer. Jno. McLennan, who drew comics for *Harper's Monthly*, and Hoppin, who made curious book illustrations in outline in Darley's time, were the artists.

Vanity Fair, started in 1859, lived eight years, and brought to the front some new names in literature, such as Richard Henry Stoddard, Edmund Clarence Stedman, Artemus Ward, Thos. Bailey Aldrich, and William Winter.

Momus was started in 1860, as a comic daily, and after a few numbers it was changed to a weekly and died.

Mrs. Grundy, started July 15, 1865, expired with the eleventh number.

Punchinello was born in April, 1870, and died in December. Among its contributors were Orpheus C. Kerr and W. L. Alden, the veteran editor of *Harper's Monthly*.

The Thistle was published for a short time in 1872 by S. M. Howard. The articles were signed by various names, but all were written by the poet Francis S. Saltus.

" LIFE "

Among the comic papers were the various publications by Frank Leslie: *Champagne*, *The Cartoon*, *Budget of Fun*, *Jolly Joker*, and others. Of various nomenclature there is mention of a paper called the *Innocent Weekly Owl*, *The Phunniest of Phunny Phellows*, and, in Philadelphia, *John Donkey*.

The first great success in comic journalism, in New York, was that of *Puck*, which began its career at No. 13 William Street in the spring of 1877. Keppler and Schwarzmann were the owners of the new paper, and Sydney Rosenfeld was the first editor. He was succeeded during the first summer by H. C. Bunner, who kept the editorial chair until his death in 1896.

Mr. Joseph Keppler left Leslie's in the summer of 1876 and began making his arrangement to start *Puck*. He was so fearful, however, of adding another to the long list of failures in comic journalism that at the last moment he offered to remain in the employ of Frank Leslie if his salary were raised from fifty to fifty-five dollars a week.

Mr. Leslie indignantly refused, asserting that *Puck* could not live six months. The Kepplers, father and son, have been the cartoonists, and C. J. Taylor was for a long time the dean of the artist staff.

Puck was not only an evolution from failure to success, but from black and white to color. This striking innovation was of itself enough to ensure the triumph of the venture. It caught the popular fancy at once, and the paper has made fortunes for its owners.

Judge, published by Arkell and Co., took the field during the candidacy of James G. Blaine, to offset the political influence of *Puck*, and has achieved a permanent success on the same lines as its great rival.

The first number of *Life* appeared on January 3, 1883, at 1155 Broadway. This second great success in the comic field was inaugurated by J. A. Mitchell and Andrew Miller. Mr. Mitchell has distinguished himself as an author, but before he became an editor he was best known as an artist of cherubs.

His contributions to the exhibitions of the Etching Club were invariably cupids and he continued to draw cupids for *Life* until the little god turned on him and landed him in the usual way.

Charles Dana Gibson has been closely identified with *Life* from his first appearance in its pages.

Van Schaick has been affixing his familiar signature,"Van," to society drawings for about the same length of time. Mike Woolf was a frequent contributor. Charles Howard Johnson did some of his cleverest work for *Life*, and "Chip," the younger Bellew, before his death, formed a peculiar link between the old and the new in comic journalism.

The Lenox Library is the custodian of files, more or less complete, of several of these old comic periodicals. The only publication of this class, preserved at the Library, not mentioned in the foregoing list, is *Yankee Notions*, which, strange to relate, appears in the familiar cover of my boyish recollection in the window of the Canandaigua bookstore. It was pleasant once more to watch the pendent figures on the side of this old cover, clinging desperately to each other above the blade of a huge jack-knife still patiently waiting to receive them.

The Lenox collection includes, furthermore, six volumes of *Yankee Doodle, six* of *Vanity Fair*, two of *Momus*, three of John Brougham's *Lantern*, and one each of *Judy* and *Mrs. Grundy*.

The cover of *Mrs. Grundy* was by Thos. Nast and consists of a broad-backed old woman with an umbrella and a cat, who is lecturing an audience of celebrities, crowding the interior of a theatre, which suggests the old Academy of Music on 14th Street.

Some of these publications, as *Yankee Notions* and *Momus*, are illustrated with sketchy drawings of the Sir John Gilbert school, then so much in vogue, cut in facsimile in the best manner of that period. Excellent examples of this school may be found in the *New York Ledger* of the fifties and in the comics in the back of *Harper's Monthly*. It was the best result at that time of the combined efforts of the draughtsman and the wood-engraver, and more artistic and sincere than the style adopted by the American Tract Society, which was a labored cross-sketching in imitation of steel engraving. Most of the comic papers of those early days are amusing because of the coarseness of the woodcuts and by reason of the deadly cheapness of the jokes.

Yankee Doodle covers the Mexican war period, and one of its cartoons shows Henry Clay brandishing a sword in front of an open cupboard in which a tiny Mexican is cowering among the shelves and the rats, with the legend below, "I smell the blood of a Mexican and I'll have it, too." The references to old New York as well as to old national issues are interesting in the extreme, and new surprises come upon you with the turning of every leaf. Henry J. Raymond appears "Trying to go ahead with the Times" against a contrary wind, and Wm. H. S--d rides through Washington seated beside Fred'k D--s in a barouche drawn by four horses having human heads—which may have been portraits.

REPRINTED FROM *ATLANTIC MONTHLY*, AUGUST 1956, 269-73.

The Humor of the Colored Supplement
By Ralph Bergengren

Ten or a dozen years ago,—the exact date is here immaterial, an enterprising newspaper publisher conceived the idea of appealing to what is known as the American "sense of humor" by printing a so-called comic supplement in colors. He chose Sunday as of all days the most lacking in popular amusements, carefully restricted himself to pictures without humor and color without beauty, and presently inaugurated a new era in American journalism. The colored supplement became an institution. No Sunday is complete without it,—not because its pages invariably delight, but because, like flies in summer, there is no screen that will altogether exclude them. A newspaper without a color press hardly considers itself a newspaper, and the smaller journals are utterly unmindful of the kindness of Providence in putting the guardian angel, Poverty, outside their portals. Sometimes, indeed, they think to outwit this kindly interference by printing a syndicated comic page without color; and mercy is thus served in a half portion, for, uncolored, the pictures are inevitably about twice as attractive. Some print them without color, but on pink paper. Others rejoice, as best they may, in a press that will reproduce at least a fraction of the original discord. One and all they unite vigorously, as if driven by a perverse and cynical intention, to prove the American sense of humor a thing of national shame and degradation. Fortunately the public has so little to say about its reading matter that one may fairly suspend judgment.

For, after all, what is the sense of humor upon which every man prides himself, as belonging only to a gifted minority? Nothing more nor less than a certain mental quickness, alert to catch the point of an anecdote or to appreciate the surprise of a new and unexpected point of view toward an old and familiar phenomenon. Add together these gifted minorities, and each nation reaches what is fallaciously termed the national sense of humor,—an English word, incidentally, for which D'Israeli was unable to find an equivalent in any other language, and which is in itself simply a natural development of the critical faculty, born of a present need of describing what earlier ages had taken for granted. The jovial porter and his charming chance acquaintances, the three ladies of Bagdad, enlivened conversation with a kind of humor, carefully removed from the translation of commerce and the public libraries, for which they needed no descriptive noun, but which may nevertheless be fairly taken as typical of that city in the day of the Caliph Haroun.

The Middle Ages rejoiced in a similar form of persiflage, and the present day in France, Germany, England, or America, for example, inherits it,—minus its too juvenile indecency,—in the kind of pleasure afforded by these comic supplements. Their kinship with the lower publications of European countries is curiously evident to whoever has examined them. Vulgarity, in fact, speaks the same tongue in all countries, talks, even in art-ruled France, with the same crude draughtsmanship, and usurps universally a province that Emerson declared "far better than wit for a poet or writer." In its expression and enjoyment no country can fairly claim the dubious superiority. All are on the dead level of that surprising moment when the savage had ceased to be dignified and man had not yet become rational. Men indeed, speak freely and vaingloriously of their national sense of humor; but they are usually unconscious idealists. For the comic cut that amuses the most stupid Englishman may be shifted entire into an American comic supplement; the "catastrophe joke" of the American comic weekly of the next higher grade is stolen in quantity to delight the readers of similar but more economical publications in Germany; the lower humor of France, barring the expurgations demanded by Anglo-Saxon prudery, is equally transferable; and the average American often examines on Sunday morning, without knowing it, an international loan-exhibit.

Humor, in other words, is cosmopolitan, reduced, since usage insists on reducing it, at this lowest imaginable level, to such obvious and universal elements that any intellect can grasp their combinations. And at its highest it is again cosmopolitan, like art; like art, a cultivated characteristic, no more spontaneously natural than a "love of nature." It is an insult to the whole line of English and American humorists—Sterne, Thackeray, Dickens, Meredith, Twain, Holmes, Irving, and others of a distinguished company—to include as humor what is merely the crude brutality of human nature, mocking at grief and laughing boisterously at physical deformity. And in these Sunday comics Humor, stolen by vandals from her honest, if sometimes rough-and-ready, companionship, thrusts a woe-begone visage from the painted canvas of the national sideshow, and none too poor to "shy a brick" at her.

At no period in the world's history has there been a steadier output of so-called humor,—especially in this country. The simple idea of printing a page of comic pictures has produced families. The very element of variety has been obliterated by the creation of types,—a confusing medley of impossible countrymen, mules, goats, German-Americans and their irreverent progeny, specialized children with a genius for annoying their elders, white-whiskered elders with a genius for playing practical jokes on their grandchildren, policemen, Chinamen, Irishmen, negroes, inhuman conceptions of the genus tramp, boy inventors whose inventions invariably end in causing somebody to be mirthfully spattered with paint or joyously torn to pieces by machinery, bright boys with a talent for deceit, laziness, or cruelty, and even the beasts of the jungle dehumanized to the point of practical joking. *Mirabile dictu!*—some of these things have even been dramatized.

With each type the reader is expected to become personally acquainted,—to watch for its coming on Sunday mornings, happily wondering with what form of inhumanity the author will have been able to endow his brainless manikins. And the authors are often men of intelligence, capable here and there of a bit of adequate drawing and an idea that is honestly and self-respectingly provocative of laughter. Doubtless they are often ashamed of their product; but the demand of the hour is imperative. The presses are waiting. They, too, are both quick and heavy. And the cry of the publisher is for "fun" that no intellect in all his heterogeneous public shall be too dull to appreciate. We see, indeed, the outward manifestation of a curious paradox: humor prepared and printed for the extremely dull, and—what is still more remarkable—excused by grown men, capable of editing newspapers, on the ground that it gives pleasure to children.

Reduced to first principles, therefore, it is not humor, but simply a supply created in answer to a demand, hastily produced by machine methods and hastily accepted by editors too busy with other editorial duties to examine it intelligently. Under these conditions "humor" is naturally conceived as something preëminently quick; and so quickness predominates. Somebody is always hitting somebody else with a club; somebody is always falling down stairs, or out of a balloon, or over a cliff, or into a river, a barrel of paint, a basket of eggs, a convenient cistern, or a tub of hot water. The comic cartoonists have already exhausted every available substance into which one can fall, and are compelled to fall themselves into a veritable ocean of vain repetition. They have exhausted everything by which one can be blown up. They have exhausted everything by which one can be knocked down or run over. And if the victim is never actually killed in these mirthful experiments, it is obviously because he would then cease to be funny,—which is very much the point of view of the Spanish Inquisition, the cat with a mouse, or the American Indian with a captive. But respect for property, respect for parents, for law, for decency, for truth, for beauty, for kindliness, for dignity, or for honor, are killed, without mercy. Morality alone, in its restricted sense of sexual relations, is treated with courtesy, although we find throughout the accepted theory that marriage is a union of uncongenial spirits, and the chart of petty marital deceit is carefully laid out and marked for whoever is likely to respond to endless unconscious suggestions. Sadly must the American child sometimes be puzzled while comparing his own grandmother with the visiting mother-in-law of the colored comic.

Lest this seem a harsh, even an unkind inquiry into the innocent amusements of other people, a few instances may be mentioned, drawn from the Easter Sunday output of papers otherwise both respectable and unrespectable; papers, moreover, depending largely on syndicated humor that may fairly be said to have reached a total circulation of several million readers. We have, to begin with, two rival versions of a creation that made the originator famous, and that chronicle the adventures of a small boy whose name and features are everywhere familiar. Often these adventures, in the original youngster, have been amusing, and amusingly seasoned with the salt of legitimately absurd phraseology. But the pace is too fast, even for the originator. The imitator fails invariably to catch the spirit of them, and in this instance is driven to an ancient subterfuge. To come briefly to an unpleasant point, an entire page is devoted to showing the reader how the boy was made ill by smoking his father's cigars. Incidentally he falls down stairs. Meantime, his twin is rejoicing the readers of another comic supplement by spoiling a wedding party; it is the minister who first comes to grief, and is stood on his head, the boy who later is quite properly thrashed by an angry mother,—and it is all presumably very delightful and a fine example for the imitative genius of other children. Further, we meet a mule who kicks a policeman and whose owner is led away to the lockup; a manicured vacuum who slips on a banana peel, crushes the box containing his fiancée's Easter bonnet, and is assaulted by her father (he, after the manner of comic fathers, having just paid one hundred dollars for the bonnet out of a plethoric pocketbook); a nondescript creature, presumably human, who slips on another banana peel and knocks over a citizen, who in turn knocks over a policeman, and is also marched off to undeserved punishment. We see the German-American child covering his father with water from a street gutter, another child deluging his parent with water from a hose; another teasing his younger brother and sister. To keep the humor of the banana peel in countenance we find the picture of a fat man accidentally sitting down on a tack; he exclaims, "ouch," throws a basket of eggs into the air, and they come down on the head of the boy who arranged the tacks. We see two white boys beating a little negro over the head with a plank (the hardness of the negro's skull here affording the humorous *motif*), and we see an idiot blowing up a mule with dynamite. Lunacy, in short, could go no farther than this pandemonium of undisguised coarseness and brutality,—the humor offered on Easter Sunday morning by leading American newspapers for the edification of American readers.

And every one of the countless creatures, even to the poor, maligned dumb animals, is saying something. To the woeful extravagance of foolish acts must be added an equal extravagance of foolish words: "Out with you, intoxicated rowdy," "Shut up," "Skidoo," "They've set the dog on me," "Hee-haw," "My uncle had it tooken in Hamburg," "Dat old gentleman will slip on dem banana skins," "Little Buster got all that was coming to him," "Aw, shut up," "Y-e-e-e G-o-d-s," "Ouch," "Golly, dynamite am powerful stuff," "I am listening to vat der vild vaves is sedding," "I don't think Pa and I will ever get along together until he gets rid of his conceit," "phew." The brightness of this repartee could be continued indefinitely; profanity, of course, is indicated by dashes and exclamation points; a person who has fallen overboard says "blub;" concussion is visibly represented by stars; "biff" and "bang" are used according to taste to accompany a blow on the nose or an explosion of dynamite.

From this brief summary it may be seen how few are the fundamental conceptions that supply the bulk of almost the entire output, and in these days of syndicated ideas a comparatively small body of men produce the greater part of it. Physical pain is the most glaringly omnipresent of these *motifs*; it is counted upon invariably to amuse the average humanity of our so-called Christian civilization. The entire group of Easter Sunday pictures constitutes a saturnalia of prearranged accidents in which the artist is never hampered by the exigencies of logic; machinery in which even the presupposed poorest intellect might be expected to detect the obvious flaw accomplishes its evil purpose with inevitable accuracy; jails and lunatic asylums are crowded with new inmates; the policeman always uses his club or revolver; the parents usually thrash their offspring at the end of the performance; household furniture is demolished, clothes ruined, and unsalable eggs broken by the dozen. Deceit is another universal concept of humor, that combine easily with the physical pain 'motif'; and mistaken identity, in which the juvenile idiot disguises himself and deceives his parents in various ways, is another favorite resort of the humorists. The paucity of invention is hardly less remarkable than the willingness of the inventors to sign their products, or the willingness of editors to publish them. But the age is notoriously one in which editors underrate and insult the public intelligence.

Doubtless there are some to applaud the spectacle,—the imitative spirits, for example, who recently compelled a woman to seek the protection of a police department because of the persecution of a gang of boys and young men shouting "hee-haw" whenever she appeared on the street; the rowdies whose exploits figure so frequently in metropolitan newspapers; or that class of adults who tell indecent stories at the dinner table and laugh joyously at their wives' efforts to turn the conversation. But the Sunday comic goes into other homes than these, and is handed to their children by parents whose souls would shudder at the thought of a dime novel. Alas, poor parents! That very dime novel as a rule holds up ideals of bravery and chivalry, rewards good and punishes evil, offers at the worst a temptation to golden adventuring, for which not one child in a million will ever attempt to surmount the obvious obstacles. It is no easy matter to become an Indian fighter, pirate, or detective; the dream is, after all, a daydream, tinctured with the beautiful color of old romance, and built on eternal qualities that the world has rightfully esteemed worthy of emulation. And in place of it the comic supplement, like that other brutal horror, the juvenile comic story, that goes on its immoral way unnoticed, raises no high ambition, but devotes itself to "mischief made easy." Hard as it is to become an Indian fighter, any boy has plenty of opportunity to throw stones at his neighbor's windows. And on any special occasion, such, for example, as Christmas or Washington's Birthday, almost the entire ponderous machine is set in motion to make reverence and ideals ridiculous. Evil example is strong in proportion as it is easy to imitate. The state of mind that accepts the humor of the comic weekly is the same as that which shudders at Ibsen, and smiles complacently at the musical comedy, with its open acceptance of the wild oats theory, and its humorous exposition of a kind of wild oats that youth may harvest without going out of its own neighborhood.

In all this noisy, explosive, garrulous pandemonium one finds here and there a moment of rest and refreshment,—the work of the few pioneers of decency and decorum brave enough to bring their wares to the noisome market and lucky enough to infuse their spirit of refinement, art, and genuine humor into its otherwise hopeless atmosphere. Preëminent among them stands the inventor of "Little Nemo in Slumberland," a man of genuine pantomimic humor, charming draughtmanship, and an excellent decorative sense of color, who has apparently studied his medium and makes the best of it. And with him come Peter Newell, Grace G. Weiderseim, and Conde,—now illustrating *Uncle Remus* for a Sunday audience,—whose pictures in some of the Sunday papers are a delightful and self-respecting proof of the possibilities of this type of journalism. Out of the noisy streets, the cheap restaurants with their unsteady-footed waiters and avalanches of soup and crockery, out of the slums, the quarreling families, the prisons and the lunatic asylums, we step for a moment into the world of childish fantasy, closing the iron door behind us and trying to shut out the clamor of hooting mobs, the laughter of imbeciles, and the crash of explosives. After all, there is no reason why children should not have their innocent amusement on Sunday morning; but there seems to be every reason why the average editor of the weekly comic supplement should be given a course in art, literature, common sense, and Christianity.

Glossary of Comic Strip Terms

Action strip   A comic strip whose chief appeal is adventure and suspense rather than humor or human interest. Synonym of adventure strip.

Adventure strip   A comic strip featuring a hero (or a group of heroes) involved in exciting and usually exotic adventures. Classifiable into a number of subcategories: the *aviation strip* features a pilot-hero in situations related (often remotely) to airplanes and flying (e.g., *Scorchy Smith*, *Barney Baxter*, and *Michel Tanguy*); the *science-fiction strip* uses themes that are grounded in scientific conjecture or implausibility, such as interplanetary expeditions and time travel (e.g., *Buck Rogers*, *Jeff Hawke*, and *Saturno contro la Terra*); the *detective strip* deals with stories of crime, detection, and suspense (e.g., *Dick Tracy*, *Secret Agent X-9*, and *Buck Ryan*); the *Western strip* takes place in the American West (e.g., *Red Ryder*, *Lieutenant Blueberry*, and *Tex Willer*); and the *superhero* strip stars a protagonist who is naturally or artificially endowed with superhuman powers (e.g., *Superman*, *Cyborg 009*, and *Garth*).

adventure strip: *"Dickie Dare,"* Coulton Waugh. © AP Newsfeatures.

Animal strip   A comic strip with an animal, or a group of animals, as its main protagonist. Animal strips are of two types: one completely excludes people from its cast, but presents what are essentially human characters in animal guises (e.g., *Tiger Tim*, *The Pussycat Princess*, and *Pogo*); also known as "funny animal strips"; the other features recognizable animals in identifiable human environments (e.g., *Napoleon*, *Fred Basset*, and *Cubitus*).

Animal strip: *"Pogo,"* Walt Kelly. © Walt Kelly.

Assistant A person hired to help a comic strip artist with such tasks as lettering, inking, laying color, etc.

Backgroundman An assistant who draws the backgrounds of a comic strip.

Balloon An enclosed white space issuing from the lips of comic characters, generally used to convey dialogue, but can also enclose a variety of signs and symbols. (A discussion of the role of the balloon in comics can be found in the analytical summary contained in this work.)

Ben day (or benday) **1.** A transparent screen, usually dotted or crosshatched, pasted over a panel to add shading. **2.** The process itself: to benday a drawing.

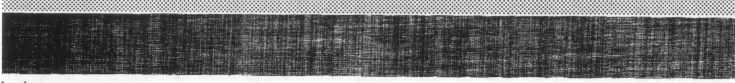

benday: *two screen patterns.*

Cartoon (from the French *carton*, a sketch or study on pasteboard) A drawing of political, satirical, or humorous intent, containing within one frame a self-explanatory scene or composition accompanied by a caption or brief text. *Animated cartoon:* a series of drawings photographed on film and shown like a motion picture. (A detailed discussion of the animated cartoon can be found in the analytical summary contained in this work.)

Cartooning The art of drawing cartoons; the art of doing comics.

Cartoonist **1.** An artist who draws cartoons. **2.** A comic strip or comic book artist.

Cartoon strip (British) Synonym for comic strip.

Color scheme Indications given by a cartoonist for the coloring of a comic strip or page.

Comic art The comics considered as an art form.

Comic book An individual magazine, usually printed in color on pulp paper, containing stories or gags in comic strip form. A comic book may reprint previously published comic strips (reprint comic book) or original material.

Comicdom **1.** An ensemble of those people (cartoonists, publishers, editors, etc.) engaged in the creation, production, and distribution of comics. **2.** The world of comics treated as a separate and self-contained entity.

Comic magazine (or comics magazine) **1.** (U.S.) The official name for a comic book. **2.** (Europe) A magazine (usually weekly or monthly) featuring gag strips, story strips, and other comic material.

Comics A narrative form containing text and pictures arranged in sequential order (usually chronological). Name derived from the first examples of the form, which were all of a humorous nature; it has since become a misnomer, since the comics now encompass narratives that are not primarily comical but involve suspense, adventure, human interest, etc. The term "comics" applied to the form has also proven unwieldy, as it does not easily lend itself to grammatical derivatives (e.g., there is no comic equivalent to the word "cinematic"). The Italians use the word *fumetto* (literally "little cloud," the traditional term for balloon), from which they have been able to derive such neologisms as *fumettare* (to arrange in comic strip form), *fumettologo* (a student or scholar of the comics), and *fumettistico* (pertaining to the comics). It would be a great advance in the study of the form if such a simple word (preferably from a Greek root) could be coined in the English language.

Comic strip **1.** A comic sequence arranged in strip form (e.g., horizontally); synonym of daily strip. **2.** Synonym of newspaper strip. **3.** Any story told in comic terms. **4.** Synonym of comics in general.

Comic supplement A separate section of a newspaper, usually published in color on Sundays, containing a number of comic features; also called a Sunday or weekly supplement.

Continuity Comic strip plot that unfolds over more than one installment.

Continuity strip A comic strip featuring day-to-day and/or week to week action.

Crossover The appearance of one character in another character's comic-book title.

Daily strip A comic feature appearing across a daily newspaper page, usually in a horizontal arrangement of panels. *Mutt and Jeff* is usually considered the first daily strip of any significance.

daily strip: *"Peanuts,"* Charles Schulz. © United Feature Syndicate.

Doubletone Chemically pretreated paper consisting of two imperceptible patterns of lines or points, more or less widely spaced and regular, according to the model. A yellowish developer can then be applied to the paper with brush or pen to bring out both patterns, or a different solution can be applied that will reveal only one of the patterns. Roy Crane is acknowledged as the master of this delicate technique.

Drop Panel in a Sunday page designed to be discarded to accommodate a limited layout.

Drybrush Use of a nearly dry brush in order to achieve a gray, rather than a black, quality.

Episode **1.** A complete plot occurring in a continuity strip. **2.** A single installment (daily, weekly, or monthly) of a comic feature.

Family strip A comic strip centering on the adventures of a fictitious family group (e.g., *The Gumps, Blondie,* and *The Potts*).

doubletone effects: *"Buz Sawyer,"* Roy Crane. © King Features Syndicate.

family strip: *"Blondie," Chic Young. © King Features Syndicate.*

Fandom   Term used to describe the group of devotees of a particular form, medium, or activity; specifically, enthusiasts of the comic medium.

Fantasy strip   A comic strip whose main purpose is to appeal to the readers' imaginations or fancies (e.g., *Little Nemo, Krazy Kat,* and *Barnaby*).

Fanzine   Amateur publication (often of a cultish nature) devoted to some aspect of popular culture; specifically, a publication aimed at comic enthusiasts. Contraction of "fan magazine."

Feature   Any comic story (whether appearing in newspapers, magazines, or comic books) with a separate and continuing title. Synonym of comic strip.

Funnies   Synonym of comics. (While still widely used, the term is generally shunned by specialists and has acquired a slightly pejorative meaning.)

Funny strip   Synonym of humor strip.

Gag man   Writer who contributes gags or situation ideas to cartoonists.

Gag strip   Humor strip that makes a different point in each installment, without recourse to continuity (e.g., *Hagar the Horrible, Sturmtruppen,* and *Andy Capp*).

gag strip: *"Old Doc Yak," Sidney Smith. © Chicago Tribune-New York News Syndicate.*

Ghost   Person who draws and/or writes a comic strip for a cartoonist who gets the public credit. Unlike an assistant who only does well-defined chores, a ghost carries a strip in its entirety. One of the most contemptible practices in the comics, it is particularly widespread among syndicated strip cartoonists (comic books usually do not pay enough to allow their practitioners to hire a ghost). In Europe the practice is illegal, and there is some question of its legality in the United States. The practice seems to violate the "truth in advertising" laws because the actual author of the strip is not the one advertised in the byline.

Girl strip A comic strip featuring the (usually romantic) adventures of a young and unmarried girl or a group of young girls (e.g., *Tillie the Toiler, Winnie Winkle, Dot and Carrie,* and *Apartment 3-G*).

girl strip: *"Connie,"* Frank Godwin. © Ledger Syndicate.

Graphic novel An extended comics narrative published in book form.

Humor strip A comic strip whose staple is comedy—slapstick or burlesque—and which makes its point in one installment (gag strip) or uses continuity (e.g., *Alley Oop, Tintin,* and *Patoruzú*).

Illustrated strip A comic strip whose drawings are related to illustration rather than to cartooning.

Inker Person who inks over the pencilled drawings of another cartoonist.

Kid strip Comic strip having a child, or a group of children, as its protagonist. From *The Katzenjammer Kids* to *Dennis the Menace*, the kid strip has been one of the staples of the comic medium.

Letterer Person who does the lettering in a comic strip.

Lettering The handwritten dialogues and/or text contained in a comic strip. Lettering is more important to the overall effect of a particular comic strip than it superficially appears; it should harmonize with the style of the specific comic strip for which it is devised. Some cartoonists, conscious of this prerequisite, do their own lettering (e.g., Charles Schulz).

Logo The distinctive word or group of words formed by the title of a comic strip. Contraction of logotype.

Manga Japanese word for comics; by extension, a comic story following Japanese conventions of narrative and style.

Miniseries (or **limited series**) A comic-book title published in a finite number of issues.

Montage panel A series of space-unrelated pictures arranged or superimposed within one comic strip panel.

kid strip: *"Zig et Puce,"* Alain Saint-Ogan. © Saint-Ogan.

MORE ABOUT THE COMICS

Narrative 1. Plot line or story line of a comic strip. 2. Synonym of continuity.

Newspaper strip Any comic feature carried by a newspaper.

One-shot Comic book title issued only once (usually for tryout purposes).

onomatopoeia: "Broom Hilda," Russ Meyers. © Chicago Tribune-New York News Syndicate.

Onomatopoeia Imitative sound words (e.g., vroom, bang, zap, gasp, argh) widely used in the vocabulary of the comics.

Open panel Any panel not enclosed within a frame; also called borderless panel.

open panel: "Pedrito el Drito," Antonio Terenghi. © Universo.

Page A weekly newspaper comic feature usually printed in color (few Sunday comics are now full-page size, but the name is still traditionally used, regardless of actual format); also called weekly or Sunday page.

Panel **1.** A single drawing, most often enclosed in a rectangular or square frame, that is part of a comic strip or page. **2.** A daily or weekly gag feature consisting of just one panel (e.g., *Out Our Way* and *Our Boarding House*); sometimes called a panel strip.

panel (*definition 2*): *"Outdoor Sports,"* Tad (T. A. Dorgan). © King Features Syndicate.

Pantomime strip **1.** Comic strip in which no dialogue is used; silent strip. **2.** Comic strip in which the protagonist remains mute, although dialogue may occasionally be used by secondary characters (e.g., *The Little King* and *Henry*).

Penciler Person who sketches the drawings of a comic strip in pencil.

Presentation strip A specially prepared strip that serves to introduce the feature's characters to new readers; also called an introduction strip.

Reprint A run of newspaper or comic book features issued after the date first published. Reprints may appear either in the original format or (more often) in magazine or book form.

Scripter **1.** Synonym of scriptwriter. **2.** Person hired to write the dialogue and/or narrative of a comic strip on a synopsis provided to him by the strip's author, syndicate, or comic book company.

Scriptwriter Person who writes the continuity and/or dialogue of a comic strip. (Lee Falk and Allen Saunders are two of the best-known American scriptwriters.)

Sequence **1.** A chronological grouping of comic strips. **2.** Synonym of episode.

Silent strip A comic strip using only pictures to the exclusion of dialogue or narration (e.g., *Adamson* ["Silent Sam"], *Max*, and *Ferdinand*).

silent strip: *"Ferd' nand,"* H. Dahl Mikkelsen. © PIB.

Splash panel   A large panel appearing at the beginning of a comic-book story; also called a bleed panel.

Sports strip   A comic strip built around some facet of the sports scene (e.g., *Joe Palooka*, *Michel Valiant*, and *Kyojin no Hoshi*).

Story strip   Comic strip that tells a story over a number of installments. Synonym of continuity strip. Story strip plots vary widely from burlesque (*Li'l Abner*) to soap opera (*Mary Worth*) to adventure (*The Phantom*).

Strip   **1.** A single installment of a daily strip. **2.** Synonym of comic strip.

Sunday page   A newspaper feature appearing only once a week, usually on Sunday.

Syndicate   An organization involved in the distribution of individual features (comics, columns, news items, etc.) to subscribing newspapers. (For more information, see "The History of Newspaper Syndication" included in this work.)

Thought balloon   Device used to convey the unspoken thoughts or musings of a character. (This kind of balloon is traditionally scalloped with tiny bubbles issuing up from the character's head.)

thought balloon: *"Carol Day," David Wright. © Associated Newspapers Ltd.*

Vignette   A comic strip drawing fading out of its space, with no definite border.

Zip tone   **1.** Shading effect obtained by a series of parallel strokes of the brush. **2.** Synonym of doubletone.